There Was and There Was Not

There Was and There Was Not

A JOURNEY THROUGH HATE

AND POSSIBILITY IN

TURKEY, ARMENIA, AND BEYOND

Meline Toumani

METROPOLITAN BOOKS

HENRY HOLT AND COMPANY

NEW YORK

Metropolitan Books
Henry Holt and Company, LLC
Publishers since 1866
175 Fifth Avenue
New York, New York 10010
www.henryholt.com

Metropolitan Books® and ▥® *are registered trademarks of Henry Holt and Company, LLC.*

Portions of chapter 7 previously appeared, in substantially different form, in the journal n+1.

Library of Congress Cataloging-in-Publication Data
  Toumani, Meline.
    There was and there was not : a journey through hate and possibility in Turkey, Armenia,
  and beyond / Meline Toumani.—First edition.
      pages cm
    ISBN 978-0-8050-9762-7 (hardback)—ISBN 978-0-8050-9763-4 (electronic book)
  1. Toumani, Meline.   2. Toumani, Meline—Travel—Turkey.   3. Armenian Americans—
  Ethnic identity.   4. Armenian massacres, 1915–1923—Influence.
  5. Genocide—Armenia—Psychological aspects.   6. Armenia—Relations—Turkey.
  7. Turkey—Relations—Armenia.   8. Turkey—Social conditions—1960–   9. Social
  change—Turkey.   I. Title.
    E184.A7T68 2014

    327.5610566'2—dc23   *2014018362*

Henry Holt books are available for special promotions and premiums. For details contact:
Director, Special Markets.

First Edition 2014

Designed by Meryl Sussman Levavi

Printed in the United States of America
10 9 8 7 6 5 4 3 2 1

This is a work of nonfiction. The names of some individuals have been changed, particularly when describing private conversations with people who were not expecting to have their remarks published. Identifying details have not been altered, with one exception where privacy was of the utmost importance. There are no composite characters or scenes, but in a few cases individuals who were present for a given conversation have been left out of the narrative for the sake of clarity.

For Mom and Dad

Contents

There Was and There Was Not

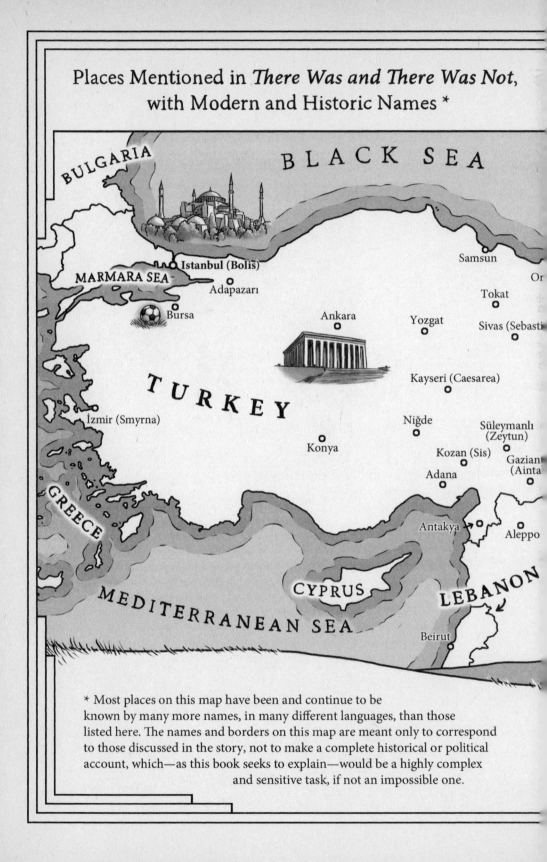

Places Mentioned in *There Was and There Was Not,* with Modern and Historic Names *

BULGARIA

BLACK SEA

Istanbul (Bolis)

MARMARA SEA

Adapazarı

Bursa

Samsun

Or

Tokat

Ankara

Yozgat

Sivas (Sebasti

TURKEY

Kayseri (Caesarea)

İzmir (Smyrna)

Niğde

Süleymanlı (Zeytun)

Konya

Kozan (Sis)

Gazian (Ainta

Adana

GREECE

Antakya

Aleppo

CYPRUS

LEBANON

MEDITERRANEAN SEA

Beirut

* Most places on this map have been and continue to be known by many more names, in many different languages, than those listed here. The names and borders on this map are meant only to correspond to those discussed in the story, not to make a complete historical or political account, which—as this book seeks to explain—would be a highly complex and sensitive task, if not an impossible one.

RUSSIA

GEORGIA

CASPIAN SEA

Trabzon

Tbilisi

Kars

Gyumri

Shaki (Nukha)

Baku

ARMENIA

AZERBAIJAN

ebinkarahisar

Erzurum (Karin)

Yerevan

Iğdır →

Ararat

NAGORNO-KARABAKH

emaliye
gin, Agn)

Tunceli (Dersim)

Kapan

lâzığ (Harput, Kharpert)
+ Palu

NAKHICHEVAN

Muş

Van

Agulis

Qara Dagh

alatya

Bitlis

Tabriz

Akdamar
(Akhtamar) →

Diyarbakır
(Dikranagerd)

Maragheh

Mardin

nlıurfa (Urfa)

To Tehran →

SYRIA

IRAQ

IRAN

N

W   E

ԿԱՐՈՒՀԿԱՐ

S

Map by Elisabeth Alba

Notes on Language

Because the issues I've written about in this book are highly sensitive for Turks and Armenians, every choice I've made is doomed to be a political act, even decisions on spelling. In my research, I have often lamented the frequency of error in the Turkish and Armenian media with regard to name spellings of members of the other ethnic group, and even as to whether a given name is male or female. Generally the mistakes are unintentional; but often they seem like evidence of a larger failure to engage, or to attempt to understand the other culture and take seriously its symbols. With this in mind, I've chosen to spell all Turkish names with Turkish spellings and diacritical marks, even though this may seem cumbersome to an Anglophone reader.

GUIDE TO TURKISH PRONUNCIATION:

The Turkish language uses Latin characters, a handful of which take special diacritical marks. Approximate pronunciations are as follows:

c – hard *j* sound, as in "jar." Turkish example: Cemal, often spelled in English as "Jemal."
ç – *ch* sound, as in "chicken." Turkish example: Çarpanak Island.
ğ – similar to *w* sound, but in practice nearly silent, such that Erdoğan sounds like "Erdowan" or "Erdo-an."
ı – similar to the "schwa" vowel sound, as in the first syllable of "again." Turkish example: the final syllable of Diyarbakır.
ş – *sh* sound, as in "share." Turkish example: Paşa ("Pasha" in English).

ABOUT ARMENIAN TRANSLITERATIONS:

Armenian uses a distinct alphabet, so all transliterations of Armenian words into English are subject to debate. In some cases I have deliberately chosen to render a word in a specific dialect, or opted for the spelling most likely to be used by the group I am describing. For example, the word "Hai," which means "Armenian," is spelled as such in "Camp Haiastan," but in the word "Bolsahay" I have kept the "hay" spelling typical in Turkish-Armenian usage. The most attentive Armenian-speaking readers will notice inconsistency in my rendering of the Armenian *oo* vowel sound. I have rendered it *u* in some cases and *oo* in others, depending on my own sense of how a given spelling will be interpreted by an English-speaking reader.

PART ONE

Diaspora

- 1 -

When We Talk About What Happened

I HAD NEVER, NOT FOR A MOMENT, IMAGINED TURKEY AS A PHYSICAL place. Certainly not a beautiful place. But it was all I could do to get through my first taxi ride from the Istanbul airport into the city—the first of perhaps a hundred on that route, as I came and went and came back again and again over the span of four years before I was finished—without letting the driver see me cry. I shifted a bit so that my face would not be visible in the rearview mirror.

The sight of water was what did it. Istanbul is a city laced by three seas: the Marmara, the Bosphorus Strait, and the Black Sea. This struck me as utterly absurd. From as early as I knew anything, I had known Turkey only as an idea: a terrifying idea, a place filled with people I should despise. Somehow, through years of attending Armenian genocide commemorations and lectures about Turkey's denial of the genocide, of boycotting Turkish products, of attending an Armenian summer camp whose primary purpose seemed to be to indoctrinate me with the belief that I should fight to take back a fifth of the modern Turkish state—somehow in all of that, it never occurred to me to wonder what Istanbul, or the rest of Turkey, looked like. And here it was, a magnificent, sea-wrapped city, as indifferent to my imagination as I had been to its reality.

Was it anger I felt, something like what James Baldwin described when he recalled descending in a plane to the American South for the first time and seeing the stunning red hills of Georgia below him? "This earth had acquired its color from the blood that dripped down from the trees," Baldwin wrote. I felt something like that, and the thought that now formed in a place I didn't know I still had within me was: how, after everything they've done, do they get to have a place that looks like this?

No, that's not true. Anger was only what I was supposed to feel, what I perhaps even hoped to rekindle, when I arrived in Turkey, alone, looking out the window as the water chased the road all the way to my hotel. What I actually felt was loss. Not the loss of a place, of a physical homeland—that was for others to mourn. This had never been my homeland. The loss I felt was the loss of certainty, a soothing certainty of purpose that in childhood had girded me against life's inevitable dissatisfactions; a certainty that as a college student and later as a journalist in New York City had started to fray, gradually and then drastically; a certainty whose fraying began to divide me uncomfortably from the group to which I belonged, from other Armenians. The embracing, liberating expanse of Istanbul's waters, and the bridges that crossed them, and the towers on hills that rose up and swept down in every direction, made me realize upon sight that I had spent years of emotional energy on something I had never seen or tried to understand.

This was 2005. I had come to Turkey that summer because I am Armenian and I could no longer live with the idea that I was supposed to hate, fear, and fight against an entire nation and people. I came because it had started to feel embarrassing to refuse the innocent suggestions of American friends to try a Turkish restaurant on the Upper East Side, or to bristle when someone returned from an adventurous Mediterranean vacation, to brood silently until the part about how much they loved Turkey was over. I came because being Armenian had come to feel like a choke hold, a call to conformity, and I could find no greater way to act against this and to claim a sense of myself as an individual than to come here, the last and most forbidden place.

Does it sound like I'm exaggerating? Is there such a thing as nationalism that is not exaggerated?

* * *

WHEN WE TALK about what happened, there are very few stories that, once sifted through memory, research, philosophy, ideology, and politics, emerge unequivocal. But there are two things I know to be true.

One: I know that if your grandmother told you that she watched as her mother was raped and beheaded, you would feel something was yours to defend. What is that thing? Is it your grandmother you are defending? Is it the facts of what happened to her that you are defending, a page in an encyclopedia? Something as intangible as honor? Is it yourself that you are defending? If the story of the brutality that your grandmother encountered were denied or diminished in any way, you would feel certain basic facts of your selfhood extinguished. Your grandmother, who loved you and soothed you, your grandmother whose existence roots you in the world, fixes you somewhere in geography and history. Your grandmother feeds your imagination in a way that your mother and father do not. Imagination is farsighted; it needs distance to discern and define things. If somebody says no, what your grandmother suffered was not really quite as heinous as you're saying it is, they have said that your existence is not really so important. They have said nothing less than that you don't exist. This is a charge no human being can tolerate.

Two: I know that if somebody tells you that you belong to a terrible group of people, you will reject every single word that follows with all the force of your mind and spirit. What if somebody says to you that your history is ugly, your history is not heroic, your history does not have beauty in it? Not only that, you don't know your history. What you have been taught by your mother and your father and your teachers, it's false. You will retreat to a bomb shelter in your brain, collapse inward to protect yourself, because what has been said to you is nothing less than that your entire understanding of who you are is in danger. They will have said to you that your existence is without value. You, who wondered now and then what the meaning of your life was, who made a soft landing place for those worries by allowing yourself to feel a certain richness about where you came from and who and what came before you, will be left empty. The story you thought you were a part of does not exist. Neither do you exist.

Those accusations and their consequences are the first truths we must recognize when we talk about what happened between Armenians and Turks in the Ottoman Empire in 1915. A century after those events,

Armenians and Turks—in Turkey, in Armenia, and especially in the widespread diasporas of both countries—believe in two radically different accounts of what happened. "Believe." It is not a matter of faith, yet it might as well be for the power that these clashing narratives hold.

What did happen? I will tell you—but I am Armenian. It is almost impossible for me to talk about this history. Not because I find it painful to talk about—for me to claim that particular pain would be self-indulgent—but because the terms of the conversation have evolved to leave me no satisfactory options. To tell the Armenian version of the story goes against every instinct in me, not because I disagree with it—I do not—but because I know that even if I wanted to believe that the thing in question did not fit the definition of genocide, it would be impossible for me to find my way into that belief. Even if you wanted to believe that I am objective, it would be impossible for you to do so. I also know the pleasure of healthy contrarianism; so when I encounter an outsider who has been intrigued by the Turkish version of this history, I understand his desire to fancy himself open to an alternative point of view. But then I find myself inflamed, needing to convince him all the more. I am doomed to be what is known as an unreliable narrator. I hate the way it feels.

Newspaper articles dispense with the controversy in the first or final paragraph of any news report concerning Turkey and Armenia:

"Turkey denies that the deaths constituted genocide, contending the toll has been inflated and the casualties were victims of civil war. It says Turks also suffered losses in the hands of Armenian gangs" (AP).

"Turkey accepts that many Christian Armenians were killed by Ottoman Turks but denies that up to 1.5 million died and that it amounts to genocide, as Armenia views it" (Reuters).

"The Turkish government says massacres took place in the context of clashes that related to Armenian groups supporting Russia against Turkey during World War I" (Bloomberg).

This expository shrug is the peace that copyeditors the world over have made with the issue that, more than any other, defines the collective psychology of Armenians and of Turks, defines their educations, the development of their cultures, their political horizons, and—let me not call it any less than it is—their souls. Because what else but your soul can we speak of when, one hundred years later in your otherwise liberal and tolerant life, the very sound of the name of a country makes your head blur and your limbs tighten?

Now and then governments get involved, by participating in what Armenians refer to as "recognition." In my life, this general word, "recognition," with its various potential applications in the vast and flexible English language, had by the time I was eleven or twelve come to denote, with Pavlovian consistency, only one thing: recognition of the Armenian genocide.

Recognition: It is sought and secured anywhere possible, from the city council of Milan to the parliament of New South Wales, Australia. It has been granted in the form of official resolutions, commemorative statements, and board decisions from institutions large and small, including the European Union and at least twenty countries, forty-three US states, various American cities from Santa Fe to Minneapolis, Mayor Michael Bloomberg, and the *New York Times*. Their usage of the word genocide is tracked on lists that are ranked and counted each year in the run-up to April 24, Armenian genocide remembrance day.

For Armenians, recognition is not only institutional; tacit acknowledgment is expected on an individual basis, too. There was the thesis committee in college who reviewed my eighty-page paper about—what else could it be about?—the genocide; and there were friends (the subject has a way of coming up if you are Armenian) and boyfriends, too, and God help them if they tried to tease or argue.

Recognition means all of that, but what it really means is the United States Congress, that mysterious holdout, at once powerfully stubborn and surprisingly malleable and, as of yet, unwilling to fully appease the Armenians. Recognition means an official shift in terminology by the US president and the State Department, and one administration after another has withheld reprieve. On another level of importance, separated by an order of magnitude that straddles the realms of the possible and the inconceivable, recognition means Turkey.

To some Armenians, recognition means reparations from Turkey: to the true zealots, land; to the slightly more pragmatic, money. To most, it simply means the official usage of the word genocide. To me, it came to mean that I could no longer stand to attend any Armenian gathering, because it seemed that whether it was a poetry reading, a concert, or even a sporting match, it was always, ultimately, about the genocide.

Or was it? At some point I started to wonder. Not about what had happened, exactly, and not about whether the term genocide was applicable. It is clear that between 1915 and 1923, in Ottoman Turkey, a history-shifting number of Armenians, probably between eight hundred thousand and one million, were killed outright or driven to death on the watch of a government that was supposed to protect them; another million or so survived deportation to the Syrian desert or fled just in time to avoid it. These events echoed but exceeded earlier pogroms against Armenians, in the 1890s and 1909. The violence happened in fits and starts and was entangled with, though not fully explained by, the circumstances of World War I; and was complicated by the degrees to which different regional leaders throughout Turkey obeyed or defied central orders. In a few of the hundreds of towns and villages affected, Armenian nationalist committees seeking greater rights or independence staged violent resistance, and as a result, about thirty thousand Turks and Kurds were killed by Armenians, too. Of the 2.5 million Armenians then living in the Ottoman Empire, a few thousand men in border cities joined the Russian army against the Turks. When the fighting was over, only two hundred thousand Armenians were left in Ottoman lands, lands Armenians had called home for twenty centuries. Armenians had faced genocide. And the empire that had contained and then expelled them was itself dissolved and reborn as the Republic of Turkey.

What I started to wonder about was whether "recognition"—propagating the usage of the word genocide to every corner of the world like a smallpox shot—was what we really needed. Arguments for recognition spoke of "justice" or "honoring the memory," but these had turned into hollow platitudes for me. Claims that human rights were at stake seemed disingenuous; and when Armenian lobbying groups yoked the cause to a platform of saving Darfur, it seemed motivated more by PR than conscience. Then there was that well-intentioned but unattainable promise, the favorite argument of first and last resort, repeated over and over by scholars and laymen alike: "Never again." That if a tragedy were recognized by the world, if massacre were transfigured into punishment and compensation, such a horror would not be repeated. Doesn't all evidence suggest that this is untrue?

Let me put it less coldly: I wondered whether our obsession with genocide recognition was worth its emotional and psychological price. I wondered whether there was a way to honor a history without being suffocated by it, to belong to a community without conforming to it, a way to remember a genocide without perpetuating the kind of hatred that gave rise to it in the first place. And as I questioned the underlying needs that drove my own community, I wanted to understand what drove Turks to cling to their view. Why couldn't they admit it? This was the simple (or simplistic) question that took me to Turkey.

In both Armenian and Turkish, a particular phrase signals the start of a story: "There was and there was not." In Armenian, *Gar u chgar.* In Turkish, *Bir varmış bir yokmuş.* There was, and also there was not, a long time ago, in a place far away, an old man, a talking horse, a magical kingdom. Once there was, and once there wasn't. It is an acknowledgment not only of the layers and complexities of truth in a given story, but of the subordination of a storyteller to the tale she tells. It is my way of saying that this is where we find ourselves now—locked in a clash of narratives that confuses outsiders, frustrates officials, stifles economies, and warps identities—and no matter what was or was not, this is where we must begin.

- 2 -

Summer Camp, Franklin, Massachusetts, 1989

Wednesdays at Camp Haiastan were debate night, which I always looked forward to. We would have just finished dinner by then, an orderly affair where boys and girls aged eight to fifteen sat at picnic tables in the Mess Hall sharing platters of the menu du jour, maybe burgers or grilled cheese or lasagna and garlic bread. Inside the long, white-shingled building, at the head of each table hung a ghostly, blurred photo of a soldier wielding a gun. There was General Antranig, Kevork Chavush, Armen Garo, and even a woman, Sose *Mayrig*, Mother Sose, strapped with a vest of bullets. These were the early heroes of the Armenian Revolutionary Federation (ARF), the organization whose youth branch ran our camp. The Armenians in these photos had fought against the Ottoman army in the years leading up to World War I.

Before we ate, everyone stood and chanted the Armenian grace in a prepubescent chorus:

Jashagetsookkhaghaghootyampuzgeragoorusvorbadrasdyalehme-zeedyarnehorhnyalehdereebarkevusyoor. Amen.

Although all of us were Armenian, we were also entirely American, and many of the kids did not speak the bewildering language of their ancestors; most were descendants of Armenians who had arrived in the United States three generations prior, so a cacophony of Boston, Long

Island, and New Jersey accents lent our daily recitations all the convincingness of a Hanukkah blessing in Houston.

Camp Haiastan (the name means "Armenia" in Armenian) had been around for decades by the time I got there in the 1980s. A circle of fourteen faded wooden cabins sat at the center of a hundred acres, along with a pool, a large pond covered with lily pads, a basketball court, and cushions of fields and paths and forests that made camp feel like a kingdom apart from the Massachusetts neighbors just a few minutes down the road.

Each morning at camp began with the ceremonial raising of two flags: American and Armenian. In the cabin circle, lined up before a statue of the Armenian revolutionary fighter Karekin Nejdeh, we first sang "My Country, 'Tis of Thee." Then we sang "Gamavorin Kaylerkuh," March of the Volunteers, an anthem of the ARF:

> Forward, immortals of a martyred race!
> Armored in six centuries of unforgotten vengeance,
> Upon the far mountaintops of our fatherland
> Let us go plant the tricolored flag.

Even those who didn't understand the Armenian lyrics understood, somehow, that the fatherland we were always singing about was not merely the small Soviet republic on the map. And I, it should be said, sang louder than anyone.

In the evening, we lowered the flags to "America the Beautiful," followed by the Armenian national anthem. On special song nights, we treated the lyrics of Ottoman-era battle hymns as dramatic texts. Some of these songs were lively entreaties to action; others were slow laments for revolutionaries who had fought and died. One year, my cabin was assigned to perform "Menk Angeghdz Zinvor Enk"—We Are Sincere Soldiers—and I played a plastic flute and led my cabinmates down the aisle and up to the stage. We were twelve-year-old girls sporting Champion sweatshirts and oversized men's boxer shorts with the waistbands turned down, which was the fashion that year. After a somber procession, we lined up like a small platoon and sang all four verses.

In my normal life, at elementary school in New Jersey, I was not what you would call an outgoing child, or a popular one. I was too tall too soon, and although I see now from photos that I was thin as a winter sapling, I felt like a clumsy giant, and was too shy to be helped even by my mother's well-designed efforts at assertiveness training. ("You can have McDonald's french fries if you go up to the counter and order them yourself. All you need to say is, 'One small french fries, please.'" I couldn't do it.) At camp, I still felt awkward, but at least one of my social handicaps was removed: I looked like all the other kids—dark hair and dark eyes, and a nose I hadn't yet grown into, a nose that would have many competitors here for the nickname "Gonzo," a taunt I had suffered at school. At camp I felt, if not exactly "in," at least the possibility of belonging.

That possibility was strong enough to keep me going throughout the other fifty weeks of the year. In between summers at Camp Haiastan, during the school term, I did everything I could to conjure the place. In those days before the Internet or digital photography, I contented myself by making pencil sketches from memory—the benches under a stand of pine trees, the entry gate with a sign that said "Paree Kalousd"—Welcome, in Armenian. Once, sitting on the floor of my bedroom, I spent hours drawing a minutely detailed map of the entire campground, attempting not to miss a single detail, from the swimming pool pump to the torn basketball nets.

I trafficked in a constant stream of letters and packages with my girlfriends from camp, and I was not alone in feeling that these friends—Armenian friends—were special, more valuable. This was a sentiment that we shared bluntly in the pages of the camp newsletter, a yearbook of stories, poems, and lists of favorite things about camp, published at the end of each session. I saved all of these newsletters, storing them in a box in my parents' garage, and when I discovered them recently, thick, stapled stacks of purple mimeographs, I saw that the theme was repeated like a collective agreement that had to be constantly reaffirmed lest it be questioned: Armenian friends are different from *odar* friends.

Odar is an adjective that means "different" or "foreign"; but it is also used as a noun, a disparaging one, meaning "not one of us"—not Armenian. As in: "She married an *odar*." It was one of the handful of words that even non-Armenian-speaking children at camp loved to invoke. (Others included *vardig*, for "panties," *vorig*, for "bottom," and, for reasons too complicated to explain here, *madzun*, which is the Armenian word for "yogurt.")

"It's hard for odars to understand Camp and why we love it so much here, however if you could make any odar Armenian for two days, they would understand," wrote one camper in the newsletter. "No other race has anything like us. . . . Never lose touch with your Armenian friends because when your odar friends let you down, it will be your Armenian friends who come through in the end."

The other popular theme was collective destruction. "It is fun to be at Camp Haiastan because you can learn lots of things and learn about how the Armenians died," wrote a girl who was new that year. "Today we learned about the Armenian case and talked about our feelings and how we felt when the Turks killed the Armenians."

Many of the newsletter entries imagined genocide. Poems told of orphaned children ("A red, so red / drips so endless / Why, Daddy? Why?") or national liberation ("But just when they think they've got us all / we will rebuild / One day an Armenian will find another, / and red, blue, and orange will raise high / And not another Armenian will have to cry.").

A poem by one of the counselors, in which a billiard table served as a metaphor for Armenian history, climaxed with the lines, "Is it the stick / Behind the white ball / Which forces him to do evil? / Or is it the Turk behind the stick?"

And from a distant relation of mine, eleven years old then, now an intellectual property lawyer in Manhattan: "Keeping the Armenian nation alive is a hard task. But doesn't it bother you when they say 'What is Armenian?' If you learn the language, if you learn the traditions, and most importantly fight for your freedom, you will see positive results."

But if you stopped by at the right time of day and didn't stay too long, Camp Haiastan might have been just another wholesome East Coast retreat with a name that sounded vaguely Native American. We learned to swim and went canoeing. We made macramé bracelets in arts and crafts classes (in the colors of the Armenian flag, naturally) and attended Saturday night socials where, in between 1980s pop songs, we linked pinkies and stomped around for hours in circle dances derived from the Anatolian *halay* step but reinvented with names like the Michigan Hop or the California Run.

Athletic activities at camp featured games like Capture the Flag, in which sections of the campgrounds were named for World War I battles the Armenians had fought: we raced from Sardarabad and Bash Abaran (near the pool) to Karmir Blour (over by the infirmary), which referred to a seventh-century BC citadel outside of Yerevan, erected by the last great Urartian king. In this way we merged normal camp activities with Armenian history.

Debate night was held in the Rec Hall. Each week there was an issue to discuss concerning Armenians, usually something about the genocide. Not "was it or wasn't it"—that was not considered a question—but innumerable variations about how Turkey's denial should be fought, or once, on a lighter note, whether Armenia was ready to break free from the Soviet Union.

The Rec Hall smelled like wet wood—summer in the Northeast was humid enough without packing a hundred children and twenty counselors into a room. The youngest campers, eight-year-olds, scrunched Indian-style in tight rows on the floor, while the older kids, fourteen and fifteen, lounged against the back wall, perched atop cabinets where art supplies, board games, and Armenian grammar worksheets were kept.

I was thirteen, and it was my third summer at camp. I normally enjoyed debate night; I had a righteous streak, despite my shyness, and felt a lot more confident arguing about issues than, say, talking to boys at the Saturday night dance. Debates at camp were usually voluntary activities in which teams of campers faced off in front of the rest. But this week's debate was different. We had a special guest speaker, an ARF representative from a nearby chapter. He was an Armenian man, barely older than the counselors, perhaps twenty-five, which would have made him the most senior figure in the room aside from the camp director. And although he was dressed as casually as the rest of us, in a T-shirt and shorts, with an unshaven face and wavy black hair overdue for a haircut, he did not appear relaxed. From the moment he stood up, he twitched with impatience, bouncing on his heels and scanning the room. It seemed like we were keeping him from some clearly more urgent business.

"Tonight we are here to discuss what we are willing to sacrifice to achieve Hai Tahd," he began.

Hai Tahd is generally translated as the Armenian Cause (technically the Armenian "Case"). We treated it not as two words that somebody had decided to put together, but like a basic truth, as fundamental as gravity or the sunrise. The Armenian Cause was the official ideological platform of the ARF. Versions of it date back to the ARF's early days. The group was founded in 1890, when Armenian activists in the Caucasus began to organize to improve the lot of Armenians living in the Ottoman Empire; it quickly expanded to chapters all over the world and still takes seats in parliamentary elections in Armenia, Lebanon and Nagorno-Karabakh. Its junior branch, the Armenian Youth Federation (AYF), was founded in Watertown, Massachusetts, in 1933, and opened Camp Haiastan in 1951. Together, the ARF and the AYF are known as the Dashnak Party, shorthand for *Hai Heghapokhakan Dashnaktsutiun*.

In my camp days, Hai Tahd meant (and still means) the following: gaining recognition of the Armenian genocide, reclaiming the formerly Armenian-inhabited provinces of eastern Turkey, and reunifying the other patches of historic Armenia that are now part of Georgia and Azerbaijan. We were always talking about Hai Tahd. It was in our language lessons, our history classes, our songs, and our debates. But since we chatted only in English at camp, a non-Armenian visitor overhearing these conversations might be struck by the Tourette's-like interjection of a sudden greeting—"Hi, Todd"—making its way into otherwise intelligible sentences. Who was Todd?

Most of the campers attended Dashnak youth group meetings throughout the school year where they learned about things like Hai Tahd, but I had never attended those meetings. Each summer, when I returned from camp, I asked my parents if I could join a nearby chapter, and although they didn't reject the idea outright, my request never came to anything. (They had sent me to Camp Haiastan not for political reasons but only because some of my cousins were going there.) I understood Armenian—it was my first language—but Hai Tahd was the Western Armenian pronunciation. In my dialect, Eastern Armenian, it would be Hai Dat. Thus the words Hai Tahd did not communicate anything to me. I sometimes imagined my elementary school classmate, Todd Twersky, showing up unannounced at the perimeter of the campground. Hi, Todd.

The speaker continued. "The question is, is violence in the name of Hai Tahd justified?"

"An eye for an eye!" one of the male counselors shouted. Cheers went up.

"The ends justify the means!" somebody else called out.

Before long, the room was flaring with arguments. At first I thought of the old soldier photos hanging in the Mess Hall. But gradually, taking in the voices around me, I realized they were not talking about violence in the past. This was something new. The speaker was talking about a group called the Lisbon Five.

I had no clue who the Lisbon Five were. I was, however, a geography buff, the sort of child who made a sport of memorizing capital cities, so I knew Lisbon was in Portugal. What could this possibly have to do with us?

I looked at one of my cousins sitting to my left but got no signal of whether she was as lost as I was. I noticed a younger camper, Julie, weeping quietly while her friend rubbed her back—but then, Julie was always crying about something.

How did everybody know what this man was talking about? Although I was confused, it was clear from the intensity of the debate that asking for clarification was out of the question. I was embarrassed that my parents had not taught me such things.

I can't say for sure how much of the story I pieced together that strange evening, how close I came to comprehending the murders that were the subject of our debate, but I got the salient point: five Armenian guys blew up a building to get back at Turkey.

In 1983, these men, calling themselves the Armenian Revolutionary Army, had planted a bomb inside a Turkish embassy residence in Lisbon, Portugal. Although their primary target was the Turkish chargé d'affaires, it was his wife who was killed, along with a Portuguese policeman—and all five of the Armenian terrorists. Throughout the 1980s, the same network, and a similar group called the Armenian Secret Army for the Liberation of Armenia (ASALA), carried out more than eighty attacks against Turkish targets all over the world, including a few in the United States, killing forty-six people and injuring some three hundred. Their stated goal was to force Turkey to take responsibility for the genocide and compensate Armenians with land and money.

As the debate continued, things grew chaotic. A folded-up metal chair slid to the ground with a clatter. The glass on the sliding doors fogged up. Younger kids squirmed as the older campers and counselors argued on. Some said the men were martyrs and that Turkish denial of the genocide was too powerful for softer measures. Now and then the prevailing "eye for an eye" sentiment was challenged by something along the lines of "two wrongs don't make a right." Others spoke of the horrors their grandparents had endured, and insisted that Armenians had the right to seek retribution. I was baffled by the certainty around me. How had everybody gotten to be so sure of themselves, so sure that it was okay to kill people to make a point?

The speaker had become seriously agitated, spinning from an argument with one person to a question from another, and as the room grew hotter, his wavy hair coiled into tight curls. I was scared of him. I had never been this close to violence, even the idea of violence, before. Then he stopped talking long enough to wipe the sweat from his forehead, and all sound in the room seemed to go mute. Slowly, he looked up with an expression so hurt and raw that I wanted to enter into it. The passion in his eyes, the way he had taken on everything so personally, like it was all his responsibility, had hypnotic force. I decided to try on the idea, see how it felt. Tried to hear my own voice saying *Yes, it made sense to bomb those people. They brought it on themselves. They chose to represent Turkey. That makes them murderers, too.* I transported myself right into the speaker's eyes. I wanted to be a part of whatever was in them. That I could not quite get there felt almost, if not completely, like a failing of my own.

Suddenly one of the counselors, a young woman from San Francisco with a bohemian air about her, took a step forward. She had been leaning against a wall on the right side of the room, arms crossed, until she could no longer contain herself. When she tried to speak her voice collapsed into a sob. "You people are all crazy!" she shouted. Everybody turned to look at her. With her face swelling to a red, wet mess, hair sticking to her cheeks as she tried to wipe her tears away, she forced a path through the seated children and ran out of the room.

You people are all crazy. You people, she had said. She had been one of us, until she chose for a moment not to be. In that moment the choice revealed itself as binary. Years later, it was not the shock of learning about the Lisbon Five that defined the evening for me. It was the explosive anger of the counselor from California—or rather, not her anger, but the clarity it revealed. It was not the same as the certainty that the others had been proclaiming. Her reaction came from somewhere deeper than camp, than family, than being Armenian. We had been taught to believe that nothing went deeper than the fact that we were Armenian, but in that moment I sensed, with a feeling too hazy to identify as either disappointment or relief, that this wasn't necessarily true.

Two decades later, in Armenian communities from Los Angeles to Paris to Beirut, ARF members would still gather each July to commemorate the anniversary of the Lisbon bombing, to celebrate the five men—aged nineteen to twenty-one—who killed a Turkish diplomat's wife. A priest would say a blessing. The men would be called martyrs and heroes, and about this there would be no debate at all.

- 3 -

"How Did They Kill Your Grandparents?"

WE SAT IN THE PARLOR, WAITING. FINALLY AN OLD WOMAN APPEARED in the doorway. She wore a polyester dress onto which ivory lace had been added at the wrists, and a pink crocheted shawl covered her shoulders. Using a walker, she lurched across the small room. She tried to smile up at us while also keeping an eye on her feet. When she reached the chair that had been set up for her, two members of the nursing home staff held her arms as she lowered herself into a tentative crouch. They redirected her several times until finally she landed in the seat.

Then her gaze snapped up at the assembled visitors. With her eyes wide open, she said in Armenian, "Tajik al gah hednerin?"—Are there Turks among them, too?

"No!" several staff members called out.

The woman was Onorik Eminian, a ninety-six-year-old resident of the Armenian Home for the Aged in Flushing, Queens. It was March 2008. As part of the annual genocide recognition campaign preceding April 24, a public relations firm had invited journalists to hear eyewitness accounts from the home's elderly residents who had survived deportation. The event was put on by the local chapter of the Knights and Daughters of Vartan, a fraternal organization named for Vartan Mamikonian, an

Armenian military hero and saint who led the Armenians against the Persian army in AD 451.

I looked around at the other journalists—a few reporters from Queens neighborhood papers, one from Connecticut, and a journalism student from Columbia University. Their faces were blank; only the student and I were Armenian, and the others had not understood Onorik's opening remark. The public relations consultant, who was not Armenian, had not gotten it either until one of the aides translated for her. Her face lit up.

"Did everybody hear that? She asked whether there were any Turks present!"

Then, the sound of pens scribbling.

I had come as a reporter, but I didn't intend to write about the event for any newspaper. I'd had it in mind for some time to visit this nursing home to talk to the survivors in residence. My growing ambivalence toward the diaspora's genocide recognition efforts was starting to worry me, and I thought the quickest way to remedy this would be to cut through all the lobbying and hateful rhetoric and simply sit down with some elderly Armenians to hear what they had suffered. But before I managed to arrange a private visit to the nursing home, I received a press release inviting journalists to this event. So much for avoiding politics. That is how I found myself disembarking at the end of the subway line and wending my way, Google map in hand, to this quiet street in Queens. From a distance, I noticed an Armenian flag waving atop a pole at the end of the block. It stood alongside a redbrick colonial-style home with gabled windows, set oddly amid the tall box-buildings of Flushing.

The executive director was Aghavni Ellian (she went by Aggie), a trim, sixty-something woman who spoke with an extraordinary outer-boro rasp. The home was founded in 1948, Aggie told us. One day, at the Armenian church on 187th Street in Washington Heights, a little old Armenian lady sat crying on the steps after Sunday service. A woman named Siranoush Sanossian noticed her and asked why she was crying. "I have only one son and his wife threw me out," the woman had said. "I have nowhere to go." Sanossian took the woman in. Later, with the help of friends, she found a small house in Queens with just a few bedrooms for elderly Armenians who needed a place to live. The project was soon incorporated, and in 1954 moved to its current location, which was licensed as a seventy-nine-bed retirement home. It was an elegant old house, its huge backyard brimming with cherry trees in blossom.

The home had many genocide survivors in residence. "Every year we lose a few," said Aggie. "In fact, two of the people on your list"—we had each been given a stapled pamphlet containing the names, photos, and birthplaces of the survivors we would meet—"will not be able to join us today after all."

The day's event was not unique, she told us; it was a matter of course to involve the survivors in genocide commemoration events, whether at Times Square on April 24, or in Washington, DC. Some of the residents had attended a hearing of the House Foreign Affairs Committee on the genocide resolution a few months earlier. "We also bring some of the other elderly Armenians that like to come and who feel that they are survivors, and I think in their own way they are."

"They sit in the front row and they get recognition," added Linda, the PR consultant. "It's really great."

ONORIK EMINIAN WAS born in 1912, in İzmir, a Western coastal city in Turkey. According to the pamphlet, she was rescued by the Red Cross and put in an orphanage in Turkey, then "somehow she was transferred to Greece" before coming to the United States in 1930.

"Onorik, would you like to explain how your father died?" Aggie asked her in Armenian.

Onorik's voice emerged with the round, ringing timbre of an old-fashioned telephone. "Again, you want to hear it?" She paused and then added, "Just as long as there are no Turks here."

"No, no, there are none here!" came a chorus. A staff member explained to us that on a recent visit to Washington, the elderly had come face-to-face with Turkish protesters.

Linda, the PR consultant, tried to move things forward. "Onorik, can you please tell us what happened to you and your family during the Armenian genocide?"

"Every time I remember I start shaking," said Onorik. She drank some water, sat quietly for a bit, and then said, "Kleenex."

A whisper went up—what did she say? Linda called out for a translation.

Onorik had said "Kleenex" in English, but it had sounded like a foreign word to those who could not switch languages with the flickers of an elderly immigrant's mind. Everybody stared at Onorik.

"She said 'Kleenex,'" someone explained.

"Onorik, how old were you?" asked Linda.

"I am fifty-one." She was ninety-six.

"I was a little girl, I was playing ball, and my aunt and my uncle went to get the license, they were going to marry. It was a Saturday morning exactly, and then I saw the dogs on their horses, running, and holding knives."

"She's referring to the Turks," Aggie slipped in.

"All of a sudden my grandmother grabbed me and pulled me inside. I said what's the matter grandma? And she said it's the Turks, they'll take you! Come inside!

"So we went in. We had a beautiful big yard in the house. And next door the neighbor, they put a stepladder and she said take the kid, we can go to the church or something and be protected. So they put me in the stepladder, I climbed next door, the building to the roof. My grandmother started to cry looking for her daughter. So we went to the church. It was a Protestant church!" she remembered suddenly. Onorik had settled into English now, but her sentences rolled over one another as though someone had shuffled a set of notes and handed them back out of order.

"It was so crowded inside there was no space. We had to sit outside with my grandmother, and she was crying and crying.

"So finally I don't know how it happened, that part I don't remember, my uncle, my grandmother, my aunt, we went home. The doors closed, the windows closed. But all of a sudden they knocked the door. My grandmother says don't touch the door.

"The Turk he says to me, pulls my hair, where's your father? I said I don't know, he didn't come home yet. And he says don't you lie to me. And he holds my hair and we look in every room, underneath the beds, the closets. So there was two Turks. One started walking and the other says *efendi, efendi*, see this stepladder maybe they're hiding downstairs.

"And they take me down and say where's your father? I say I don't know, he didn't come home yet. They slapped me a couple times, pulled my hair, I had long hair. My mother says leave her, she's only a kid, why are you hitting her? So we went down those steps and my father over there says to me shhhh. And they heard him and they beat him up and brought him upstairs. And my mother was feeding the baby, we had a little baby, and they said why are you hiding your husband? And my mother says I didn't know he was home. And they beat him and he said leave my family alone. And I was there crying. And my mother sitting feeding the baby. And the baby cried. So they took the baby, my baby brother who was little, maybe one month two months old, they took the baby so my father got mad. So they slapped my father very bad. They took my father, they left, and I was crying, crying, I want my father, I want my father. The Turk said you want your father? You're gonna have it later on not now.

"So then me, my mother, my grandmother, and my baby brother we all sitting crying and my father says don't cry honey I will be back, and when I come back I'll bring you figs. They took my father they went. I don't know how long. I don't know, I'm a kid.

"Those two they came back. Listen this. They came back. And we opened the door and he said you want your father? And I said yes, where is he! And they opened a little bag and they opened the bag and they pulled out my father's jacket, the sleeve of his jacket. There's your father. And also the pants. There's your father.

"And my mother said don't you feel shamed a little bit? You're showing this little kid what you did to the father? He said you talk too much you gonna get it, too.

"They brought the jacket and the pants and it was all blood." With those words Onorik started crying. The attendants tried to comfort her.

After a moment she said, "So anyway. That's all right. So this is it. They killed my father. So my mother starts crying, my grandmother, and I was crying, too."

And then she paused, a bit confused, and a staff member prompted her from across the room: "They killed your father, they killed your mother, and they killed your little brother . . ."

Onorik repeated the part about the bag of clothes again. And then she continued, "I kept saying my father my father my father! And my mother said she's a little girl, don't hit her anymore she doesn't know what's happening and they said you have a big mouth you gonna get it, too." And then Onorik gestured a shooting motion with her hands, and in a falsetto burst she said, "pop pop pop pop pop pop they killed my mother too right in front of me." And then her grandmother and baby brother.

Then they hit her with the butt of the rifle. "I got witness for you," Onorik said, and pointed her jerking finger at a scar between her eyes.

"I go next door because I was really blood. She takes the salt and puts it with a handkerchief." She meant the neighbor, I guess.

"See, this mark, it didn't go away, and I'm fifty-one years old, very soon I'm gonna be fifty-two . . ."

Someone asked her to explain how she escaped, but things started to get really mixed up and Aggie said, "I think this is enough." But then she added, "Did they take you to an orphanage?"

"You want the orphanage, too?" said Onorik.

"How did you get to Greece?"

"Oh, long story, I'm gonna tell you."

She began a confusing chapter about disguising her uncle in a dress and a head scarf.

"Just tell us how you got to Greece."

"Now I'm going to tell you in full!" she said.

A jumble of details followed, something about her father making donations to German organizations, her sister, American flags, boats, then somehow she ended up in Greece at an American orphanage.

"God bless American navy I tell you, they saved my life, that's why I'm alive today, fifty-one years old."

Onorik was stuck on the part about how they got to go to the ship. And how on their way to the ship they saw that the young girls and the teacher—which young girls and which teacher was not clear—were tied to trees in front of the orphanage, naked, their heads shaved. She used the Turkish word for stark naked, çırılçıplak.

"The ship was there, we see it, the ship was there, we're gonna go . . ."

The story became incoherent. We sat still and waited. The staff was trying to tell Onorik it was okay. "Thanks, sweetie, that was enough." But now she was inside it completely and did not want to stop.

"American navy gave us bread, an Army blanket for five children. First they put us in a little boat that took us to the large ship. They said to us, 'Don't worry, the Turks aren't gonna get you anymore.' One blanket five children. Italian bread, the square Italian bread, we had to eat, four of us, that one bread.

"It was a lady, an American lady, Miss Kishman, she says children don't cry, I'm going to go get a little orphanage and take you over there. And they teach us 'My Country, 'Tis of Thee.'

"And the American navy says don't worry, we're here, the Turks can't come for you anymore."

She repeated these few themes over and over. The boat, the navy, the naked women in the yard. Wandering the caverns of her ninety-six-year-old brain in search of the memories of a three-year-old girl.

Then she described seeing a priest stabbed through the orphanage window. As she circled around her story, the room filled with an awareness that nobody was in control anymore. Neither was anyone in a hurry. We were with Onorik completely. But all the same, it was a Sunday afternoon in Queens, press releases had been sent out, and the organizers seemed to feel they needed to apologize for the way their painstaking preparation was unraveling into this confusing tale.

Aggie stepped in. "You know, she's told a wonderful story that has been consistent with all the stories she's told us from the onset."

Several staff members were gathered around Onorik, trying to convince her that she had done fine. Onorik felt the pressure of her mandate to perform. That much was obvious. The kindness of the staff members and their devotion to the residents was evident, too. But to set loose such a narration and then try to corral it—well, who could say what to do? Was it kinder to stop her, or to let her talk as long as she needed?

As Onorik was escorted out of the room, gripping her walker, kneading the carpet with it, she turned her head just slightly over her shoulder. "Don't forget, American people the best people!" Her voice gave way to tears again. "American navy saved my life today. And I'm not lying, I got witness, this"—she pointed to her forehead again—"I'm not lying what they did to me!"

Throughout Onorik's story, one of her elder coresidents, Adrineh, sat at her side in silence. Adrineh was ninety-eight. She was born in 1909 in Adapazarı, in northwestern Turkey. Aggie warned us that Adrineh could be ornery; whenever she was asked to repeat the story about what happened to her a very long time ago, Adrineh would get annoyed and snap, "You'd better start remembering what I say."

But the Adrineh we saw now stared dully into the distance. The bags under her eyes hung halfway down her cheeks, elongating her face in a way that reminded me of Munch's *The Scream*.

A case manager working for the home said, "Adrineh, these people are here because they want to ask about how the Turks hurt your family and what you remember about what happened."

"Ask."

The publicist tried. "What was it like during the Armenian genocide when you first saw the Turks? Do you remember what happened?"

Silence.

"How old were you?"

Silence.

"Where were you?"

She sat motionless.

"How old were you? You were a little girl, and then the Turks came. You remember?"

"Yeah." She paused. "They came and killed."

"Killed who?"

"Us, the Armenians. My grandmother had studied at Oxford. My grandfather was a bank director." The staff looked at one another. Nobody was certain what she meant by Oxford, an issue that had apparently come up before.

"So the Turks came and did what?" asked Linda.

Adrineh paused a long time again and then said, "What didn't they do?"

"How did they kill your grandparents?"

"They hit them on the head with rifle butts and threw them into the water." This streamed out of her like one long word.

Then Aggie broke in and explained that the story was really incredible, but that we might not be able to get anything clear from Adrineh today. The staff kept apologizing.

Somebody asked, "What do you want them to do to the Turks?" No answer came, and the question was repeated twice more.

"*Voch mi ban*," Adrineh finally said in Armenian—not a thing.

Then after a long silence and more apologies from the staff, Adrineh smiled broadly and said, "My mother pulled someone's tooth out!" An aide explained to us that this is how they survived, because when someone had a toothache and Adrineh's mother pulled out that person's tooth, it was assumed that the mother was a doctor, and sometimes doctors were spared because they could be of service.

How many years ago had these stories degenerated into this? I wondered. I thought of my own grandmother's long journey into dementia; there were so many switchbacks along the way, and perhaps yesterday or an hour from now Adrineh's command of her story would be entirely different.

We moved upstairs and crowded into a small dining room that held a square table set for eight or ten. It felt like some kind of tea party in an eerie dream; almost everyone in the room was female, and several of the elderly women were seated at the table smiling expectantly at the visitors squeezed before them.

Perouz Kalousdian was ninety-eight years old. She was born in 1909 in Palu, a town on the banks of the Euphrates in what is now Elâzığ, Turkey. She used to be a high-fashion designer, we were told, and she was wearing a flowing red blouse and skirt of her own creation. A murmur of compliments—"beautiful," "what a lovely outfit"—came from the guests, who had been almost entirely silent until then. Perouz nodded, then began without prompting.

"I was six years old when the war happened in my country. So they took all the men, they tied up two together, and they were gone, to Yeprat Ged"—the Euphrates. "It's a river in Armenia." Her voice had all the weight of New York, the husky vernacular to which immigrants from around the world donate upon arrival, a bit of wherever they came from layered on top of whatever they find in Rego Park or Sheepshead Bay.

"So my mother, myself, from a big family there were about four people left. The Turks they took the men, tied two together, and they were gone and never came back. I saw with my own eyes, I was, what, four or five years old?"

Aggie chimed in, "Six."

"I was asking my ma why they doing this? She started to cry, they are going and not coming back. After that they took everything away from us, we were poor for years. Everything the Turks took away from us. They took the men, killed them away, then the poor women and children were left. That's all. They took everything away from us. And this is the truth, and I remember just like today. I never, never forget that."

Perouz had a forceful tone and, unlike the others, she stuck almost entirely to English. As she continued, there were only unresolved threads. A mother disappearing and reappearing, an orphanage in Kharpert and another—or was she describing the same one?—in Aleppo, Syria, 300 miles away. The kaleidoscopic swirl of remembering and forgetting, remembering and forgetting things that you could see only through a pinhole even as they were happening a century ago. Like the other survivors, Perouz seemed to understand that some burden of proof was now teetering on what remained of her memory. What could she do? She might not have even remembered a few years after the fact, when she was ten or twelve, much less ninety years further on. An experience was trapped inside her and, as much as she insisted that she could never forget, she had neither the words nor the details to convey what she remembered. She kept saying, "This is my story. This is my life."

Later I wondered what to make of the possibility of a child walking the miles between Kharpert (the Armenian name for old Harput, modern-day Elâzığ) and Aleppo. In my research, I came across a statement dated October 16, 1915, signed by the American Consul General of Aleppo.

> On the first of June, 3,000 people, mostly women, girls, and children, left Harput, accompanied by 70 policemen. . . .
>
> On the 15th day they were again trodding their way through steep mountains, where the Kurds gathered 150 of the men . . . and taking them to some distance, butchered them. . . . That day another caravan of exiles, only 300 of which were men, from Sivas, Eğin, Tokat joined that from Harput, thus making a bigger caravan, 18,000 all counted. . . .
>
> On the 52nd day they arrived at another village, here the Kurds took from them every thing they had, even their shirts and drawers and for five days the whole caravan walked all naked under the scorching sun. For another five days they did not have a morsel of bread, neither a drop of water . . . their tongues were turned to charcoal. . . . At another place, where there were wells, some women threw themselves into it, as there was no rope and pail to draw water but these were drowned and in spite of that the rest of the people drank from that well, the dead bodies still staying and stinking in it. . . .
>
> On the 70th day, when they reached Aleppo, 35 women and children were remaining from the 3,000 exiles of Harput, 150 women and children from the whole caravan of 18,000.

The statement was dated one week later. I cannot know whether the caravan it described was the same one that Perouz was now trying to find in her own recollection. The document was cited frequently in books about the genocide. State-sponsored historians in Turkey pounced on it as an example of "Allied propaganda." But there was Kharpert and there was Aleppo, and Perouz would have been, indeed, six.

Somebody asked Perouz, "What do you want people to learn from hearing your story?"

"What can they learn? They are here, Turks are there. They feel sorry, that's it. What can they learn? We are in America, we are saved, that's it, they already forgot it. But I never forget it."

Aggie reminded her that she told a committee in Washington that she wants the genocide to be recognized officially. "Oh yeah, they took me there, that's right, I forgot, sorry, I don't remember everything."

I recalled seeing a photograph on the front page of the *New York Times* a few months earlier, the morning after the House Committee on Foreign Affairs had given preliminary approval to the genocide resolution (the bill never made it to the House floor). In the photo, a row of elderly Armenian women sat in wheelchairs in front of a roomful of wonks and lobbyists.

"So you want us to know there was a genocide?" asked Linda.

"Yes. We went to White House."

THE OLDEST WOMAN we met was Hingeni Evrensel. She was one hundred years old. She was born in March 1908 in Ordu, a city near the Black Sea coast famous for its hazelnuts. Her father had a big hazelnut store. She survived thanks to a Muslim family, we were told.

The case manager looked at Hingeni and shouted, slowly, creating the effect of a record playing on the wrong speed at full volume. "Hingeni, *hokis*"—my dear—"this group of people have gathered here today for you to explain how the Turks massacred your family."

"I don't know a single thing, I was a baby" (*Yes hich pan muh chem kider, bebek eyi*).

She said a few more things then, but it was impossible to understand her. Age had burnt the pathways connecting her brain and her voice such that what emerged had the rough texture of language but not the necessary dimensions. Her appearance, too, stood apart from the others, as if she had seen not only a few more years, but a harder life all along. Clumped locks of hair hung from her head in patches. Her face came from another epoch, like a set of antediluvian Armenian chromosomes that had not been passed on to later generations. Or maybe she was ethnically mixed; the town of Ordu had a level of diversity unusual even for the Ottoman Empire. It was the home not only of Turks and Armenians but of a Georgian Muslim minority and the Hemshin people, a mix of Christians and converted Muslims who had Armenian roots. The name Hingeni was not typically Armenian. Her last name, Evrensel, means "universal" in Turkish.

Hingeni's daughter Nadya was sitting next to her. Nadya was also a resident at the home. The director explained to the group that because Hingeni was getting upset thinking about the past, her daughter would tell the story.

Nadya looked like she was in fine health. But when she began to speak, it was incoherent, and one could see that in aging, her mind had fallen far behind the rest of her body. Suddenly she was talking with gusto about the years she spent in nursing school.

The director gently reoriented her to the matter at hand, and then, as though somebody had pressed a button and changed the channel, Nadya said, "Kurd people took the whole house."

"She doesn't know," muttered her mother.

Nadya peered up at the case manager through thick glasses. "You tell it."

"If I knew it, I would tell it," the case manager said.

Now Hingeni, the mother, lifted her head again. "*Badmem*?"—Shall I tell it?

That voice—it was as brittle as the crumbling paper of an ancient manuscript. The beginning and end of each sound she made was faded, and I struggled to detect the meaning in a pileup of half-words, each one disintegrating further into fragments of Armenian, Turkish, perhaps even Kurdish or Arabic or Georgian, I could hardly tell.

"What did they do?" somebody asked her.

"What did they do?" Hingeni repeated. Then she said something that ended with *sürgün*, Turkish for "exile."

Suddenly Hingeni's daughter blurted out, in English, "You know Atatürk? They killed Atatürk. They gave him medication and he thought that it was good medication but—"

The case manager stopped her again and turned our attention toward a woman who had been sitting primly and with excellent posture throughout the discussion, her blue eyes, neatly styled beehive of white hair, and red lipstick making her look younger than the others, something like a genteel southern lady.

She went by Charlotte, an Americanization of the Armenian name Arshalouys, which means "dawn." Charlotte was born in 1912 in a place we were told was Nikhda, possibly what is known now as Niğde, a town on the outskirts of central Turkey's Cappadocia. Like others who left Turkey before Atatürk's 1928 language reforms, she had a story marked by names of places that no longer exist, a living register of Ottoman-era sounds and spellings that are difficult to correlate with their modern replacements.

"Charlotte, now you're going to tell them about your origins and how your family was killed and how you survived and escaped. That's the story you're going to tell them, okay?"

I knew that the point was to keep the elderly speakers from straying to random topics, but I wished, if only to quiet the ready cynic inside me, that this stage direction would cease.

"I hate to go through all that," Charlotte said. "It's sad for me because my mother's children never lived. And I lived. I saw my father at wartime. And that was the end. I just saw him. I had no chance to get acquainted with him. And we suffered hunger, thirst, everything, walking and walking for miles, with my mother. My mother kept pressuring me. *Aghchigus, kich men al, kich men al.*" My girl, a little bit more, a little bit more. "That *kich men al* never ended."

Now and then, as she spoke, her dentures slipped and she paused to wiggle her mouth back into place.

"There was somewhere where we stayed overnight."

"Where did you stay overnight?" the case manager asked.

"I don't know, it was in Turkey. Thank God I had my mother. If I didn't have my mother, how would I have courage? I was eight years old. My dear daughter, she said, bear a little more, a little more, there's going to come an end of this. You're going to have comfort. You're going to have a home. You're going to be happy. So who else did I have to listen to? I never had a father, I lost him. I lived because I had a shirt that they sent to Jerusalem to be blessed. The children did not live in their own country and in their own comfort. I lived through wars and everything. And came to America at the age of ten with my mom. My mother was thirty-three years old. My mother worked so hard doing needlework and bought a house in New York City on Thirty-Third Street, four floors. She went to night school to better her English. Later on, she opened a grocery store and a house. How could she take care of it by herself? She couldn't afford to take care of it. So she asked my permission, 'I'm going to marry an old man so he'll be a good father to you.'"

"Was he Armenian?" I slid in a question. Charlotte seemed completely American to me somehow. Her enunciation in English was as careful as a kindergarten teacher's.

"Yes, of course he was Armenian! And then my mom sold the house. And I was married. I was pretty comfortable. I gave the whole thing to my brother. That house still stands now. That's the memory I live with. I had a wonderful marriage, I had four children, I sent them all to college, and I'm in this home now. That's life. And I had a wonderful life, with all that. And I brought up wonderful children in America."

"Do you ever think about seeing the place where you came from in Turkey?" I asked.

"I do, but I feel I'm in the right place. They have to live their life. I lived mine as well as I could. And I loved it. I learned from every step. And I thank America for it. Because I don't know the other side. And my wonderful mother. She was a nurse in the Kilikia orphanage, my mother, till we came here. I'm so happy I had *here*. Otherwise where would I be?"

"Was your mother being a nurse a reason you were saved?" I was asking questions eagerly now because Charlotte seemed more able than the others to move between her own thoughts and our interjections.

"Yes. My mother was a nurse in the orphanage and my aunt, a college graduate, was a teacher. So that's the way we got away a little bit, to safety. And it wasn't easy. I had an uncle. He brought us over. Otherwise we had no money, how could we come over? We were walking and walking and I was so thirsty. Mom, I can't walk anymore."

"Where were you walking?"

"*Andarneruh, anabadneruh.*" The forests, the deserts.

Suddenly Hingeni, the oldest woman, blurted out, "*Sood eh.*" It's a lie. She repeated this twice. After a while, she said, "*Cheghav*"—which can mean either "that didn't happen" or "it didn't work."

Nobody translated these interjections or asked Hingeni what she was talking about, though the staff could not be blamed for losing track. But there was something performative, even melodramatic about Charlotte's delivery, and I wondered if Hingeni, despite being senile, was responding intuitively with annoyance at these theatrics, trying to express that what Charlotte was saying didn't ring true. Another option: was Hingeni channeling an imagined Turk, denying Charlotte's story? I wish I knew why Hingeni kept saying "*cheghav*," but she seemed so much farther away than a few feet across the table, and I could not bring myself to risk making things more awkward by asking.

Charlotte ignored her. "That *kich men al* never ended," she said again.

The way Charlotte kept repeating this line depressed me, not only because the little girl had to keep walking but because her story had the fixed contours of one she had told a thousand times. It sounded like a story that over the years—and how could it not?—had been shaped by the other stories she had heard and read, and by the context in which such stories are told: a witness stand, a podium in the congressional hall, at the end of a journalist's microphone. It had condensed itself into plaintive one-liners. The rest was inaccessible. The soul wants to connect, to be heard, and to persuade. But the storyteller, having heard herself so many times before, loses faith in the innate power of her experience or in her ability to convey it. The aging brain does not yield to new pathways, and the same hard-beaten roads are trekked over and over, the same few stores of memory squeezed dry and then squeezed again.

Charlotte found another detail. "They took us to a churchyard, and they gave us a little lunch of some kind. Where was the church?" She preempted our question. "I have no idea, I just know there was a church. And we came to America when I was ten—"

"Yes, you told us that already," said the case manager.

"Yes."

THE LAST WOMAN we met was a ninety-four-year-old named Arşalos (the same name as Charlotte's—Arshalouys—but with a Turkish spelling). Her uncle, a doctor, was among the large group of intellectuals killed on April 24, 1915, in Constantinople. Arşalos was clear and direct. She said her family had been elite. She was one year old when they had to leave Şebinkarahisar. Her family, being very well-off, was saved by a wealthy

Turkish family they were friends with. They ended up in Sebastia, modern-day Sivas, and eventually Arşalos settled in Istanbul, from which she emigrated to the United States thirty years ago. She told us that after the war, her mother, an expert in the niceties of table settings, was enlisted to train the people who were responsible for setting the dining tables of none other than Atatürk himself.

At the mention of Atatürk, Hingeni began a chant from across the room. "*Atatürk Turk cher,*" she said—Atatürk wasn't a Turk. What could she possibly mean by this? What combination of brain chemistry and intention, what echo of irretrievable life was triggering these contrarian cries? Soon all the old ladies were making different comments in different languages, now Armenian, now English, now Turkish, each in her own world of time and place and self, their memories filling the room like scene-shifting, cast-swapping, overlapping dreams.

- 4 -

A Real Armenian

IT WAS A VERY LONG TIME BEFORE IT OCCURRED TO ME THAT NONE OF my own grandparents survived the genocide. Nor did any of them not survive. They were simply elsewhere, part of the two million or so Armenians in the world at that time who did not live in the Ottoman Empire. This was a surprise only because the genocide had become central to my understanding of being Armenian. It was almost disappointing to realize, as I did in the gradual and unspecific way in which one learns most things before adulthood, that my family had had nothing to do with it.

I was born in Tehran, as was my father. My mother was born in Tabriz, in the north of Iran, and so were both of her parents. My paternal grandfather came from Tbilisi, Georgia, my paternal grandmother from Mashad, near Iran's eastern edge. My great-grandparents on both sides came from all over the Caucasus region: Tabriz, Maragheh, and Qareh Dagh in northern Iran; Agulis, an ancient Armenian settlement in Nakhichevan; and the mountain town of Nukha, now Shaki, in Azerbaijan.

Yet as far back as anyone knows or can imagine, every last one of us has been Armenian. When I was younger and tried to explain to friends, or to myself, why we called ourselves Armenian instead of Iranian, Georgian, Azeri, or even Russian, I came up with this: "Armenians were always living in these places, but over the years the map changed." Everything about Armenians was always "*always.*" Time itself seemed to begin with us, as we proudly noted that Noah's Ark landed on Mount Ararat (although the mountain is now on Turkey's side of the border, it remains our national symbol).

Although some history books written by Armenians insist that we were the original Indo-Europeans, more humble accounts show that about twenty-seven hundred years ago, a group of people in southeastern Turkey branched off from a kingdom called Urartu, centered around Lake Van, and came to be known as Armenians. The earliest-known reference to Armenians was carved on a rock in northern Iran around 500 BC by the Persian king Darius. On his massive cliffside history scroll, the king described his battles against all the rebellious nations of Mesopotamia; five of those battles were against the Armenians.

For most of the next two millennia, there were Armenian dynasties and kingdoms all over what is now southeastern Turkey, the Caucasus, and northern Iran. A century before the birth of Christ, King Dikran the Great brought the Armenian kingdom to its height: for sixteen years, the domain of Armenia stretched from the Mediterranean to the Caspian Sea. But from then on Armenia shrank and struggled between empires: the Romans and the Parthians; the Byzantines and the Persians; the Ottomans and the Russians. From 1375 until the Soviet Union disintegrated—except for an eighteen-month stretch from 1918 to 1920—Armenians were under other people's rule. Today there are about eight million Armenians in the world, and a remnant of rocky country east of Turkey and north of Iran that still, or again, is called Armenia. Almost two-thirds of the world's Armenians do not live there.

We have a habit of saying that it was the stubbornness, or the wits, or the unique Christian faith of Armenians that allowed the nation to endure for so long without a state; but some historians argue that in fact being spread out and powerless ensured the Armenians' survival. After all, it is easier to invade and destroy one capital city than a thousand villages.

One way or another, when I was born in Tehran in 1975, my first language was Armenian, an Indo-European language with no direct cousins. I was baptized under the same doctrine, in the Armenian Apostolic Church, that had governed community affairs since AD 314, when Armenia became the world's first Christian state. (The only challenge to my christening came not from any existential threat to Armenian culture, but from ideological differences between my mother, the sentimental grand-daughter of a minister, and my father, the atheist son of a Bolshevik.)

We moved from Tehran to the United States when I was two, a few months before the 1979 Iranian Revolution, to a well-off township in New Jersey with streams, woods, excellent schools, and several noteworthy sites from the American Revolution. My father had attended graduate school at Stanford as a foreign student almost a decade earlier, and he won our ticket back to America in the form of a job offer from Bell Labs.

Things began auspiciously for me as well. In New Jersey, my mother took me with her to the local community college, where she was taking classes. Bubbly young women in the day care center showed me unpreju-diced warmth and fed me fascinating snacks: a cupcake with an incon-ceivable crown of pink frosting, a rolled-up ball of something sweet coated in Kellogg's Corn Flakes, fruit cocktail from a can. Entry points to a new culture that I recall registering only in terms of food. And when it was time for me to start school, my kindergarten teacher, Miss Kim-inkinen, the descendant of Finns, had an even weirder name than I did.

One afternoon, my mother appeared in the kindergarten classroom. A photo of the occasion shows her in a dark blue knit dress with white trim that flattered her slender figure, and a red-and-white flowered chif-fon scarf tied loosely around her neck. In red, white, and blue, with a glori-ous smile, white teeth against waves of black hair, she could have been a poster girl for the Immigration and Naturalization Service. After my mother spoke briefly with Miss Kiminkinen, we, a room full of five-year-olds, were informed that it was Citizenship Day, September 17, and as a new green card holder I would be feted with the case of lemon cream-filled wafers that my mother had brought in. I was as surprised as anyone by the news—although not by the wafers, which came from the Arab grocery in Paterson where we stocked up once a month. If this had been first or second grade, Middle Eastern packaged wafers would have been embarrassing. But in kindergarten sugar conquered all, and I may have even been a little bit proud.

Or was I? For years after that day, well into junior high school until I moved away, a redheaded classmate named Danielle would make nostal-gic references to the time in kindergarten when my mother had brought in the delicious lemon wafers, and each time, although I knew she meant it kindly, I felt the shame of my foreignness confirmed.

But compared to my older sisters, I was lucky. The year was 1981, and the Iran hostage crisis had ended that January. My classmates were too young to make the connection, but my oldest sister had entered the fourth grade in New Jersey just a few weeks before Americans were locked up in the embassy in Tehran. The other kids called her Ayatollah Toumani. (Since everybody in school mispronounced our last name as Toe-may-nee, this coinage rhymed perfectly with Khomeini.)

That my sister's classmates identified her as Iranian rather than Armenian was inconvenient, but it made sense: we had never lived in Armenia, the Armenian we spoke was riddled with Persian vocabulary, and many of the foods we ate were Iranian. While most Armenians in Tehran went to special Armenian schools, my father had attended an Iranian high school. He spent his college years in Beirut with Iranian roommates, which gave him an intimacy with Iranian culture that many Iranian-Armenians did not share. My mother, though educated in Tehran's Armenian schools (it was unthinkable for an Armenian girl to be mixed up with Muslims), imparted to me a great enthusiasm for Iranian customs, the exaggerated grace of which suited her character. Neither of my parents were encouraged to participate in Dashnak youth groups, even though such groups were active in the Armenian community in Tehran during those years; my father's father, as a once-active Communist, was unmoved by Dashnak nationalism, and my mother's father considered the group's activities inappropriate because they were coed.

But many Armenians, no matter where they came from, had a tendency to conflate Iranians with Turks, Azeris, Arabs, and all other Muslims, considering them one large and undesirable group. This first occurred to me during a conversation I had with one of my cousins the summer we were ten, when she was visiting with her family for the weekend. Standing in the driveway of my house in New Jersey, we were ranking ethnic groups by the order in which we guessed our parents would not want us to marry someone from them.

At first it was a given that black would be at the top of the list, but then my cousin changed her mind. "I think my parents would rather I marry a black guy than a Muslim."

I was shocked. If she had said Turk, I would not have been surprised—but I thought we liked Muslims in general. It turned out my parents' equanimity was unusual.

Recently I asked my parents whether Armenians in Iran had lived comfortably as Christians within a Muslim majority.

"There was no problem," they both said at first. "We were very comfortable with our Muslim neighbors."

We were sitting at our round kitchen table drinking tea. But then my mother's face changed as she remembered something. She set her cup down on its saucer and looked out the glass door to the yard. "When I was a child," she said, speaking slowly, surprised by what her memory was offering up, "if one of the Iranian neighbors came over for tea, we would sit and talk and have a very nice time, and then the cup the guest had drunk from would be put aside so that it could be washed out with bleach."

My father stood up and crossed the room, shaking his head hard as if to cancel her comment, and placed his cup in the sink. "No. My parents never would have done such a thing," he said. "Mom's family were snobs."

I believed him about the last bit. But then he sat down and as the two of them started to puzzle over my question, it became clear that there was no easy answer. On one hand, people said that Armenians were held in a certain regard in Iran—"If there were two Iranians making a business deal," I had heard more than once, "they would ask an Armenian to be their witness." On the other hand, there was a school yard taunt familiar to all the Tehran children of my parents' generation: giggling, they sang it to me in unison. "*Armani sag Armani, jar-u-kesheh jahanami!*" It meant "Armenian, Armenian dog, the sweeper of hell." My father reassured me that it was playful—the sort of thing you would shout if you lost a soccer game. Armenian kids sang an equally appalling verse in reply: "*Mosalmun, shekleh meymun, khaket konam tuyeh meydun*"—"Muslim, looks like a monkey, I'll bury you in the town square."

It was difficult for me to understand the subtleties of normalized separation that they grew up with, but I had absorbed something of them. I had always felt that Iran was a fond part of our family story, and since I was born there, the administrative attachment could not be assimilated away, a fact I am reminded of frequently in airport security lines. But I had never called myself Iranian. It wouldn't have occurred to me to call myself anything but Armenian.

* * *

ONE DAY, I was summoned from my fourth-grade classroom to the principal's office. Mrs. Green, the secretary, said to me, "Meline, you speak Armenian, don't you?" I nodded, and wondered how she knew. I had no accent in English and had recently entered a phase of pronouncing my name as "Melanie" instead of Meh-lee-neh, its arduous, proper form.

"We may need your help with something," she said. I was sent back to class.

A few days later, another teacher came to my classroom and took me into the hallway. There was a boy standing there, a bit younger than I was, and I understood immediately by looking at him that this was why they needed my help.

"Meline, this is Artun. He has just come to America. He speaks Armenian. Can you tell him that on Tuesdays he needs to bring gym clothes for PE?"

It was a big deal to see another Armenian child in my school. It had never happened before. I did not say hello but looked into Artun's hazel eyes, which resembled my sister's, and wondered where, exactly, he had come from. Armenians typically stated their geographic affiliations by way of introduction: Beirutahai (Armenian from Beirut), Suryahai (Armenian from Syria), Parskahai (Armenian from Iran), or the grand prize, Hayastantsi—Armenian from Armenia—sometimes adding in the name of the town in Turkey where their ancestors had lived before 1915 (Vanetsi, Urfatsi, and so on). My thoughts were stuck on the fact that the teacher had not said that Artun *was* Armenian, but that he *spoke* Armenian.

I needed to know where he was from. Armenians from Armenia were not emigrating to the United States in those years; they couldn't leave the Soviet Union very easily, and the few who did were more likely to end up in Los Angeles than in New Jersey. Neither were they likely to arrive, in those years, from Iran; we had gotten out just before the revolution, and those who hadn't been as lucky generally had to wait a few years longer until things loosened up (unless, like some families we knew, they escaped through the mountains and sought asylum). As for Armenians from Lebanon or Syria, they had, in my mind, a swagger about them that did not match with the sight of this quiet, awkward boy standing before me in pants that were belted too high. I knew all this intuitively in a way that made Artun's presence fail to add up.

What I did not know was that right around the time that Artun arrived at my school, in the mid-1980s, Armenians from Turkey—from Istanbul's small, leftover Armenian community—were leaving in droves and settling in New Jersey. Discrimination against them had flared in Turkey after the Armenian terrorist groups whose activities we debated at camp started assassinating Turkish diplomats all over the world. I had no idea there were still Armenians living among Turks at all. In my own life, another twenty years and a long journey later, it would be obvious to me for a constellation of reasons that Artun Danis was a Turkish-Armenian name. But at the time I only stared at this boy's face and wondered what journey had brought him to Randolph, New Jersey.

I paused for a moment to think about whether we had words for "gym clothes" or "PE," and then I said, in an Armenian as stripped of dialect as I could devise, "On Tuesdays you must bring short pants for exercising."

Artun nodded.

"Does he have any questions?" the teacher asked me.

"Do you have any questions?"

Artun shook his head.

Later I noticed that Artun turned up on my school bus line; in fact, he lived just a few streets away from my family. Every time the bus approached the cul-de-sac at the end of Shady Lane, his mom was waiting for him, a small crime of social sabotage typical of an immigrant parent. When I told my mother about Artun, she told me to get his telephone number so she could make contact with his mother.

My mom had become a one-woman welcome wagon of the West; the consulates of various Middle Eastern countries should have been paying her a retainer for resettlement aid to foreigners who found themselves in the northern New Jersey suburbs. People would come over for dinner—I never understood where my parents collected these embarrassing new arrivals, Armenians as well as regular Iranians, with bad hair and inexorably alien names—and my mother would set to work matchmaking or career coaching; if they couldn't get to our house because they didn't have a car, we would drive long distances to pick them up.

My parents had lived in Palo Alto, California, in the late 1960s, while my father earned his doctorate in engineering, before returning to Iran for a brief spell during which I was born. They both spoke English well and moved gracefully through the barbecues and potluck dinners of our new American neighborhood within months of emigrating. But the bonds of culture were nonetheless a source of survival. One of the first things my mother had done upon arrival in New Jersey was to get a copy of the Morris County telephone book and page through it in search of any conceivably Armenian last name; she finally struck gold in the S's. She wrote down the address, checked a map, drove across town, and knocked on the front door to introduce herself. "Hello, I'm Armenian," was the long and the short of what she said. The Surenians remain among my parents' dearest friends to this day.

But I did not inherit even enough of her limitless courage to get Artun's phone number. I felt sorry for him, because he was so much more immigrant than I, but it was the kind of sorry where you avoid the person. Artun seemed nothing like my Armenian friends at camp, and besides, my tenuous social standing at Shongum School couldn't accommodate any additional burdens.

* * *

ALL FIVE MEMBERS of the Toumani family—my parents, my two older sisters, and I—had, in our own ways, quickly integrated ourselves into American life. My father was earning a string of patents at Bell Labs, my mother was finishing a business degree at Rutgers, and my sisters and I were Brownies and Girl Scouts (although my parents found the cookie-selling ritual disgraceful and forbade us to go door-to-door asking for money). But our weekends were Armenian. The Saturday and Sunday afternoons of my youth elapsed in traffic jams on the Long Island Expressway or the Garden State Parkway, as we drove an hour or two each way to see other Armenian families.

Some Sundays, we went to a place we called "agoomp." *Agoomp* means "club," in Armenian. The club met in a pair of freshly cemented buildings in Saddle Brook, New Jersey, belonging to an Armenian charity. My parents and their friends had organized this club as an alternative to the more politicized or religious Armenian groups in the area. A handful of families showed up each weekend. It was an informal gathering place, like a village contrived from a suburban New Jersey parking lot. As in a village, at *agoomp* people idled in clusters, simultaneously ignoring and scrutinizing one another, simply being together, which was what immigrants did, creating for themselves a comfortable pocket of society within the larger, less comfortable one. While kids ran around the corridors and the yard, the men played backgammon and the women brewed coffee and gossiped. There were cultural and social events now and then—including, once, a yogurt-eating contest, a diversion crafted by my mother on a lazy summer day. Another time she brought in a stack of brown paper bags and had the children make "Michael Jackson vests" with sequins, glitter, and glue.

Occasionally the club held panel discussions. At one of these, the topic was "What makes somebody a real Armenian?" Speaking the language and attending church and sending money to Armenia were the obvious answers, but each one met with debate. Finally somebody spoke up with an idea that everyone could agree on: a real Armenian was the one who, at the end of a film, sat through the credits to search for an Armenian name.

DOES THIS SOUND quaint, or warm, like it gave me a cozy sense of belonging to counteract the relentless mortifications of being foreign? The problem is that belonging and not belonging are so intricately linked. Once the lines are drawn, there is a possibility that you may fall on the wrong side of them. This is what I learned at Armenian school at St. Mary's Church in Livingston, where we went now and then for Sunday services and special events. We also visited the church one evening a week for Armenian language lessons. My mother taught the older students, and my eldest sister was in her class. But my middle sister and I were stuck in a class down the hall where the teacher spoke a different dialect than we did: she spoke Western Armenian.

Western Armenian is the dialect of Armenians who originated in Turkey. This meant that in the northeastern United States, where most Armenians were descendants of genocide survivors, Western Armenian was dominant. My family spoke Eastern Armenian, the official language of the Republic of Armenia and the one used by Armenians from Iran and Russia. The Western and Eastern dialects have big differences in grammar, vocabulary, pronunciation, and spelling. They are mutually intelligible with some strain; but the issue is not merely comprehension. Coded in the difference between the two dialects is a difference of histories: Western means your parents or grandparents probably suffered unspeakable horrors. Eastern means they probably did not. It was clear to me from an early age that each side considered theirs the "real" Armenian: Western Armenian speakers had claims on the national tragedy; Eastern Armenian speakers could argue that theirs was the official language of modern Armenia.

In our class in the church basement, my sister and I were the only Eastern Armenian speakers. Nobody had explained to us why there were two different dialects or that both were legitimate. It seemed like a zero-sum game: if theirs is right, ours must be wrong, and vice versa. We already knew Armenian conversationally; the class focused on learning to read and write. (The Armenian alphabet has thirty-eight letters; as a friend would note many years later, and rather accurately, it looks like somebody has thrown a pot of spaghetti in the air and walked away.) Paging through glossy workbooks, we muddled through an Armenian version of Dick and Jane—featuring Ara and Maral, their dog, and their family members, to whom they showed great respect. Sometimes the differences in dialect were manageable: their word for spoon, *tekal*, was, in our dialect, *ketal*. Their good night—*kisher paree*—was *baree gisher* for us. But not all the differences could be resolved with just a dyslexic shimmy.

One day my teacher asked me how to say egg, and I gave her the obvious answer: *dzu*. She howled with laughter and then, catching her breath, corrected me: "*havgit!*" she shouted across the room. Her word for egg meant "came from the chicken." Ours meant something like "came from the ovary." I was humiliated. The ridicule did not end with eggs, and little by little I refused to speak Armenian to anyone.

My parents bothered me about this now and then, but they went easy compared to other Armenian parents, who refused even to respond to the sound of English. I lived in terror of some of those fathers; the memory of turning into the driveway of one family's home in Westchester, where English was officially banned, still fills me with dread. It was all I could do to endure a silent rush of kiss-kisses in the front hallway on our arrival before I could run to the yard or the playroom with the kids. *Why aren't you speaking Armenian? Why don't you make them speak Armenian? Aren't you ashamed that you don't speak Armenian?* Once, after a concert in Manhattan given by a famous Armenian soprano, my sister and I ran into the diva herself in the ladies' room. She blocked our exit and said, as if we were her own grandchildren, "You *must* speak Armenian, my dears.

It is your responsibility to our people." Incidents like this were cause for giggles or rolled eyes when they happened—but the pileup of them, the accrual of moments of falling short, of disappointing, of letting down parents and strangers, and potentially an entire posterity, took its toll. It felt like a debt that could never be paid.

My phobia around speaking Armenian became even more unbearable when, in the years after the Iranian revolution, relatives who had remained in Iran began making their way to the United States. They all wanted to know why I didn't speak Armenian. "She can," my parents would say. "She just won't."

My mother's mother, Shushan, who we called Shushumama, was my only refuge; she was fluent in English. She had attended an American high school in Tabriz and later taught English at the British Council in Tehran. For a few months when I was seven, Shushumama, fresh off the plane, occupied the extra bed in my room. She carried a tiny yellow notebook, spiral-bound across the top, and wrote down every new English expression she learned, whether at the grocery store or the post office, or while reading the newspaper. Together, we recited nursery rhymes as if they were high theater, taking pleasure in perfect English articulations and the satisfying patterns they yielded: Jack Sprat could eat no fat, Hickory dickory dock. Once, Shushumama asked me to teach her all the words for "My Country, 'Tis of Thee," schooling me on the British original in return, and we stood together singing to my shelf of stuffed animals as though the queen herself were nestled among them. But after Shushumama moved on to Los Angeles, where most of my extended family had migrated, my father's mother took her place as my roommate.

Arammama—we called her that after my grandfather Aram, although her name was Siranoush—spoke very little English. I figured I could get by on smiles and kisses when the rest of the family was around to carry the conversation; but I worried about what would happen when my grandmother and I were going to sleep in my bedroom at night and there would be nobody else to fill the silence. At the time of her visit, I had a nightgown that I was fond of, pink cotton, with a picture of a rainbow streaking out from a wide paintbrush, and the words "Paint a Rainbow Day." For several days preceding Arammama's arrival, I focused my anxiety on this nightgown. What if, some evening as we climbed into bed, she asked me to tell her what was written on my nightgown?

To prepare, I asked my eldest sister to tell me the Armenian word for "rainbow." *Dziadzan*, she said. *Dzi-a-dzan*. I repeated it to myself like a protective spell. *Mi hat dziadzan or nerki*. Paint a rainbow day. (This made as little sense in Armenian as in English.) I imagined Arammama's reaction. It got to the point that I was almost looking forward to the moment when she would ask me about my nightgown, so that I could impress her with my feigned impromptu translation. But she never did ask. (It turned out she needed cataract surgery and could hardly see.) We never had a real conversation at all, not then or later, Arammama and I. My older cousins, who grew up with her in Iran, describe Arammama as nothing less than a saint; as love incarnate. But I was so ashamed of my refusal to speak Armenian with Arammama that I somehow assumed she was ashamed of me. When I was much older and Arammama was no longer alive, relatives sometimes said I must have gotten my love of language from her. Despite not having finished high school, she had been known for her talent in reciting poetry, for telling elaborate stories, and for writing long, sensitive letters in Armenian.

At family gatherings over the years, nobody knew what to make of the fact that I answered them only in English, whether it was as simple as hello and how are you, or as complicated as an argument over current events. Nobody knew this, either: that from the time I got my driver's license at sixteen, I developed a habit of taking the car for long solo drives during which I would describe, out loud to the steering wheel and the windshield, everything I saw—in Armenian. *There are many trees here. We're getting close to the city. I'm going to the store to buy food.* I didn't want anybody to hear me, but I wanted to make sure I didn't forget.

My parents never stopped addressing me in Armenian, but more than twenty years would pass before they heard the language from my mouth again. And for a long time, I blamed my teacher at St. Mary's for this, but I suspect she was only a small part of a larger problem: the problem of not feeling entirely at ease in either the American world or the Armenian one. It amazed me that Armenians, as few as we were and as doomed as we liked to imagine ourselves, separated at every opportunity into endless subdivisions, including this loaded divide over language. The entire experience of being Armenian in the diaspora was a bizarre fluctuation between sweeping, unconditional unity and irrational, hostile fragmentation. The reality was that we came from different host countries that had treated us with varying degrees of respect or intolerance; we spoke different dialects (and within both Eastern and Western Armenian there were many local variations), ate different foods, and represented different classes of wealth and levels of education. Among ourselves, these differences had a way of chafing. As the diaspora evolved and assimilated, there was only one thing that everybody agreed on: the Turks hated us and we hated the Turks. This trumped everything.

Hostility toward Turkey came in various forms, but in the American suburbs opportunities for conflict were limited, so it skewed toward the trivial. We referred to Turkish coffee, which we drank every day, as "Armenian coffee," steered clear of shops rumored to have Turkish owners, and refused to buy products labeled "Made in Turkey." My mother once spent weeks trying to buy a new bathrobe, but at store after store, every robe declared its Turkish origins: the Turks had cornered the market on terry cloth. One evening, my mom returned home, exhausted, with a large bag from Sears. "Don't tell anyone," she warned me. She clipped the label and then held out her plush, pale yellow purchase.

* * *

DIVISIONS AMONG DIASPORA Armenians were not merely implied; there was an explicit, institutionalized divide that extended to communities all over the world and mattered more than the differences between dialect or origin. It was whether or not you sympathized with the Dashnak Party. This determined which schools you would send your children to, which youth groups, and especially which church you would attend. "Which church are you?" we used to ask each other. This was not a question about which building your family drove to on Sundays—it was a question of whether or not your church was Dashnak. None of the children knew what this meant or why it mattered, only that it did.

But the reason for the church schism was, even as these things go, pretty strange and had nothing to do with religious doctrine. It was the result of long-simmering political differences between Armenian diaspora clubs (and their newspapers). These differences exploded in an incident involving the Soviet Union, the Chicago World's Fair, a murder in New York City, and, at heart, Turkey.

In 1918, as the weakened Ottoman Empire fought against Russia, most Armenian provinces of eastern Turkey were held by the Ottoman army. All of Eastern Armenia, meanwhile, was under Russian control. Armenians, led by a Dashnak committee headquartered in Tbilisi, managed to take over a sliver of eastern Turkey that they would control from 1918 until 1920. Armenians call this the "Thousand-Day Republic," and still celebrate its brief existence every year as a national holiday, the first time in six hundred years that Armenians had an independent state.

When this land was divided between Turkey and Russia in 1920, many Armenians saw Russia as the lesser of two evils—the greater being Turkey. But for the Dashnaks, already the most nationalist among Armenian parties, Soviet rule looked like intolerable subjugation, while for other Armenian parties, it was safe shelter in lieu of better options. The thousand-day republic had a flag—red, blue, and orange stripes—and brandishing this flag instead of the Soviet one became standard Dashnak practice even after the short-lived republic was dissolved.

Thirteen years later in Chicago, in 1933, the highest-ranking Armenian priest in the United States, Archbishop Leon Tourian, was invited to give an invocation at the Chicago World's Fair. But there was a problem. The archbishop refused to speak until a red, blue, and orange Dashnak flag was removed from the stage. His boss was the Patriarch of All Armenians at the Holy See of Etchmiadzin, the Armenian equivalent of the Vatican, in Soviet Armenia. Archbishop Tourian feared that standing beside the Dashnak flag at the World's Fair would be an unwise public rejection of Soviet leadership, which some Armenians believed was all they had to protect them from further invasion and massacre. This decision would cost him his life. A few months later, during a Christmas Eve service at the Holy Cross Church in New York City, as the archbishop proceeded up the aisle toward the altar, a group of Dashnak activists sprang from the pews and stabbed him dead.

Following the murder, Armenian churches began to affiliate as Dashnak or non-Dashnak. A dual narrative was born: In one version, the Dashnaks had secured a precious window of Armenian freedom in the thousand-day republic, and for snubbing it, Archbishop Tourian got what he deserved. In the other version, the thousand-day republic was a sloppy accident, and Armenians were lucky to have been saved from themselves by the Soviets, a powerful opponent to Turkey; the priest had been prudent in his choice at the World's Fair, and a reckless gang of nationalists had committed unforgivable murder. Congregations in the northeastern United States reshuffled themselves along political lines, sometimes going so far as to lock their opponents out of the building during Sunday services, and soon the divisions spread to Armenian churches all over the world. In 1956, the schism was formalized after the Armenian Patriarchate of Antelias (based in Lebanon) broke away from the Mother See at Etchmiadzin, and took the loyalty of Dashnak churches with it. Where previously all churches answered to Etchmiadzin, now Dashnak churches answered to Antelias.

In the 1980s, Armenian church leaders made gestures toward reunification, and today the divide is not as charged. But still we asked each other that question: which church are you? Many Armenians would sigh and say, "You know, it really doesn't make any sense. Why should we be divided like this?" And yet we loved being divided. The most important thing was to belong to something, but it only worked when you had something or someone to fight against, an inch of air that could surround you and let you feel yourself not overly but just slightly separate. The scale of us-ness versus them-ness was amazingly fluid and could shift with the circumstances.

The Dashnak Party, and groups affiliated with it, sponsor perhaps half of all organized Armenian activity in the world: schools, charities, arts organizations, sports teams, youth groups, even New Year's Eve parties. Nearly anything Armenian that is not connected to the Dashnak Party is affiliated with another group, the Armenian General Benevolent Union, or AGBU. A nonprofit with a thirty-six-million-dollar budget, the AGBU also sponsors schools, camps, and, indeed, New Year's Eve parties, but its ethos is more humanitarian than political. And yet, while the two groups pursue different agendas, it should be noted that involvement in either group is often passive, merely circumstantial. That is, a Dashnak New Year's Eve party might just be the nearest one around, and attendance does not necessarily make one an aspirant to the lands of Eastern Turkey. Which is the only way to explain how I ended up spending five summers of my youth at Camp Haiastan.

* * *

IN THE SAME box where I found my old camp newsletters, I found a paper that I had written in the ninth grade for my English class. The assignment had been completely open-ended as far as subject matter; our task was merely to demonstrate that we had learned how to make a proper outline. I called my paper "The Survival of a Nation," quietly stealing the title of a book about Armenia that I had found on my parents' bookshelf.

My outline begins like this: "Purpose—To show that although some people would disagree, the Armenian Genocide of 1915 did occur."

As the outline proceeds, I describe the genocide with numbered points such as: "1. Armenians starved, soon became inhuman. 2. World closed its eyes." I end the outline where it began: "Conclusion—As horrible as the story of the Armenian Genocide is, it is the truth."

Then comes the paper itself, thirteen pages about life in the Ottoman Empire as I imagined it: "Much of Turkey's business dealings were in the hands of Armenians, because the Turks, as a whole, have always been a poorly, if at all, educated people, and very barbaric and untactful in their methods."

I go on to depict the genocide as a continuous, two-year-long death march—the picture was clear to me, an unbroken column of Armenian women and children dragging their feet across the whole of Turkey— offering that "the march came to an end only when there was nobody left to march."

Turning to current events, I write: "Because of the blindfolded hordes who side with the Turks, it has become necessary to recognize that the events of the Armenian Genocide are not affirmed by all."

In the final two sentences, I use the word "truth" five times. In the bibliography I cite as a source the Armenian national anthem.

- 5 -

False Assumptions

IT WAS MY SENIOR YEAR OF COLLEGE AT UC BERKELEY, AND ARME-
nian genocide memorial day number 83: April 24, 1998. On Sproul Plaza,
in front of the main entrance to campus, we set up several easels holding
black-and-white photographs of corpses. Blown up to poster size, the old
pictures had become so distorted they looked like patchy shadows interrupted by eyes and teeth. Above them we strung up a banner made of
dot-matrix printer paper, the kind with holes along the edges, bearing a
message handwritten in black Sharpie, capitalized strategically to catch
the eyes of passersby: "'Who today remembers the extermination of the
Armenians?' SAID ADOLF HITLER."

There was a long table with flyers explaining what happened on
April 24, 1915, along with lists of institutions all over the world that
had recognized the events as genocide. The Berkeley Armenian Student
Association, of which I was an active member, put together a display like
this every year.

It was a windy day, this particular April 24, and with each gust, one
or two of the posters fell over. My assigned task was to reset them on the
easels whenever they fell, and as I lifted one back into place, I noticed a
middle-aged man who looked like a professor approaching our table. I

picked up a flyer and prepared to tell him about the importance of geno-cide recognition.

But he stopped a few feet away and shook his head, waving his hands in a crossing-out motion. "This is pathetic," he said.

How did we know so instantaneously that he did not mean the obvious—that the massacre of the Armenians had been pathetic? It was as if our mythological demon—Turkish denial—had suddenly taken liv-ing form before us and we sensed it the way animals in the wild recog-nize their enemies for the sake of survival.

Within seconds, one of our members, Patrick, was in a shouting match with this man. They were only five feet away from me, but over the wind and the chronic rattle of the drum circles of Berkeley I could not make out what they were saying. As students streamed past, unaware, Patrick and the professor lurched at each other with their shoulders and chests and yelled in each other's faces. Then it was over, and the professor paced toward a nearby classroom building.

A particularly disorienting kind of shock sets in when you have acted as if in anticipation of something, even though that thing was always more an abstraction than a real threat, but then it actually happens—like a fire drill that isn't just a drill after all. A Turkish professor had brought genocide denial directly into our liberal collegiate utopia. Even if our goal with the April 24 display was to combat precisely this, we had never expected such a confrontation—certainly not here. This was UC Berkeley, bastion of truth-telling, pride of a city so politically correct that the parking meters listed as a holiday "Indigenous People's Day" instead of honoring Christopher Columbus.

We circled around Patrick. Because it was lunchtime, between classes, many more club members were arriving to help with the commemoration. Breathless with confusion and excitement, we rushed to replay for them what had happened.

At the same time, privately, I considered a different problem: it was Friday, and every Friday the California Golden Overtones, an a cappella singing group of which I was the musical director, held a performance at one p.m., at a spot twenty feet away from our genocide display table. It was almost one o'clock. I felt slightly sick at the prospect of leaving the scene of my Armenian club's drama and joining my other group, a group I spent considerably more time with, to sing doo-wop tunes and the occasional Indigo Girls number. I also worried what the others would think about my priorities.

When I had arrived at the Armenian Student Association table that morning, I had noticed that somebody brought black armbands for us to wear, so that people might stop us throughout the day and ask what they signified. I had opted not to put one on—the idea struck me as melodramatic. But now it seemed like my best shot at compromise. Watching my singing mates assemble across the walkway, I grabbed an armband and tied it on over my red thrift-store shirt, a men's button-down with a butterfly collar, apologized feebly to my Armenian friends, and went to sing, facing the corpse posters all the while. At the end of the performance I thanked the audience and then invited them to take a look at the genocide display behind them.

That Sunday, we had an emergency meeting of the Armenian Student Association. The purpose was to plan our retaliation against the Turkish professor. In the four years I had been with the club, we had never faced a politicized situation like this. Usually we carpooled to church picnics around the Bay Area or held potluck dinners where the most excitement one could hope for was that somebody would bring a bottle of Armenian brandy. Now, about twenty of us were collected in a living room south of campus, and Patrick took the floor.

Patrick was a slight fellow, not the type you would imagine getting into a fight. He was the picture of responsibility—like a hired efficiency expert roaming the campus, he wore loafers, khakis, and button-down shirts, the sort of attire one did not often see on Berkeley-dwellers below the age of fifty. It was not entirely surprising that he would take charge in a crisis, but his was not a charismatic leadership; it was more like the bottled-up aggression of a hall monitor.

For the benefit of those who had not been there, he described in detail what had happened at the display table. The professor had stopped in front of the genocide photos and said, "I wish it were true, you lying pigs." Then the professor said that the Armenians had deserved to be massacred.

I wondered whether Patrick was embellishing the professor's words— the part about pigs strained belief—but since I had heard only bits of the shouting, I kept my mouth shut.

The offender, Patrick told us, was a professor of Near Eastern Studies.

In order to confirm the man's identity, Patrick had tracked him down to his office and waited outside with a newspaper shielding his face.

Patrick had also spoken to the campus police and had filed a complaint for physical assault. At this news, audible gasps went up in the room. But it made no sense; I had watched the argument from beginning to end. While I hadn't heard every word, I had seen the entire thing clearly, and recalled no physical contact. Over murmurs of anger from the others, I asked Patrick what, exactly, he meant by physical assault.

"He spat at me," said Patrick. "That qualifies as physical assault."

I didn't know Patrick very well, but I had never liked him. A few weeks earlier our group had attended a reading on campus by the Armenian writer Peter Balakian, and the first question after the applause had come from Patrick: "How do you think Armenian writers can use their work to fight Turkish denial of the genocide?" I had found his question embarrassing—there were non-Armenians present who had come with the impression that they were there to discuss literature—and more important, depressing. I was an English major—a small but hard-won personal triumph since my parents saw this course of study as impractical—and I had come to the event eager to discover some aspect of Armenian culture that wasn't defined by politics.

The same attitude that allowed Patrick to see literature as only a means to a political end now revealed a willingness to bend the truth for the same purpose. I didn't even pause to think before blurting out a response.

"Patrick, I was right there. I didn't see the professor spit at you."

Patrick glared at me. "I know when I've been spat on," he said. "He spat in my eye. I could have gotten a disease."

"But you were shouting in each other's faces. Do you mean that a drop of spit from his mouth flew into your eye by accident? That's not the same as spitting on you intentionally," I said.

Patrick ignored me. The spitting question, while it raised a few eyebrows, was put aside. The conversation turned to the problem of how we could get media attention. In my head, meanwhile, I reviewed my memory of the event carefully, trying to determine whether I could have missed an overt act of spitting.

Then the telephone rang, and everybody went silent. This call had been scheduled, it became clear; somebody had arranged for a lawyer from San Francisco to advise us as to how the matter might be pursued in court. He was an Armenian lawyer, naturally. Or was he even a lawyer? Was he even Armenian? He was only a voice on the phone, and he told us by way of greeting that he could not speak long and that he could not be identified to the group.

As we knelt on the floor, heads bent toward a speaker phone that sat on a desk in the corner, I started to feel the way I had as a child at Camp Haiastan on debate night: that either I had missed something important or that something was very wrong. The voice at the other end of the line was speaking only of media strategy and legal ramifications—albeit with an inflated urgency that felt menacing—yet we imbibed his words like loyal operatives receiving our next set of instructions, genuflecting to a chief whose face we couldn't see.

But there was a difference between summer camp and college: this time I trusted my reaction. Who was this voice on the end of the phone and how important could he possibly be that he couldn't risk identifying himself? How valuable was his input that twenty undergrads and graduate students at the University of California, Berkeley, could not plan a course of action without him? And how could we look each other in the eye and talk about using a claim of physical assault by stray saliva fleck to get the Turkish professor in trouble? I was enraged by the professor's comments, but if we wanted to see him penalized for his crude treatment of a student group, this was no way to handle it. We could not fight genocide denial by creating new lies of our own.

The matter held the attention of the college paper for some time, and soon the *San Francisco Chronicle* was weighing in, condemning the professor of Near Eastern Studies as well as the university for not taking swift action against him. The UC Berkeley student senate, at the ready for any battle of the people versus power, passed a resolution calling on the school to fire the professor and to draft new standards against hate speech on campus. A university ombudsperson investigated the affair and concluded that the professor's remarks, although obnoxious, were protected by free expression policies. Patrick was quoted in the *Daily Californian* describing the confrontation. "I will not change my story—it's the truth," he said. "If somebody comes and says there was no genocide, then that's going to be my response time and time again."

Meanwhile, the university police came to the same conclusion as I had about the spitting: that an accidental droplet had crossed the inches separating two shouting men. The case was closed.

I OFTEN WONDERED what became of the Turkish professor, whose name, Hamid Algar, had never left my mind. Thinking back on the incident a decade later, I consulted the Internet. What I discovered, at my desk in my living room, the sounds of Brooklyn traffic screeching outside my window, left me dazed: the offending professor was not Turkish. He was an Englishman.

How was this possible? It had seemed obvious that a man named Hamid Algar who harassed a group of Armenian students, who said there had been no genocide, must have been a Turk. I wasn't aware that Hamid had fallen out of fashion as a name for Turkish boys around the time that Abdul Hamid II, the last real Ottoman sultan, lost his grip on the empire and became a symbol of irredeemable decline. On the Internet, I learned that Professor Algar had converted to Islam while a student at Cambridge, and had changed his first name to Hamid. As for Algar, it had struck my ear like as Turkish a name as any, a cousin of Altun or Altınay, or maybe something with an Arabic twist—Al-Qar? But no: Algar is an old Anglo-Saxon name meaning "noble spearman." Its variants include Elgar, as in Sir Edward, the British composer, or Alger, like Horatio.

I couldn't square this new information with the image that in the course of a decade had developed in the darkroom of my mind—a room dark enough that I had been positive that the man I'd seen storming up to our table had a face with the stereotypically Turkish blend of yellow-olive skin tone and faintly Asian eyes. Now I saw that Hamid Algar's students had made him a fan page on Facebook, and in his photograph he had round eyes and blushing cheeks and a rusty speckle of a beard. He might have stepped out of any London pub.

There were so many layers of confusion in what had happened. For starters, the content of the fight between Patrick and the professor was a clash of narratives. In addition, they reported the incident differently. As a bystander, my version was different still. Then there were media accounts and official statements. But beyond all of that, when I realized the most basic assumption I had made—that the professor was ethnically Turkish—had been wrong, and that this inaccuracy had been curing in my mind for ten years, only fortifying my contempt for Turkey, I saw that the entire mess was even more toxic than I had feared. How easily certainty took shape. How hard it was to dismantle.

What other hazards of perception, what other false assumptions were at play between Armenians and Turks? What else might we, or they, need to reconsider, and which questions were too dangerous even to entertain?

- 6 -

"With This Madness, What Art Could There Be?"

My first trip to Turkey happened quickly and with little planning. I bought my ticket only two weeks before leaving, hardly enough time to read a book or study a map—not that doing either of those things had occurred to me; I was operating on instinct. Looking back, I can see that instinct had been leading me away from the Armenian community for a while already, but this did not mean I was any more comfortable with Turks or Turkey than I had ever been. It was as if I had been moving in a certain direction without knowing it, until suddenly I realized I was on the edge of a cliff. My decision to go to Turkey was a surprise even to myself.

I was well traveled by then. I had spent the two previous summers working in a provincial Russian city as a journalism teacher, had enjoyed a few precious weeks rediscovering Iran with my parents, had done all the usual backpacking through Europe with my sister the summer I finished college. I had beloved relatives in Paris whom I visited anytime I could find an excuse. I had made a first, obligatory pilgrimage to Armenia, getting there by car from Georgia, where I stayed in Tbilisi as a guest of the presidential family—long story—and I had taken trips to Singapore, Hong Kong, Malaysia, and other places that could make me seem adventurous, open-minded, savvy. How was it possible, then, that I never even paused on the fact that Turkey was a country that could be visited? How did curiosity never move me, especially after the Internet had made curiosity as cheap as breath, to consider that I could enlist Google's help, buy a plane ticket, get some kind of visa, or at the very least read an article in the Travel section of the *New York Times*, skim a dispatch from Istanbul or some colorful Turkish seaside resort? Would you believe me if I said those small exploratory endeavors would have felt, right up until the moment they didn't, like something acidic spreading through my insides? But this was irrelevant. When you don't want to see something, you don't look for it, don't even know you are avoiding it.

It suited me to believe that the first trip happened without much planning because a whim required less justification than a quest. But it was a quest, a quest that would eventually be disguised in the finery of important-sounding freelance writing assignments, and ultimately supported by the best excuse of all: a book contract. But that was all later.

I couldn't have seen it then any more than you can see a leaf growing if you stare at it, but a very definite series of events had led to the day that I arrived in Istanbul, and those events began with an evening three years prior—a night at the movies.

"ON NOVEMBER 15 WE ALL HAVE THE SAME PLANS." In the fall of 2002, I received an e-mail from a stranger that began with this capitalized decree. I had just moved from California to New York for graduate school, a writing program at NYU, and already the local Armenian e-mail networks had me in the loop. You didn't question how an Armenian organization had gotten your e-mail address; our e-mails were collective property, and unsubscribing was useless as it would quickly be overruled by a new list that someone compiled.

This particular e-mail went on to explain that on the evening of November 15, all Armenians in the New York area would attend the premiere of the film *Ararat*, by the Canadian-Armenian director Atom Egoyan. It was touted as the first-ever feature film about the genocide. Anticipation had been building in diaspora newspapers and magazines for at least a year. And now, the logic went, if enough Armenians attended the limited opening run in New York and Los Angeles, we would help guarantee wider distribution of the film.

Here it was again: the expectation, the obligation, that if a thing were good for the Armenians—which could only mean good for the cause of genocide recognition—nothing else mattered. We would support this film whether we liked it or not.

I went, of course, as much to see the movie as for the spectacle of an Armenian mass descent upon the Angelika Film Center in SoHo. In the hallway outside the screening room, Armenian women in dresses and heels kissed one another on both cheeks and sized one another up as though it were the red carpet at the Oscars.

It was not until the lights went down that a problem emerged: this was Atom Egoyan, director of peculiar, nonlinear films best appreciated by film buffs in art house cinemas. Although he had been nominated for two Academy Awards and five Palme d'Or prizes, he was not known as a crowd-pleaser. And so it turned out to be not so clear that the film was good for the Armenians after all.

The plot centered on an Armenian director (played by French-Armenian luminary Charles Aznavour) making a movie about the genocide, focusing on the Siege of Van, one of the few incidents in which the Armenians put up serious resistance against Turkish forces. Parts of the story are told through the eyes of the Armenian painter Arshile Gorky. The genocide scenes take place on a cartoonishly colored film set, with crew and cameras visible, creating a sense of unreality and encouraging the audience to maintain critical distance. Mount Ararat is transplanted to the wrong side of the set, geographically, because the showbiz-minded film producer (another Armenian performer, Eric Bogosian) feels it looks better there. Throughout the film-within-the-film, scenes of bloody fighting between Armenians and Turks are shown at length and then interrupted by the director's commands to the cast, which serve as abrupt reminders that the scenes are not the thing itself, but a story under construction. Death marches, rapes, the torching of a circle of Armenian brides doused in kerosene and forced to dance, all are started and then stopped short, with the equivalent of a "Cut! Let's run that again" or "Let's break for lunch and then redo the rape scene."

A half-Turkish character named Ali, an aspiring actor who happens to be gay, wins the role of Jevdet Bey, a notoriously brutal Turkish governor during the genocide era. (Ali is actually played by a Greek, Elias Koteas.) We see Ali at home preparing dinner, chatting with his boyfriend about the film. At first he feels uneasy playing such a villain, but when he begins reading about the history, he finds there are people who argue that the Armenians had it coming, a notion that helps him embrace his part more freely.

Several intense side plots explore the theme of manipulating stories to serve emotional needs. An Armenian art historian named Ani (played by Egoyan's wife, Arsinée Khanjian) is hired as a consultant on the film; she is obsessed with Arshile Gorky's life, and especially with explaining his death. She herself has been widowed twice; her first husband was an Armenian terrorist, and their son, Raffi, is seeking a way to honor the legacy of his father, whom he prefers to call a "freedom fighter." Ani's second husband, not an Armenian, supposedly killed himself, but his daughter Celia (Ani's stepdaughter) believes Ani killed him. Both offspring are consumed by their fathers' deaths. The two of them have an affair that threatens to destroy Raffi's relationship with his mother. (Given the extreme sexual repression in Armenian culture, a graphic sex scene between the stepsiblings could have been the film's undoing if the stakes were any lower.)

But the most haunting story line unfolds when young Raffi returns from a secret trip to what he calls "Western Armenia"—Turkey—where he has gathered footage for the film-within-the-film. At the airport in Canada, a customs officer (played by Christopher Plummer) interrogates him for hours about whether his sealed film canisters might actually contain heroin. The interrogation drags on well beyond what the conventions of entertainment would seem to allow and generates a creeping confusion for the viewer about where Raffi has been and what he has done; Egoyan seems to be demonstrating the inherent instability of a narrative whose goal is to persuade—such as the narratives on both sides of the Armenian genocide. When Raffi tries to tell the truth about his trip—and to explain why the film's director can't bail him out, because Raffi did not tell him he was going to gather this footage—his story sounds so convoluted that he resorts to lying to make it seem more true. In the end, the officer turns off the lights, opens a film canister, feels for the contents, and—leaving mysterious what was inside—lets Raffi go. Later, telling his son (who happens to be the boyfriend of the half-Turkish actor Ali) about the incident, the officer muses on the question of whether the canisters indeed contained heroin. "What difference does it make?" he says. "He didn't believe he could do something like that."

Through all of these threads, the film grapples with a question that Egoyan later articulated in an interview: "How do you know what you know?"

AT THE ANGELIKA Film Center, for a brief spell after the credits rolled, the Armenians allowed themselves their disappointment. Many said they wished it had been a more clear-cut rendering of the story of 1915, that Egoyan blew our big chance—to secure genocide recognition via Hollywood, that is.

"Why couldn't he have done something normal, like *Schindler's List*?" people asked.

"It was too confusing" was a frequent refrain, another way of saying that the film wasted its capital on ideas and emotions that were not politically instrumental.

Meanwhile, in the *New Yorker*, the critic Anthony Lane concluded his review of *Ararat* with an observation that explained perfectly the Armenians' sense of a lost opportunity: "If I were a Turkish official, I would not be too worried by this picture. Nothing so slippery can stir up indignation."

But the critic Brandon Judell from Indiewire took this further, accusing the filmmaker of abdicating a moral duty. "If only Egoyan took a chance," he wrote. "The main problem with his *Ararat* is that it's a subject that should overwhelm us intellectually and emotionally. Egoyan's already made his point time and again that modern technology has increasingly distanced us from experiencing the joys of life and the ability to cope with everyday sorrows. But the Armenians don't need any more intellectual game-playing with their past. They need a catharsis."

How enormously this missed the point. We had no shortage of catharsis. I had been reading tragic memoirs and gruesome eyewitness accounts from genocide survivors since I was old enough to read Dr. Seuss. I consumed them greedily and bawled like a professional mourner. I had attended awful theater by Armenian playwrights in which young actors faked the accents of genocide survivors in kitschy attempts at representing trauma, tugging the heartstrings of audiences who handed them over expectantly, as if in a prearranged bargain. Egoyan had taken a huge artistic risk by diverging from this well-worn path, whereas attempts at catharsis of the sort Judell recommended had catered to our most super-ficial feelings for years already and had led to something very much the opposite of relief.

In any case, the Armenian community's dissatisfaction with *Ararat* was short-lived: within a few months all was forgiven, and Egoyan and his leading-lady wife, Arsinée Khanjian, were honored at a black-tie affair at the New York Yacht Club sponsored by the Armenian Prelacy, the leadership council of the Dashnak-affiliated arm of the church. The head of the Armenian lobby from Washington served as master of cere-monies and spoke about how the film might aid in the campaign for genocide recognition. The Archbishop His Eminence Oshagan Choloyan admitted that it was the first film he'd seen in seventeen years. Then, apparently willing to overlook not only the movie's challenges to the party line, but also its depiction of homosexuality, incest, and nudity, he blessed the project with a prayer and bestowed a medal of honor.

Was this reversal of attitude governed more by cold political strategy or was it shaped by a kind of denial, denial of the uncomfortable feelings, complexities, and questions that Egoyan had tried to articulate? Either way, it amounted to a neatly tautological lesson: First, there is only one acceptable way to talk about the genocide. Second, what you actually say is irrelevant because no matter which questions you ask or what answers you give, you will either be ensnared, appropriated, and controlled, or sim-ply rejected. Even an artist of Egoyan's stature could not escape this system entirely. It was some kind of clan velocity, some law of ethnic physics by which everything would be swept into the same story in the end. You're either with us or against us. In the case of *Ararat*, the balance had fallen toward the first option, a calculation reached, no doubt, because of Egoy-an's clout in the wider world; the solution was to ignore the "slippery" mes-sage and replace it with a less confusing one.

These forces left little room for individuality, which meant they left little room for art—a high price to pay for membership in the group. (And speaking of high prices: the Yacht Club event, a few hours on a weeknight, cost a hundred dollars per person to attend. The prohibitive admission fee was typical for Armenian community gatherings, a kind of tithe that all but guaranteed the absence of artists, since only those with corporate salaries would be able to pony up on a regular basis. Each time I received an invitation to another of these black-tie affairs—whose ticket prices served to underline the message I had struggled against all my life, that my passions were merely hobbies and that a real job needed to have the initials MD, JD, or CPA attached to it—I felt a wave of rage.)

Yet somewhere in the midst of all this, a possibility had taken root in my imagination. I had spent a couple of hours of private time with a Turk—a Turkish character on the screen, a fellow named Ali. In the safety of a dark theater, I had been allowed to observe him and consider his behavior, his humanity or inhumanity. Wait—to consider whom? This Turk, whose character was somebody's thoughtful gay boyfriend one minute and an actor playing a genocidaire the next, this Turk whose actor-character was only half-Turkish, this half-Turkish character played by Elias Koteas, an actor who was Greek, of all things? But his name was Ali, and he was tall, with broad shoulders, black hair, and a pasted-on mustache. He was as Turkish-seeming as I needed him to be in order to carry out what my professors in grad school would have called a thought experiment—a thought experiment that could be summarized as follows: so, there's a Turk. So what?

* * *

ONE WEEK AFTER the Yacht Club event, I attended an academic conference about the film, sponsored by the City University of New York. A few scholars of Armenian descent spoke analytically about the film's complex handling of narratives. Some compared it to Egoyan's other work. There was a discussion about the reaction of Armenian audiences to the film. Confounding my expectations, the conference was riveting. But the biggest shock came when a man named Taner Akçam took the floor.

Akçam was Turkish. How this was communicated I cannot remember—but since the proceedings took as a given the idea that the Armenians had faced genocide, his participation was strange enough that there might as well have been a flashing purple neon sign that said "TURK" with an arrow pointing at the small man with glasses and thinning gray hair who stood alone behind the podium.

Now a historian, Akçam had fled Turkey in the 1970s after getting in trouble as a political activist. He would later explain to me that it was while he was in exile in Germany, pursuing his studies at the Hamburg Institute for Social Research and working alongside Holocaust scholars, that he went "through a certain process" to become comfortable referring to the Armenian massacres as genocide. He was one of the first Turkish scholars to have done so openly, and for that he was facing death threats from Turkish diaspora nationalists in the United States. If he seemed out of place in a conference hall filled mostly with Armenians, it was nothing compared to the alienation he risked among his compatriots.

This was a kind of alienation I was testing out in my own life, not exactly by design. I had begun publishing my first articles as a journalist, and although I thought I wanted to write about anything but the Armenians or the genocide—and although a favorite professor in graduate school warned me that the subject of Armenians and Turks and their "little quarrels" (which cost several million dollars a year in lobbying money and inspired the occasional assassination) would interest no magazine editor—the *Ararat* events had lured me back in. Even as I cast about my journalistic bait, pitching articles on health care in prisons and immigration reform, I kept coming back to the same story.

Except that for me, the story was changing, and within a year of the *Ararat* screening, I was writing about the issue with a new outlook, interviewing Armenian scholars and politicians, and, starting with Taner Akçam, communicating with Turkish historians as well. In the fall of 2004, I wrote an essay for the *Nation* arguing that the Armenian diaspora's obsession with genocide recognition had become its raison d'être, that it had become inextricable from a general hatred toward Turks, and—here was my big hook—that this was actually harmful to the fledgling post-Soviet Republic of Armenia, which desperately needed the economic benefits of diplomatic relations with Turkey.

Turkey had sealed its border with Armenia in 1993, ostensibly in response to Armenia's war with Azerbaijan, a Turkic nation and thus Turkey's national next-of-kin, if there could be such a thing. But I had interviewed Armenian officials who were concerned, privately, that the diaspora's vilification of Turkey—the lobbying, the protests, the boycotts—was the real obstacle to Turkey ever opening the border. Thus Armenia was in a bind; diaspora philanthropists were financing everything there—new streets, schools, hospitals, and an array of NGOs—but the diaspora also fueled a climate of animosity that prevented Armenia and Turkey from establishing neighborly ties. The diaspora obsessed with its homeland was in fact hurting that homeland with its efforts.

With that essay, I had crossed a line, arguing—more or less, and not directly but implicitly—that the genocide recognition campaign was destructive. Several Armenian publications ran articles saying that my moral fiber was damaged, that I had no understanding of the diaspora, and that I was playing right into the hands of Turks. The author of one of these retorts began almost chivalrously, before going on to dispute everything I had written: "I choose to believe that [Toumani] did not intentionally insult the diaspora and demean the citizens of Armenia. Her conclusions indicate that she generally contacted sources who would provide her with answers she apparently was programmed to hear."

While a few friends and relatives confessed they agreed with me, most expressed something like fear.

"Why did you have to publish it in the *Nation*?" several people asked, wishing that I had raised the issue in a community magazine rather than in a national, American one.

"The people on the Hill read that shit," one of my old camp friends told another, who reported the concern back to me.

I told her that the *Nation* had seen better days. But the truth was that I had no interest in community magazines. While there were countless Armenian-American publications that circulated through their diaspora audience with an efficiency and reach that the *New York Times* might have envied, I wanted to make a name for myself outside the community.

As for my parents, they encouraged me, more or less, and this meant a lot, even if it wasn't clear how much of their attitude was simply relief that my ambition of being paid as a journalist was bearing fruit (kumquat-sized fruit, in the case of pay rates at the *Nation*, a nonprofit affair). But they had to answer to their friends, too. *What happened to her?* whispered the men and women gathering in living rooms for tea. *She was always such a nice girl.*

MY ARGUMENT ABOUT the effect of the diaspora's genocide recognition campaigns on Armenia's economy was probably flawed, or at the very least incomplete. But it was as close as I could come to finding an argument that would justify a feeling I didn't know how else to defend: that our obsession with 1915 was destroying us. Emotional logic seemed feeble; I thought I needed geopolitics to make the case. But the case, at its heart, *was* emotional; it was about the cost to our spirits and our imaginations, to our psychological well-being, and to our ability to flourish creatively as individuals.

The Armenian poet and scholar Leonardo Alishan framed the problem twenty years earlier, in an essay called "An Exercise on a Genre for Genocide and Exorcism": "Without art, there was madness. But with this madness, what art could there be?"

Alishan argued that telling the story of the Armenian genocide was impossible because the Armenian artist was always partly a propagandist, always struggling between serving his art and serving his community. Until the world, and Turkey, recognize the genocide, he wrote, Armenians (and especially Armenian artists) cannot digest it. Until it is digested, the story cannot be told in a way that preserves artistic objectivity.

Artistic objectivity: the ability to see a problem or an experience from multiple points of view, to tell a story for the sake of a deeper understanding, not to further an agenda. To inhabit the mind of the villain as fully as that of the victim.

The villain, for me, had always been the Turk. It was time to try to understand him.

PART TWO

Alternate Realities

- 7 -

"So You Are a Bit Mixed Up Now"

I HAD ONLY ONE FULL DAY IN ISTANBUL BEFORE I WAS TO LEAVE FOR Van, a city in southeastern Turkey. I had gotten myself invited to travel through the southeast with a small group of researchers who wanted to find out what remained of the region's formerly Armenian villages. The group was led by a Turkish sociologist named Fatma Müge Göçek.

I had called Müge (she went by her middle name) at the suggestion of Taner Akçam, the Turkish historian I'd first encountered at the academic conference about *Ararat*. I didn't know anything about Müge's travel plans when I called her; the mere fact that she, like Taner, was an ethnically Turkish person analyzing the genocide issue outside of the standard Turkish framework was reason enough for us to speak. After some telephone interviews, I wrote an article for the *Boston Globe* about how Taner and Müge were working with a small group of Armenian and Turkish scholars in an initiative called the Workshop for Armenian-Turkish Scholarship (WATS), an unprecedented effort at cooperating across ethnic lines.

Talking to Taner and Müge on the telephone had been its own adventure; as I took in the sound of the Turkish accent in English—previously unknown to me, even though I prided myself on having a keen ear for the music of each Middle Eastern ethnic group's speaking style—I recognized how preposterous it was, and also how undeniably real, that the mere fact of their Turkishness made each conversation feel frightening as well as thrilling. As a corollary, it amazed me—and disturbed me a bit—that their willingness to acknowledge that the Armenians had faced genocide could so completely alter my sense of them, make them seem safe enough. We were researchers talking on the telephone and yet it was not so great a leap to imagine the effect the same dynamics could have if we were young men in neighboring villages.

Müge and I hit it off. She immediately made me feel comfortable asking questions about Turkey so elementary I hardly knew how to phrase them. I learned that she was raised in a Turkish family that was secular and nationalistic—her grandfather had built his fortune on a flag-making business. Growing up, she had always understood that the Armenians had second-class status, but she had never really known why. Despite having the best education Turkey could offer—Robert College (a liberal, private high school in Istanbul established by missionaries) and then Bosphorus University, which was Istanbul's answer to Berkeley—she knew little about 1915. It was only when she came to the United States, for graduate school at Princeton, that she began to hear about the genocide. "Suddenly I had to account for why I had killed all the Armenians!" Müge told me. As with Taner, a mysterious alchemy of self-questioning, scholarly work, and chance encounters had moved Müge away from the mainstream narrative she was raised with.

After we had spoken on the phone several times—occasionally I would call with a question, or she would get in touch to report an interesting development—Müge told me she was planning a trip to Turkey's southeast, to see for herself what remained of the Armenian villages, as part of her research on what she called "the silences in Turkish history."

To make such a trip was a quietly radical act; Turks who were not from the southeast did not visit the region unless their military duty took them there. It was a far-off place only heard of when state media issued news briefs about roadside bombs and clashes between the Turkish army and Kurdish guerrillas in the PKK (Partiya Karkerên Kurdistan, or the Kurdistan Workers' Party). If a visit there, in 2005, to track down the ghosts of the Armenian population, was not quite on par with taking a bus to the American South during the freedom rides of the 1960s, it was not so far off, either.

Müge would travel with a seventy-year-old man from Istanbul named Sarkis Seropyan. Seropyan was ethnically Armenian but had lived in Istanbul all his life. He was a former appliance salesman and now the publisher of *Agos*, an Armenian newspaper there. Müge had gotten to know him when she approached the newspaper's editor, Hrant Dink, looking for someone to help her with such a trip. Keeping track of Armenian ruins in the southeast was a sort of hobby for Seropyan, so he agreed to come along as a docent.

Müge called him Sarkis *Bey*, combining his Armenian first name with the Turkish honorific, which was a respectful way of addressing a man. Sarkis had been my grandfather's name, and its juxtaposition with a Turkish title was, to my ear, a tiny scandal in itself.

I asked Müge to tell me more about—I tried out the pairing myself— "Sarkis Bey."

What's an Armenian still doing living in Istanbul? I asked her. How could there be an Armenian newspaper there? Wouldn't they get in trouble for tracking down Armenian sites?

Müge laughed and said I should find out all of this for myself. She suggested I come along.

By then, I had mostly gotten used to the strange exhilaration of talking on the phone with a Turk—not just that, but admiring and trusting her, considering her a friend. But to actually go to Turkey?

"Can I bring a tape recorder?" I asked Müge.

"Bring a whole camera crew," she said, with a tone at once dead serious and slightly sarcastic, and followed by the full-spectrum, unencumbered laughter I would come to think of as inextricable from the sound of her voice.

IMMEDIATELY, I APPLIED to a Washington-based think tank for a small grant to fund my trip, proposing to interview the residents of formerly Armenian villages to understand how Turks made sense of the Armenian issue. The think tank was an international organization with an interest in European Union expansion, and the grants director there, an enthusiastic German woman, all but promised me funding; the genocide issue was a recurring snag in Turkey's EU membership talks, and anything that could shed light on the controversy would be relevant. But then she called to say it wouldn't happen. They had recently opened an office in Ankara, and their Turkish program manager there discouraged the support of my

project "in the strongest possible terms," arguing that it was too dangerous and that the timing was not right.

When I told Müge, she was furious, and immediately looked up the
Turkish program manager. A quick Google search told her all she needed
to know about his politics. She offered to write to the grants director
explaining why allowing that particular Turk to vote on my proposal
was equal to guaranteeing its rejection. But the idea of some unseen Turk
in Ankara being aware of my pursuits had already shaken my nerves and I
opted to move on quietly.

Next I tried to get an assignment to write about the trip for a magazine, pitching it as a covert mission with a radical Turkish historian and
a courageous Armenian newspaperman. Each editor I spoke to had the
same response: interesting, but where's the action?

"We're not convinced enough is going to *happen*," a Waspy young
editor at *Harper's* wrote to me, propping the last word up on double
asterisks.

This was difficult for me to understand, since I was expecting that
nothing less than a seismic shift in my internal universe would happen.

Eventually, the editor of a new literary magazine was intrigued enough
to ask me for a dispatch. Even if the only funding would come from my
American Express card, now I had something that passed for a reason.

"So I HEAR you're going to Bolis," an Armenian acquaintance said to me
as I was preparing for the trip. Bolis was the Armenian name for Istanbul, short for Constantinopolis.

"I'll start out in Istanbul, but then I'm going to Van," I replied.

"Oh," she said. "You mean you're going to Western Armenia."

"Actually, Van is in Turkey," I said.

But she knew that.

* * *

IT WAS MIDDAY when I reached my hotel in Istanbul. Müge had recommended the place, an airy, marble-clad little building on the edge of the
old city, and I had reserved a budget room—priced lower than all the other
rooms, it turned out, due to its window being mere inches from the loud-
speaker of the adjoining mosque. I had been up until three a.m. the night

before with last-minute preparations, and had stayed awake through the entire overnight flight, so before I did anything else, I put down my bag, took off my shoes, and lay down on the pristine white bedspread. Labile with fatigue and uncertainty, I wept until I fell asleep, then dreamt wildly until I was awoken at dusk by the call to prayer, its volume so deafening that it sent me into a private giggling fit. Behind these manic emotions was the discovery that all these years, nothing but an ordinary airplane ride and a hotel reservation had separated me from seeing Turkey.

I sat up on my bed—it was the width of a cot and higher than normal, like a doctor's examining table—and for several minutes tried to decide how to deal with the fact that I had to eat. The restaurants immediately outside the hotel were gaudily desperate for tourists. And although I probably knew less about Turkey at that point than the average backpacker, I had a strong urge to seem like I belonged. Exiting the lobby, I walked into a tiny market across the street, tried to indicate with a forceful turn toward a particular shelf that I knew what I was doing, and in less than ten seconds selected a miniature can of Pringles and a peach yogurt. When the man at the register said something short and incomprehensible, I did not have to speak a word before he held up from under the counter a plastic spoon. I only nodded, relieved, and carried my small white plastic bag back to my room with still more feigned assurance. As if anybody cared what I was doing except me.

THE NEXT MORNING, I called Müge on her cell phone to tell her I had arrived, and she surprised me with the news that she had arranged a meeting for me with an old family friend of hers, a man named Nihat Gökyiğit, the founder of one of Turkey's largest corporations. After building a business empire that had made him very wealthy, he had started an environmental protection fund. He was also a patron of the arts and had created a multicultural music group called the Black Sea Orchestra. Müge knew that I sometimes wrote articles about classical music, so she suggested I interview Nihat Bey about his orchestra. He had attended college in the United States and spoke good English.

"I think you will find him very interesting," said Müge.

I felt awkward arriving at the office of someone I'd never heard of, without any specific purpose, but it seemed rude to refuse Müge's offer, so I went. Everything I saw in Turkey, after all, I took as data: this is how roads look in Turkey; this is a Turkish breakfast; this is a brand of Turkish soap; this is the upholstery on the seat of a Turkish car. This will be a Turkish millionaire, I told myself, and handed the driver a slip of paper on which the concierge at my hotel ("this is a smiling Turkish woman who deals with tourists") had written directions.

Thinking back on that first, naive morning, and the weight of the trust I immediately had to hand over to so many strangers, Turkish strangers, I get a fragile, porous feeling in my chest. I recall the white brightness of the day's light, the surprisingly modern buildings, the taxi ascending a hill, and the driver's unspoken understanding that it was up to him, not me, to confer with the security guard and find the appropriate entrance to the large corporate compound where that slip of paper had pointed us.

NIHAT BEY, WHO was nearing eighty, had white hair, a white mustache, and bright blue eyes. We sat in his palatial office, facing each other on velvet armchairs, with a vast, square coffee table between us. An assistant brought in cups of Turkish coffee on a tray, and Nihat Bey told me that his Black Sea Orchestra brought together Iranians and Iraqis, Greeks and Turks, Israelis and Palestinians, Armenians and Azeris.

"Why should these civilizations, East and West, ever clash?" he said. "They can get together and share their talents! You see that painting?" He pointed to one of the forty or so canvases covering his walls. "I got that at the outdoor market in Yerevan."

When Müge told me about Nihat Bey, I had resisted asking her the main question on my mind: had she told him I was Armenian? I was playing it cool; I didn't want Müge to think she'd brought an amateur along on this expedition, and it seemed unsophisticated to let on that I was still basically afraid of any Turk other than her.

Now it was clear that she had indeed told Nihat Bey. The painting he indicated was of Mount Ararat, the twin-peaked mountain that Armenians consider their own. Mount Ararat, which Turks call Ağrı, lies on the Turkish side of the border. In Yerevan, it is how the locals assess the weather: on a clear day you can see Ararat; when it's hazy, you can spy only a bit of the peak. New condos in Yerevan go for a premium if their windows face Ararat.

I examined the painting. When one looks at the mountain from

Armenia, the smaller peak is on the left. From Turkey, the smaller peak is on the right. Nihat Bey's painting looked from Armenia. This seemed like a good sign, so although I hadn't expected to talk about politics with Nihat Bey, I suddenly found myself asking: "Do the Armenian and Turkish musicians in your orchestra ever discuss the Armenian issue?"

He regarded me for a moment.

"I'll tell you a story," he said. "I came from the town in Turkey called Artvin, near the Black Sea. About 1921, the Armenians started leaving for Batumi, in Georgia. My grandfather told me that he wanted to buy a store in town from an Armenian. He wanted it for his two sons. So he went to the Armenian and said, 'I want to buy this store,' and the Armenian said, 'Sixty golds.' My grandfather gave him the money. But later my grandfather thought about it and he said, 'That was not the proper price for this store.' It was not enough. Probably the Armenian wanted to be sure that he could sell it because he had to leave anyway. So he went back to the Armenian and said, 'I have changed my mind. I do not want to buy this store.' 'But why?' the man said. And my grandfather said, 'You did not ask for enough money. I do not want my two sons to live with this on their hearts. I have brought thirty more golds. If you take this, I will buy. Otherwise the deal is off.'"

Nihat Bey waited, to let his message sink in, then he asked me, "How could such people make harm to each other? Impossible!"

"That's a nice story," I said, but I was annoyed by it. His grandfather was the hero, and the Armenian guy was a poor schmuck. The fact that the Armenians "had to leave" did not seem to have troubled Nihat Bey's imagination.

I tried again. "Did you know all your life that there was this question—this issue about what happened to the Armenians?"

"In my family it was not an issue," said Nihat Bey. "We always talked about how good the Armenians were."

"Really?"

"All of the woodwork in my house was done by an Armenian. Very talented woodworkers."

I nodded appreciatively as he motioned to a finely carved molding along the doorway.

I would have to be more direct. "Do you believe that the Turkish government is being honest about the information they have?" My English had already taken on a stilted, simplified quality, recalibrating itself to maintain some kind of polite subordination to my host.

"It is my sincere belief."

"So, what do you think is motivating the Armenians who say that it was genocide and ask for recognition?"

"Hmm?"

"Why do you think they would—"

Nihat Bey cut me off. "I don't know. It doesn't make sense. If they want to be friendly with their neighbors, they shouldn't bring up old issues and go into every parliament in Europe and the United States and always try to push it. Why? I'm asking the question to you now. Why repeat these sad stories over and over? The Turkish side never makes an issue of this with the Armenians.

"It's history," he went on. "So what do the Armenians want to do? They want the Turkish government to accept that we have done such a terrible thing, and that we are going to pay for it? They will never have that."

I didn't say anything.

"They will never have that," he repeated.

And then he talked about Armenian terrorists and Armenian assassins, and how there are two sides to every story.

"So you are a bit mixed up now," Nihat Bey concluded.

And I was. Nihat Bey's words weren't so far off from my own. I had written that the genocide recognition campaigns were hindering diplomatic relations between Armenia and Turkey. I had started to question the value of repeating the same sad stories over and over. But coming from him, the message sounded very different.

Nihat Bey had been educated in the finest and most liberal schools in Turkey and in the United States. He was elegant, generous, and unusually well rounded. He had used his tremendous business success to fund initiatives to protect the environment—his ecology foundation had reforested half of Turkey and was the engine behind the country's new environmental standards. With the orchestras he sponsored, he promoted peace through music. The man had built a sprawling botanical garden on the outskirts of Istanbul, an extraordinary haven for quiet reflection, in memory of his late wife. He had been alive in the world since 1925. He had even been to Armenia. But none of this meant he believed that what had happened was a genocide.

Did it matter? He was a good person, and he was doing remarkable work. I didn't enjoy meeting Nihat Bey, and I wouldn't so much as break the seals on the publicity DVDs he gave me for his various projects. But there was some kind of relief in this meeting—like losing one's virginity, an experience not pleasant but not as bad as one feared it could be, a first time whose chief virtue was that it was over and that I had survived it.

* * *

WHEN I FINALLY met Müge in person, at the airport gate for our flight to Van, she was exactly as I had pictured her during our phone conversations: her easy smile, wavy golden brown hair, bronzed skin, and broad frame made for a powerful physical presence that matched her bold personality.

Sarkis Bey, on the other hand, was not as I had envisioned him at all. In my imagination he was a gentle old man bent over a cane; a sage who had seen things, who dispensed wisdom with a patient glint in his eye. Instead he was a thickset fellow wearing a Yankees cap (a gift from Müge) over his curly though thinning hair, and a fanny pack stretched over his ample belly. He had a jowly, ruddy complexion, and his default expression was something between grumpy and bored.

When Müge introduced us, Sarkis Bey nodded, unsmiling, then handed me a package of cookies he had been powering through.

"Take these," he said to me in Armenian. "The rest of us don't need them."

Sarkis Bey's son Vagharshag was also along for the trip. At thirty-five years old, Vagharshag was in training as a deacon at the Armenian Patriarchate of Istanbul, and he already sported the long, kinky beard of an Orthodox priest. The irony was that I had imagined Sarkis Bey himself as a spiritual figure of some sort; but despite his obsession with the whereabouts of churches throughout the southeast, Sarkis Bey was not among the devout. Later in our trip, when I asked him if he was religious, he did not answer my question directly but said that in Turkey, "atheist" was the worst thing you could call yourself—worse than being Christian or Jewish. He added that he considered a church service to be a wonderful concert. Müge, less circumspect, told me that Sarkis Bey had warned the

Armenian Patriarch that if he were to ordain Vagharshag, Sarkis Bey himself would convert to Islam.

AFTER A THREE-HOUR flight to the other end of the country, we would spend the next eight days wandering in and out of abandoned Armenian churches. We drove a span of six hundred miles, through Van, Bitlis, Muş, Elâzığ, Malatya, Süleymanlı, Adana, and Antakya, our chariot a white minivan caked in dust, driven by a shy-mannered local Kurd named Refik. Half-collapsed monasteries and chapels seemed to appear around every mountain pass, and much of our work, under Sarkis Bey's direction, was simply to find them. Once we found them, our further purpose became vague. We climbed around their broken walls, took a few pictures, and moved on.

Sarkis Bey was an amateur archaeologist of sorts who for years had been collecting old maps, books, postcards, and photographs to help him track down and identify Armenian sites. In reaction to a massive body of literature produced by the Turkish state to retell centuries of history with no mention of the Armenians, there had arisen a kind of volunteer brigade of enthusiasts working to record evidence of the former Armenian population. Their efforts were not exactly coordinated, but in his office at *Agos*, Sarkis Bey acted as a one-man clearinghouse. People wrote to him with bits of information—the partial name of a village or an old document in Armenian that they couldn't read—and he wrote back.

There was an awkward paradox here. It turned out that finding the Armenian sites did not exactly require detective skills. On the contrary, southeastern Turkey was like a giant, open-air museum. In all the ramshackle towns and remote villages, hints of the Armenian past were there like a thousand elephants in the room. Locals were always willing to point out a nearby Armenian structure—occasionally for a fee—even if they knew little else about its origins. In some villages, salvaged gravestones carved in Armenian script held up the sides of homes, reduced to the function of building materials and ornaments. The stones were frequently mortared into place upside down or sideways, their particular hieroglyphics meaningless and irrelevant to the Muslim villagers who had heaved them into position.

But at the same time that Armenian ruins were everywhere if you looked for them, sorting out precise names or other details was nearly impossible. Maps and booklets about the region—glossy freebies from the Turkish Ministry of Tourism piled high in every hotel lobby—told of Anatolian relics and Byzantine-era churches without ever using the word "Armenian." The names of Armenian kingdoms and dynasties were transliterated into Turkish spellings and mentioned with no context, as if they were science fiction galaxies that had never really existed at all: "ASOT III FROM BAGRATS" built the walls at the citadel of Ani, one learned from a sign at the entrance to the ruins near Kars; that would be Ashot the Merciful, king of Armenia during its golden era in the tenth century, who made Ani the capital of the Armenian Bagratuni dynasty.

The Van Museum, like those upside-down gravestones in village walls, turned history on its head. An airy "Massacre Section" on the second floor contained displays describing how Turks were killed by Armenians. Thus the Armenian genocide became the genocide committed by Armenians against Turks. One exhibit included a lengthy pseudoscientific statement about the contents of various mass graves, detailing how Turkish skull shapes would have differed from Armenian ones (the bones in question were said to be Turkish, naturally). The museum gave no indication that any Armenians were ever killed at all.

Despite a lifetime of the words "Turkish" and "denial" being linked together in the deepest center of my brain, I found the brazenness of all this incredible.

Adding to the cognitive dissonance was the fact that the entire southeast was populated by Kurds. The hand of the Turkish state was omnipresent, but there were no ethnic Turks anywhere. Everywhere we went, people spoke in Kurdish, while banners, monuments, and texts carved into buildings and hillsides offered reminders in Turkish from the government: How Happy Is He Who Calls Himself a Turk. The Motherland Cannot Be Divided. A Land Is Not a Nation Until Blood Has Spilled There.

And yet the mood in our car after each day's discoveries betrayed little of the gravity of what we were taking in. Sarkis Bey told us stories about various sites, and Müge kept up a running commentary on the political significance of everything we saw, but none of us ever so much as said out loud, "This is crazy." And as the days went on, I worried that the editor in New York who had doubted that anything would "happen" on this trip was right. My seismic shift had yet to take place. In fact, at times I felt that I was simply on a wonderful vacation.

We sang songs as we drove, pulled peaches from trees that lined the road, cut up a watermelon every afternoon, and every night we sat down to platters of kebab or fresh lahmacun—a savory flatbread my family often bought in batches from the Middle Eastern grocery store under the label "Armenian pizza."

The countryside had the kind of beauty that made you wish you could hold back every modern encroachment—the entire Internet, if not the telephone or even the automobile. In every village, gaggles of smiling children surrounded me, bringing me wildflowers or a circle of fresh bread, and it was only in such moments that my nonchalant demeanor failed. The kids' gap-toothed grins and blameless curiosity left me with a lump in my throat each time we got back in our van. One little girl, an eight-year-old named Ayfer—her name meant "moonlight"—followed me with a gaze of such complex wonder that even Sarkis Bey was moved out of his usual reticence to comment on her old-soul aura. Then again, it was probably just that my uncovered arms and legs made me seem to her like an alien.

Instead of a seismic shift, I was undergoing a kind of exposure therapy. In the same way that people who are afraid of flying might be led by a skilled therapist onto a grounded airplane, sitting back in its quiet seats for several minutes, walking up and down its empty aisles to get comfortable with the environment before taking an actual flight, I was developing the beginnings of a sense of comfort with Turkey. Simply being there in the country's most forgotten reaches, under that sky and sun, eating the food, hearing the music, had a normalizing effect.

ONE DAY, WE set out to visit Çarpanak Island, a distant spot on Lake Van where an obscure church was said to stand. At the dock, a group of men and boys turned up to help us. The oldest, a reserved, white-haired fellow, I assumed to be some kind of boat-hand, but I found out a few hours later—when we were sitting around his dining table—that he was a member of the Turkish parliament representing the Van region. This is how my days went: I scrambled after Müge and Sarkis Bey, trying to understand what was going on, but sometimes—too often—I understood wrong. The parliamentarian was ethnically Kurdish, like everyone else in the area, and I was told his family controlled much of the region in one way or another.

After a leisurely glide across the water in a rusty motorboat, we reached Çarpanak, and I found myself talking to the parliamentarian's twenty-eight-year-old nephew, Renas, who told me he had learned English while studying in Ankara. Tall and thin with pale skin and hair the same almost-black shade as mine, he could have passed for my twin brother. It was a relief to speak to a local person in English, but I had the uneasy feeling that our afternoon-long acquaintance was going to make too great an impression on Renas. In the course of several days, I had not seen one woman out in public. We had encountered them only when we were invited into village homes or yards, and then they were draped in layer upon layer of skirts, often over loose pants, further covered up by aprons or long tunics and vests. The closest we came to seeing an actual female in town was when we found a garish white wedding dress for sale at a convenience store, hanging from the rafter of the shop's porch, in the open air, like a headless bride.

Renas led me through the abandoned church. It was dark inside, but streaks of light sliced through from cracks and windows to reveal that the dirt floor was covered with hundreds of dead birds. The island was nicknamed "Bird Paradise," Renas said, chuckling, as we inched around rotting seagull carcasses. Apparently bird-watchers took boats to the island now and then, but the church itself, an impressive structure from the tenth century, was completely deserted.

As we emerged from the cool interior to the sun outside, my chat with Renas was interrupted by a shout from Müge, who stood on the sand.

"Meline, I'm going for a swim! Come in!"

It had been over one hundred degrees every day, and everything from my toes to my eyelashes was powdered in dust. A swim sounded wonderful. Lake Van, ringed by volcanoes and said to have medicinal waters rich in saline, was as dazzling as any Armenian patriot might have hoped; the lake was mythologized in Armenian literature, and one of its islands, Akdamar, had briefly been a seat of the Armenian kingdom. Of all the things we saw in Turkey, Lake Van was the one sight that impressed me in the way it was supposed to, made me want to be able to say that I had been there and felt its waters on my skin. Hoping we'd get our chance, Müge and I had put on our swimsuits that morning under our clothes.

At the same moment that Müge announced her intention to take a dip, Renas asked me if I was married. I almost said yes, but it seemed like bad karma to lie, so I shook my head no while I watched Müge pull her long sundress over her head, revealing her swimsuit, and jump into the water.

With the sound of the splash, the men on the dock turned their heads and stopped their conversations.

"You like swim?" Renas ventured, grinning.

Swim? I was frozen, stunned by the boldness with which Müge had bared her limbs in front of a group of provincial Muslim Kurds. It was her country, so I could only assume that she knew what she was doing. But I suddenly saw that there was no way I could follow her lead. I could not bring myself to step out in a bikini in front of a group of men who might have only ever seen that much skin on the Internet. No way, I could not do it. This wasn't what I had in mind when I imagined swimming in Lake Van.

Müge called out again, "Meline! It's amazing in here! You have to come in!"

I watched her frolicking in the water, and I could not move.

Ten men and two little boys stood in a line, beaming, their gazes now fixed on me.

Oh no, this would not do. I was not about to fulfill anyone's fantasies about trashy Western women prancing around half-naked. I was a proper Armenian girl. This role that I'd grown to resent was remarkably easy to reclaim.

But then I worried that if I didn't go in, I'd be insulting Müge herself—Müge, without whom I wouldn't be standing on the edge of Lake Van at all—by making her look like the lone hussy while I blushed sweetly from the shore. It was Müge's bravery, after all, that had drawn me to her in the first place. Maybe this was just another front in the battle.

I walked quickly to the edge of the water, stepped out of my sandals, pulled off my top, dropped my skirt, and ran into the cold, beautiful lake.

Müge splashed playfully as I approached her. Once I got close, she lowered her voice and said, "Let me tell you something, Meline." She dunked her head under the water and came back up, shaking out her hair. "You've got to let them know who's calling the shots."

I THOUGHT ABOUT her words for a long time. It could not be said, by any definition, that I was calling the shots. A trip that had started as an act of defiance had so far involved a minor steamrolling by an eighty-year-old Turkish millionaire, a leisurely jaunt through the countryside, and, a few moments after our Lake Van swim, the relinquishing of my e-mail address to a satisfied Renas (he would send me short missives for months to come).

The problem was, I could hardly call the shots when I could not so much as ask someone their name in Turkish. For the most part I trailed behind Müge and Sarkis Bey like an overgrown child, smiling benevolently whether someone was describing last year's grape harvest or the way the next village had been torched in a PKK battle. I had questions to ask and could not find a way to ask them. I worried that I was wasting my only chance.

I wanted to know whether the people we encountered—anyone would do—had ever suspected Turkey's position on the genocide was false. Did they ever feel uncertain? Did they think, maybe, they would be more open to another point of view if it weren't for the Armenian diaspora's protests? Did they know any Armenians? Didn't they think it was strange that a whole nation would carry on for so long if they didn't, ultimately, have a reasonable case to make? Did they spend any time thinking about such things at all?

Sarkis Bey kept asking me to write an article for *Agos* about what we were finding. He used the request as a kind of gentle blackmail: if I tell you about this village, if I tell you about this church, you have to write something about it in *Agos*, he would say. And I kept promising I would, but I knew I wouldn't. Although he himself betrayed little sentimentality, I had a sense that he wanted me to play the role of the awestruck diaspora Armenian returning to lay eyes on the ancestral homeland. But I couldn't write about an awe I didn't actually feel. I thought of some famous lines from an Armenian poem, "Speak, Mountains of Armenia," by the poet Hovhannes Shiraz:

> *Asek lerner, khosek lerner*
> *che vor Vana liche mern er.*
> Go on, mountains, tell them:
> Lake Van was ours, after all.

I was having the opposite impulse, though. I knew, and it didn't bother me, that the lake and the mountains were there for whoever needed them, no more mine than the sky or the sun could be.

NOW AND THEN I asked Sarkis Bey, in Armenian, to pose a question for me or translate a remark, and he tended to wave me off. "It wasn't important," he snapped after a village security guard at Süleymanlı, formerly Zeytun, tried to recite to us a poem he had written about the disappearance of the Armenians.

If that wasn't important, what was? I was interested in people, not churches. For that matter, I was interested in Sarkis Bey, but how could I write in *Agos* that what I discovered on this trip was him?

When Müge described to me this passionate protector of Armenian history, his love of architecture and his penchant for literature and music, I had envisioned somebody easygoing and open—somebody like Müge herself. But Sarkis Bey's enthusiasms seemed tightly controlled. And although he was sometimes visibly angry about the way Armenian traces in the villages were being erased, his outbursts came in private, when we were back in the car. Even then, he was a man of few words. In contrast to the brash, boisterous Armenian men I was used to at gatherings back home, holding forth on any subject, dispensing opinions as facts, this was like discovering a new phenotype. Armenians living in Turkey among Turks nearly a hundred years after the genocide: what had they seen, and what did they have to teach us?

ON SOME LEVEL I had always known that there were Armenians still living in Istanbul; now and then we referred to someone as Bolsahay, which was a contracted version of the words "Istanbul Armenian." Still, by calling them Bolsahay, we never had to say the word "Turkey"; this encouraged a kind of dissociation.

In fact, there were about fifty thousand Armenians remaining in Istanbul, and not one but three Armenian newspapers. *Agos* was the newest of them, created in 1996, and the only one that was explicitly political. Its mission was to expose the problems of the Bolsahay community to the rest of Turkish society. Its name meant "furrow" in Armenian, as in the trench drawn by a plow; something priming the field for new growth. *Agos* was founded after the ASALA era, when Armenians in

Istanbul faced extreme suspicion and pressure. Unlike the two other Armenian papers in Istanbul, which were printed in Armenian script, *Agos* decided to use Turkish, with only a small Armenian-language insert, so that it could reach a wider audience. It gradually earned respect from a particular circle of Turkish intellectuals, the radical liberals who tended to be anti-state and pro–minority rights; a few prominent non-Armenian figures were *Agos* columnists.

By the time I got to Turkey, *Agos* was at the heart of the country's minority-rights debate—a debate that was itself something new. Since 1923, when General Mustafa Kemal—later called Atatürk, which meant "father of all Turks"—had come to power, the country had been run according to Atatürk's decree that every citizen of Turkey was Turkish. This was heralded as an inclusive vision, but in practice it was a rationale for squashing any expression of ethnic or religious difference. The 1923 Treaty of Lausanne had recognized only Armenians, Greeks, and Jews as official minorities, but about 20 percent of Turkey's population considered itself Kurdish. Kurds were not acknowledged in the treaty because they were Muslim—religion, rather than ethnicity, was the distinction that mattered—and as a result it had been illegal until the 1990s even to use the label Kurd; the acceptable term was "mountain Turk."

More than eighty years after Lausanne, Armenians, Greeks, and Jews (the latter two groups by then almost extinct in Turkey) were still living under separate-but-equal rights that were not actually equal at all. Armenians were allowed to operate grade schools that taught their language, but they were required to hire non-Armenian administrators and history teachers; their curriculum was mandated from above, such that Armenian children in Istanbul were taught from an early age that they were traitors and that the state had merely deported some of their ancestors during World War I to protect itself from their betrayals.

The Armenian community also faced restrictions in managing property holdings—churches and school buildings, mostly—a bureaucratic snarl of discriminatory regulations that recalled earlier hardships, such as the 1944 wealth tax in which the country's property owners were taxed to raise funds for national defense. Minorities were taxed disproportionately and arbitrarily, and those who could not pay were sent to labor camps. These misfortunes, it should be noted, were hardly acknowledged in Turkish society; they were not entirely unknown, but rather stored in a deep, collective unconscious along with a handful of other taboos—the Kurdish issue, the power of the military, any criticism of Atatürk—that, according to Taner Akçam, were part of the very foundation of the post-Ottoman-era Turkish Republic.

THE EDITOR OF *Agos*, a man named Hrant Dink, was a well-known figure in Turkey. He had become "that Armenian guy" who spoke on television anytime there was a controversy relating to Armenians. He and his paper had created havoc in 2004 when they printed a scoop whose degree of scandal for Turkey would be hard to overstate: they had evidence, they said, that a woman named Sabiha Gökçen, one of several children that Atatürk had adopted after World War I, had been Armenian. Apparently orphaned during the genocide, Gökçen had been taken in by a Muslim family before becoming Atatürk's little girl.

This would have been bad enough in itself, since one of the most offensive insults you could levy in Turkey would be to say that someone had Armenian origins—the accusation was used casually and metaphorically to complain about bad politicians, naughty children, or even the Kurdish PKK chief, Abdullah Öcalan. In 2008, President Abdullah Gül threatened to sue a Turkish parliamentarian for libel because she had asked, in a fit of pique over some disagreement, whether his grandmother had been Armenian. It was not an accusation befitting the president, and certainly not befitting the daughter of Turkey's immortal leader Atatürk, even if it were true. But to make matters worse, Sabiha Gökçen was a national hero in Turkey in her own right; she was the world's first female fighter pilot, and the subject of classroom reports, school plays, and the namesake of Istanbul's newest airport.

The claim, which was never independently investigated although Dink had offered up his evidence, had shifted *Agos* from being a marginal ethnic paper in Istanbul to being the target of Turkish nationalist wrath. At times the paper's detractors stole whole piles of issues from newsstands, and they once left a black wreath at the office door.

* * *

AFTER THE SOUTHEAST, I had just a few more days to spend in Istanbul. While there, I paid a visit to the office of *Agos*. The newspaper was housed in a small, unmarked building in Istanbul's central business district. A stone staircase curved up to the second floor, where Sarkis Bey welcomed me and showed me his workspace: a large room filled with paintings and posters of important Armenian sites, historical figures, and events. A black-and-white photo taken in the 1920s showed orphans at an Armenian hospital that was still functioning in Istanbul, where Sarkis Bey was a volunteer. He had a collection of crumbling old atlases, which we paged through using a magnifying glass. I saw, now, how he had planned our trip. He had postcards, catalogs, calendars, hand-drawn maps—anything that showed an image or a name could provide a helpful clue to match historical sites with current ruins.

Then Sarkis Bey introduced me to Hrant Dink, the paper's editor. Several people I'd met in Istanbul in the course of two days—mostly journalists and academics that Müge connected me with—had told me I should meet him; he was known for welcoming all sorts of unexpected visitors to the newspaper: reporters who needed information, European anthropologists, and once, I was told, a young Turkish fellow who wanted to marry his Armenian girlfriend and needed advice on how to win her family's support.

Hrant ambled out into the hallway looking like a middle-aged teenage boy: at fifty-one, he was taller than any Armenian man I knew, with an athletic frame and an enviable head of hair that could still be called black. Instead of sitting in his large office, which was lined with stacks of old *Agos* issues, he told his assistants to continue working in there; we went to a small empty room. A young woman rushed in with chairs, and a much older one appeared offering tea. The goofy, faux-modest smile Hrant wore throughout these preparations seemed to hint at an underlying bravado.

Although it was summer, and much of Istanbul was vacationing on the coast or the Prince's Islands, Hrant was working long hours. He apologized if he seemed distracted. He was busy dealing with a lawsuit for something he'd written. He explained that in 2003 and 2004, as part of his regular column, he had written a series of articles called "On Armenian Identity." The series focused on the psychology of the Armenian diaspora. Hrant wrote that diaspora Armenians hated Turkey so much that this hatred had become like a poison in their blood. Rather than waiting for Turkey to change, he said, they should work to rid themselves of hateful feelings toward Turks; they should put aside the genocide recognition campaigns and focus their efforts on helping the country of Armenia. For his series, he had been accused of violating the Turkish penal code by insulting Turkish identity.

"It's just a misunderstanding." He laughed. "They thought I was saying that Turkish blood is poisonous."

I asked him several times to repeat this story. I thought I must have misunderstood something. It was easy to see why his argument would inflame the diaspora, but I couldn't understand why he would be in trouble in Turkey for writing such things.

Hrant said he wasn't worried; an expert commission had been appointed by the court to analyze his articles, and he was confident that when they read the complete text, they would understand that the group he had meant to criticize was the Armenian diaspora.

Changing the subject, Hrant told me he had read and appreciated the essay I had written in the *Nation*. I learned only at that moment that it had been translated into Turkish and published in a local journal. I was mildly disturbed by this flagrant copyright violation, but flattered that Hrant had liked my piece. After several days spent trailing around after Sarkis Bey, trying with little success to figure out what was going on in his mind, now Hrant made me feel as if I had gotten something right after all. At the same time, my argument in the *Nation* seemed to have missed an important point: it wasn't just Armenia that was suffering because of the diaspora's attitude toward Turkey; it was people like Hrant and Sarkis Bey and the entire Istanbul Armenian community.

Many diaspora Armenians found Hrant's ideas offensive in the extreme. I heard that the editor of an Armenian newspaper widely circulated in Europe refused to meet with him altogether when he visited her city. Later, after my trip to Turkey, when I interviewed diaspora leaders for their thoughts on the Bolsahay community, they all repeated the same thing: "The Istanbul Armenians have Stockholm syndrome." The term refers to a phenomenon first identified during a bank robbery in 1973 in Sweden, when several employees were taken hostage, then became emotionally attached to their captors and rejected offers for rescue. Applied to Istanbul Armenians, this struck me as a narrow, coldhearted assessment. When I heard it some months later from an Armenian activist in Brussels, who believed that living among Turks at all was a form of treason, he added that he would "not step his tiniest toe on Turkish soil until Turkey recognizes the genocide." Good luck with that, I thought. Whose loss would it be?

Hrant was sympathetic to the circumstances of the diaspora, even if the diaspora was not sympathetic to his circumstances. "I can really understand their strong emotions," he said. "But we were a productive community for thousands of years. We shouldn't just rely on our hearts and lose our heads."

I studied Hrant, who sat across from me in a plastic office chair, too large for it, leaning forward into an acute angle and suddenly seeming vulnerable with no table between us to contain his long limbs.

One of his younger colleagues came in, a woman my age. She sat down and put the matter to me bluntly: "Without any contact, the diaspora maintains the image of the Turk as a murderer. They assume that Turks know all about 1915 and deny it; but of the ninety years, it has been eighty years of silence." And when the silence was broken for Turks, it was in the form of bombings and shootings in Turkish embassies all over Europe, murders by ASALA and other Armenian terrorist groups. Those murders in the name of avenging the genocide were the first time many Turks heard anything about the genocide at all. A controversial political scientist named Baskın Oran, who wrote for *Agos*, would later put it to me like this: "For Turkey, the ASALA murders were like being woken up at three a.m. with a hand grenade." It was hardly a surprise that the message was not well received.

Hrant jumped in again, speaking with a kind of showmanship—was it masking something?—that made me feel he had given his spiel a thousand times. "Do we have any doubts about what happened? Will it be any more real if they use this word? Everything Armenian in the world is a document."

Before I left, we took a photo together. He gave me copies of the issues of *Agos* in which his controversial columns had appeared, and I left with a pile of them in a shopping bag, feeling inspired by Hrant's optimism. Later I would hear through the grapevine that the editor's confidence was something of an act. He was a lot more worried than he let on.

* * *

BACK HOME IN New York, I stacked those folded newspapers neatly on my dresser, where they remained for months. I couldn't read them, since they were in Turkish, but just knowing what they represented gave me a sense of validation. Before having met Hrant or learning about his ideas, I had come to similar views of my own, and I took comfort in this as I struggled with the confusion of explaining to Armenian friends what I had seen in Turkey and why I had gone in the first place. Hrant was an Armenian living in an oppressive system, but he had not given in to hatefulness. Despite the challenges he faced, he projected clarity and hope.

By October 2005, an expert committee appointed by the Şişli District Criminal Court of Istanbul had reviewed Hrant's articles. As he had expected, the committee understood: it wrote in an unambiguous statement that within his columns, there had been no insult to Turkish identity.

But that did him no good. On October 7, the court, ignoring the committee recommendation, sentenced Hrant to six months in prison for violating Article 301 of the penal code, which prohibited insults to the Turkish nation. The verdict said he had insulted Turkish identity by suggesting Turkish blood was poisonous. It was a "suspended sentence," which meant that he would only have to serve the time in jail if he were found guilty of the same offense again.

The force behind his indictment was a nationalist lawyer named Kemal Kerinçsiz, who had already tried to press charges against Turkish novelists Orhan Pamuk and Elif Shafak for comments each had made about the Armenian issue. But the Turkish media was undoubtedly complicit. All the major papers and TV news programs had reported Hrant's story in just the way the lawyer Kerinçsiz had argued it—"Hrant Dink says Turkish blood is poisonous"—without explaining what Hrant had actually said.

On Christmas Day 2005, there was more bad news from Turkey. A new lawsuit was opened against Hrant because he'd written an editorial in *Agos* criticizing a court decision to cancel an academic conference about the Armenian issue earlier that year (the conference, unprecedented in its openness, eventually took place, but that did not mitigate Hrant's legal problems). The charge this time was "interfering with the judicial process." As publisher of the paper, Sarkis Bey—despite all his carefully crafted discretion—was also named in the suit. If found guilty, they could face up to four and a half years in prison.

I e-mailed Sarkis Bey expressing my concern about the lawsuit; it was impossible to imagine such a thing. "Please send good news," I wrote. He wrote back and didn't mention the charges at all. He told me he had just returned from Switzerland, where he had visited his daughter and her husband and their brand-new baby—a boy. "Finally, we are grandparents," he said. He also asked me why I'd never written that article for *Agos* I promised him.

- 8 -

"Armenians Are Killers of Children"

I HAVE JUST TURNED THIRTY AND AM WORKING AS AN EDITORIAL assistant at the *New York Times*. Standing a block away from my office, in Times Square, I take note of how perfectly the Turkish flags blanketing this intersection today match an overhead billboard for Target, the department store—Atatürk's crescent and star on crimson beneath the red-and-white bull's-eye of American consumerism.

The Turks carry signs on pickets: "ARMENIANS ARE KILLERS OF CHILDREN." A projection screen the size of a truck flashes photos of brutalized bodies along with the words "ARMENIANS! YOU'RE GUILTY OF GENOCIDE!"

One hundred yards south stands a crowd of Armenians, a brigade of young and old, their shoulders caped in the Armenian tricolor, all holding the same sign: "TURKEY GUILTY OF GENOCIDE."

For a few hours of a Saturday afternoon, Times Square has taken on the contours of an Ottoman village. Turks and Armenians, side-by-side but separate. Back then, a passerby might have known a Muslim district from a Christian one by the sound of dialects or the style of turbans, veils, and other garments—clothing was regulated on the sultan's orders to keep distinctions clear. Now, the language all around is English. There are pants and sweaters on both sides of the Forty-First Street parallel, and the only head coverings are hooded raincoats drawn tight to shield against the wind and drizzle of a Manhattan spring. Each of the two groups is penned in by metal police barriers. They would be indistinguishable but for their signs and flags.

For twenty-one years and counting, the Armenians have held a vigil in Times Square on the Sunday closest to April 24. On this date in 1915, two hundred Armenian intellectuals in Constantinople were arrested and deported, an incident that was a kind of Kristallnacht in the way it foretold the years of deportation and massacre that would follow. The commemoration doesn't vary much from year to year. There are elected officials on hand to praise the Armenians' contributions to American society, clergy to lead prayers, perhaps a children's choir, and as many centenarian survivors as are still around to hobble to their feet and receive an ovation.

But today is Saturday, April 22. The Armenian event was planned for the following day, but the Federation of Turkish American Associations and the Young Turks Cultural Association organized today's rally as a counterprotest preempting the vigil. And learning of the Turkish groups' plan at the last minute, the Armenians put together a counter-counterprotest. Both sides hired buses to bring in their members from throughout the tristate area.

The Turkish groups are not, strictly speaking, representing just Turkey. They are joined by Azerbaijani-Americans, who carry banners about the 1990s war between Armenia and Azerbaijan over Nagorno-Karabakh. That was a bloody ground war that saw massive losses on both sides, but in which Armenians, ultimately, came out on top, still controlling the territory in question two decades later. Many of the signs accusing Armenians of genocide actually refer to pogroms within the Karabakh war. If this is confusing for outsiders, it is perfectly clear for those involved; Turks and Azeris consider themselves cousins, and Armenians consider all of them Turks. The definition of "us against them" can expand to contain this, too.

THAT DAY I stood among the Turks. I wanted to see how it would feel. Nobody could tell by my appearance that I was not Turkish. The challenge was only to act natural when a young woman on a small stage in front of me, a woman about my age, with black hair dyed blond and straightened, concluded her speech in clean, unaccented English.

"In summary, we are here today to prove once and for all that there never was an Armenian genocide."

The audience applauded, cheers mingling with the whirring, honking noise of midtown traffic.

I looked at the faces of people around me and tried to imagine their thoughts. The man standing next to me caught my eye and smiled. I smiled back. Another tried to sell me a self-published book titled "False Armenian Allegations." I handed him seven dollars and put it in my bag.

Then I walked south toward my clan, the Armenians. At the front of the group, I saw one of my father's old friends. Beside him, a girl I recognized from summer camp.

An empty stretch of puddles and potholes served as a neutral corridor between the protests, and as I crossed it I was met by a young man with dark brown hair and thick eyebrows. He whipped a flyer toward me and said in a rapid monotone: "Recognize the Armenian genocide."

"What does that mean?" I asked, accepting his flyer.

"It's the first genocide of the twentieth century," he replied, looking beyond me for the next passerby.

"I know," I said. "What does it mean to recognize it?"

"It's the first genocide of the twentieth century."

Another young man moved in from the opposite direction, holding a stack of glossy, colorful postcards. "It's all lies, don't believe him," he said. He handed me a postcard that promised to clarify the "erroneous claims of Armenians." These words were printed in a font more suited to promoting a nightclub.

The Armenian fellow tried to block his hand. "He's got the wrong flyers," he said. "You don't want those."

With that, the two of them began to shout at each other past my face, a script so familiar I could have recited it in my sleep.

"It was a war. The Armenians were traitors—"

"My grandmother was not a traitor—"

"They fought with the Russians—"

"You've been brainwashed by your government—"

Now and then they gestured to me, as though the debate were for my benefit. Despite my black hair and brown eyes and a nose that defied European proportions, it didn't seem to occur to anyone that I might have a stake in the matter, and I knew why: it was unimaginable that if I were Armenian or Turkish I would have been wandering between the two demonstrations, allowing myself to be in that kind of intolerable physical proximity to the other side—whichever side that may have been.

As I considered whether to tell them I was Armenian—I felt somewhat guilty, and ridiculous, and irritated, and also tempted to startle these fellows with my willful calm—another guy walked up. More dark hair and eyebrows, and I couldn't guess which side he was on, until he handed me a flyer and invoked the Armenians' favorite trump card: "Go look up what Hitler said about the Armenian genocide before he killed all the Jews!"

I did not need to look up what Hitler had said. It had been my catechism as much as his, but it was no longer enough for me.

I WAS ALREADY planning my return to Turkey. A few months after that April 24, I finished a book proposal, and soon I had offers from several publishing houses to take on my project for a sum that would enable me to spend time in Istanbul doing research. I would stay there for a month or two, maybe three at the most—I bought a one-way ticket just to keep my options open—and talk to people, but more importantly listen.

It would be an act of diplomacy in the form of a book. I wanted to set out new rules of engagement that actually involved engagement. I would find a way to present each side to the other that would move people toward connection rather than continued animosity. I would learn to speak Turkish, and I would meet with Turks from all walks of life, and I believed—truly believed—that if I spoke to them in a certain way, with a certain kind of tact and with precisely the right words, I would be able to make some sort of breakthrough. I was sure I would discover that many Turks did actually know how much the Armenians had suffered. And that maybe they even wanted an opportunity to let the denial go. I felt that my ability to be self-critical as an Armenian—to question the dynamics of diaspora activism and to see Turks as human regardless of their views—would help me win people's trust. I would also go to Armenia and show that Armenians there wanted open borders and an end to the relentless focus on 1915. I believed all this, and the people who pay for the creation of serious books apparently believed it, too, which gave me the confidence (and the resources) I needed.

Soon I had an apartment reserved in Istanbul and a growing list of contacts gathered over e-mail and telephone, people in Turkey who could help me pursue my work. Since returning from the trip with Müge, I had become more involved with WATS, the Workshop for Armenian-Turkish Scholarship, which was expanding to include human rights activists in Turkey, and it seemed there were plenty of people on the other side who were eager to connect with an open-minded Armenian from the diaspora. I planned to spend more time with Hrant Dink, who perfectly embodied the approach I was interested in. I wanted to understand the Bolsahay community better; they had lived alongside Turks throughout everything, and there would be wisdom in this experience, I was convinced. But I also planned to spend time with ultranationalists, military wives, government officials, anyone who would be willing to sit down with me—the greater the challenge, the better. (I was not entirely sure how I would get some of these people to oblige, but my book proposal promised, with no sign of doubt, whole chapters profiling such individuals.)

Over e-mail I informed Sarkis Bey that I was coming back, and through Müge I lined up a translator for myself. I read everything I could get my hands on. This time I would be prepared.

- 9 -

January 19, 2007

HE HAD JUST GONE OUT FOR A MINUTE. HE HAD SOME BUSINESS AT the bank. The bank was right on the corner so he didn't even tell his colleagues he was leaving. They had just finished a meeting to plan the next week's paper. During the meeting, a young man wearing a white ski cap rang at the *Agos* office door. He was a university student from Ankara, he told the secretary, and he wished to meet with Hrant Dink.

Hrant is busy today, the secretary apologized.

Later, the bank's video camera would reveal shadowy images of a young man in a white cap watching Hrant make his transaction.

Hrant walked back toward the office. He was just a few feet from the door when the shot was fired. It came from behind him, piercing the back of his head.

Sarkis Bey saw the body first. He had heard the commotion and ran downstairs, and then immediately turned around and told some of the younger staff members that it was nothing, to stay back. He was in a state of shock. He told me later that he could not imagine he had said such a thing.

In minutes, other members of the *Agos* staff would be doubled over behind the railing of the balcony of their editor's office, shielding their eyes from the sight of a white tarp on the sidewalk below. From one end of the tarp a pair of shoes extended, heels bent outward. At the other end blood soaked through as it pooled around Hrant's head, which rested facedown on the pavement.

A crowd formed immediately. The sound of the words "Hrant Dink" piled up from overlapping voices as bystanders dialed their cell phones to pass on the news. "Hrant Dink, that Armenian guy."

Police put up tape to clear a large space around Hrant's body. Then a man burst through the crowd screaming "Abi!" Turkish for big brother. Police tried to hold him back, then let him through. Yervant Dink crouched beside his older brother's body and sobbed, clasping his hands over his eyes.

A few men and women from the *Agos* staff huddled together nearby, unable to turn toward the body, unable to go inside. "I was fixated on the bullet casing," Sarkis Bey later recalled. "It rolled back and forth, making an arc on the sidewalk. Should we take it inside and hide it?" he wondered. "Why don't I take off my jacket and put it under Hrant's head? But I couldn't do even that. I see myself in the news videos just standing there."

It was January 19, 2007. The wind was strong that afternoon, and the tarp kept blowing off. Somebody placed bricks at the corners to hold it in place. This made the center of the tarp rise like a sail so that for a while the body was again visible to the growing crowd. Even when the breeze settled, the tarp could not cover his shoes. Hrant's towering height had always given him an air of invincibility, but now it meant that the image of his skyward soles, one of them torn, would be broadcast again and again for months and even years whenever the murder of the Armenian journalist was in the news once more.

By evening, thousands had gathered, Istanbul dwellers of all backgrounds, filling the six-lane boulevard in front of *Agos* and the expanse of nearby Taksim Square. On pieces of cardboard people scrawled a few words in Turkish that had never been put together before: *HEPIMIZ HRANTIZ. HEPIMIZ ERMENIYIZ.* "We are all Hrant. We are all Armenian."

Days later, tens of thousands of mourners of all ethnic and social backgrounds would carry the same message on placards in a silent funeral march.

THE FOLLOWING NIGHT they caught the killer. His image was there on the security cameras of nearby shops as well as those of a public surveillance system that continuously monitored Istanbul's streets. When the pictures were broadcast on television, the boy's own father, sitting in the living room of the family home, at the other end of the country in the Black Sea city of Trabzon, recognized his son. He called the police. "He told us he was just going to his uncle's house."

The gunman was a seventeen-year-old high school dropout named Ogün Samast. After completing his task in Istanbul, Samast had boarded a bus back to Trabzon, but about ten hours in, a little more than halfway there, as the bus neared the city of Samsun, the driver received a call from the police: you'll stop at Samsun. They told him why.

Once the Samsun police had Samast in custody, they asked him if he had killed the Armenian newspaper editor. He confessed immediately. They asked him why and he answered that he had read on the Internet that Hrant Dink said Turkish blood was poisonous. He was defending the honor of the Turkish nation.

Before they sent him back to the Istanbul authorities, a few junior officers posed for souvenir snapshots with Samast. They positioned him in front of a poster of Atatürk and handed him a Turkish flag.

The killer's personal motives, it would soon come to light, were incidental; he was merely the henchman for a network of people—including some with ties to Turkish intelligence and security forces—who had been planning the murder for some time. Hrant himself knew he was in danger. A search of his computer turned up thousands of e-mailed death threats.

Hrant's lawyer had worried about his client's growing anxiety, he later told me. "We met at his office one evening. I told him it was time for him to keep his distance—go to Europe for a month or two," he said. "But he told me he can't stand being away. 'After two days in Europe I find I just want to come home.' Then he asked me if he should write an article about the threats he had received. I said yes, I've been telling you for more than a year to do that. Write it step by step. Explain the trials, how you were summoned by the governor, the demonstrations in front of *Agos*, and publish it in all the liberal newspapers. But as we came down the steps and kissed each other on the cheeks to say good-bye, I was thinking there's no way he'll write it. Then he looked into my eyes and he said 'I'm going to write it.'"

The column ran in the issue of *Agos* that came out a few hours before the murder. The title was "Why Have I Been Targeted?"

SOON HRANT'S ENTIRE life story was encapsulated in media coverage. He was born in the eastern town of Malatya. His father had a gambling problem that tore the family apart. He and his two brothers were sent to an orphanage in Istanbul run by the Armenian Protestant church. He met his wife, Rakel, at the orphanage summer camp. Decades later, pious Christians both, they helped rebuild the camp with their own hands. They had four children and a second grandchild was on the way.

"Hrant Dink Is Turkey" was the headline at the top of *Milliyet* newspaper.

"The Biggest Treachery" came from the front of *Sabah*, another major mainstream daily.

For the first few days the TV cameras did not leave the scene of the crime. This media reaction might be understood as repentance, considering what had come before. It so happened that the morning of the murder, all the major papers had run provocative stories reporting that Sylvester Stallone was rumored to be making a movie about the "so-called genocide." *Sabah*'s front page said, "Rambo Is Like an ASALA Militant." This sort of gratuitously charged presentation of any fragment of news about Armenians was as regular an occurrence in the Turkish press as the soccer scores and weather reports that abutted it. References to ASALA were shoehorned into seemingly unrelated stories as often as possible.

Yet even as politicians, journalists, and other public figures condemned the crime and sent condolences to the family, many of their comments had a particular emphasis: "It Is Turkey That Was Shot" was the banner headline on *Hürriyet*, the country's largest paper. "Turkey will be blamed for everything," wrote a prominent columnist. Prime Minister Recep Tayyip Erdoğan made a statement on the evening of the murder saying that dark forces had once again chosen Turkey. He went on to note that it was significant that the murder occurred at the same time that parliaments around the world were considering resolutions about the "so-called genocide."

International media outlets covered the murder extensively and suggested that judging from the hundred thousand people shouting "We are all Armenian," the awful crime might be the catalyst for bringing Turks and Armenians together. It would seem that way, wouldn't it? They were words nobody could have imagined hearing and their echo would not soon fade. But the opposite sentiment could not be drowned out so easily. The night of the murder, a message in blue spray paint appeared on the wall of an Armenian church in Istanbul: "One Hrant killed, here's to many Hrants. Die, filthy Armenian."

A couple days later a group marched down İstiklâl Street, Istanbul's pedestrian avenue, chanting, "We are all Mustafa Kemal. We are all Turks." One of the protesters was questioned by a reporter. "When our ambassadors were killed by ASALA, did any Armenian say 'We are all Turks'?" the protester said.

The leader of the Nationalist Action Party made a statement: they were not all Hrants, they were all Mehmets. "In some circles this event is being used to paint a picture of Turkish society as guilty. We do not accept this." (His party would double its popular support in that summer's elections, winning 15 percent of the vote.)

The weekend after the murder, a widely beloved singer, Bülent Ersoy, shared a similar view while serving as a judge on the popular music show *Popstar Alatürka*. Ersoy, a transsexual dressed in gaudy gowns that showcased giant breast implants, announced condolences to the family but then said, "I absolutely don't accept that 'We are all Armenian' slogan. If it were only 'We are all Hrant' that would express our unity. But I am not Christian, so even if you tied me up I could never say that I am Armenian. I'm a Muslim girl and I will die a Muslim," the transgendered pop star said.

The same weekend, at a soccer match between teams from Trabzon and Kayseri, young fans sported white ski caps similar to the one that had been the killer's identifying feature. A pep rally leader shouted into a megaphone, "Get up on your feet or else be Armenian!"

And in the city of Sinop, a small-time journalist named Mete Cağdaş decided to sue the mayor of Şişli, the Istanbul district where the funeral march began. Turkish law allowed private citizens to initiate such lawsuits. "They carried placards saying 'Hrant's murderer is Article 301.' They branded the laws of the Turkish Republic as murderers. Shouting 'We are all Armenian,' they violated the constitution. They insulted the unity of the nation with separatism based on race. They caused traffic congestion. With live broadcasts, they encouraged others to take part in the demonstration. They did not carry even one Turkish flag. What more do you need? Treason, provocation, separatism and extreme disturbance. I am complaining and am a plaintiff. Honorable Prosecutor, please start an investigation."

* * *

THE NEWS OF Hrant's murder reached me by e-mail when I woke up in New York that morning. The e-mail came from an American, a distant acquaintance who ran a hedge fund that did business in Turkey.

"This doesn't sound like good news," he wrote, forwarding me an alert sent less than an hour after the murder from a Turkish investment bank to its clients:

"Hrant Dink, the Turkish-Armenian editor of Agop newspaper is assassinated. Last year he was tried under Turkey's freedom of expression laws regarding his comments on the so-called Armenian genocide. The identity of the murderer is not identified yet. The market reacted to the assassination by a sharp fall in the afternoon session."

January 19, the day of the murder, was supposed to be my last Friday of work at the *New York Times*. The following week I would leave to spend some time in London and Vienna, then go on to Turkey. My department had arranged a little going-away party for me for that afternoon, champagne in the conference room. Somehow, I got dressed and arrived at the office. In the hour between receiving that first e-mail at home and reaching my computer at work, my brain had constructed the possibility that there was a mistake and that the news was inaccurate—not just in the shell-shocked way one rejects information when grief first explodes, but in a rational sense, because I could imagine nearly any magnitude of falsehood being generated by the Turkish or Armenian media. Maybe this was just a really heinous rumor.

But by the time I sat down in my cubicle, my in-box was flooded with e-mails that eradicated any doubt. My boss passed by and said good morning, and I stared right past him, then started to sob. I tried to explain what had happened. Colleagues gathered around to find out why I was hysterical, and I heard somebody say, "Her friend was shot."

Hrant wasn't my friend. He was a person I had spoken to for an hour, more than a year before. In the days and months to come, anybody who had ever shaken the man's hand would claim the honor of his friendship.

He didn't need to be my friend: what was unbearable was that the person who had tried harder than anyone to use love to fight hatred, to believe in the power of patience and compassion, was the one they had killed. And something even simpler: that they hated us—Armenians—that much. For the first time in a long time, I felt like a part of that "us." I was terrified.

THAT E-MAIL FROM the investment bank had contained a mistake: "Hrant Dink, the Turkish-Armenian editor of Agop newspaper is assassinated." The misspelling of *Agos* was an oversight, but not necessarily a random one. "Agop" is a common Armenian name, the Turkish-Armenian spelling of Jacob. In Turkey, the name Agop is sometimes used as slang for any Armenian man—an average Armenian Joe. Or maybe not quite average: the name is tied to a range of cultural references in which Agop is an unfortunate character for one reason or another—now blind, now missing an arm, now a hopeless glutton—but always a good guy. A good guy with bad luck. A person who would do well to be more careful.

PART THREE

Turkey

- 10 -

Paradoxes

ERTAN, MY INTERPRETER, TOLD ME TO MEET HIM AT THE OFFICE OF the publishing house where he worked. When he gave me the address on İstiklâl Street, he offered two different numbers. "It is either 465 or 231," he said.

In the past few years, the municipality of Istanbul had renumbered all the addresses in the historic Beyoğlu district, a decision made to account for new buildings and other problems of urban evolution. But it was unrealistic to expect everyone to adjust overnight, they reasoned, so the old address numbers had not been removed. On each building up and down İstiklâl Street, a mile-long pedestrian stretch that was the heart of Istanbul's social and retail life, one set of numbers was in blue and the other in red. After a while, people lost track of which were old and which were new, so it was typical to hear addresses including both. Ertan had also said to look for the doorway next to Starbucks, but there were three Starbucks just on the ten-minute walk from my house to his office.

When I finally found 465 or 231, I searched the jumble of business signs tacked up around the entryway but saw no mention of Aras Publishing. Inside, at the end of a long corridor, a man carrying a tray of tiny glass teacups—the building *çaycı*, or tea seller—pointed me to the right office.

Aras Publishing specialized in books about Armenian subjects; this explained its inconspicuous entrance. What was strange was that Ertan, who was not Armenian, had been working there for several years, translating English-language books into Turkish. Since Hrant's death, he had also been working as an editor at *Agos*. Ertan was a Turk—not a Kurdish Turk or a Greek Turk or even a Jewish Turk, although he did like to point out that he had roots in Salonika, so who knew?—but just a regular Turk. Müge had helped me find him when I told her I needed an interpreter, somebody with excellent English skills and experience with the Armenian community.

Ertan was thirty-four years old and skinny to the point of looking malnourished, with profound eyes, bristly brown hair that grew out rather than down, and a beard that was getting thick enough to seem like some kind of statement. The first time I met him, he told me, unbidden, that he had stopped cutting his hair after Hrant's death. I assumed this was a custom of mourning, but as I got to know him better I realized he meant he was simply too busy to go to the barber. Ertan was the kind of person who did not waste time on ordinary vanities when there was more important work to do. If that had a way of becoming its own sort of vanity, it was nonetheless clear that in this season of his life, there always was more important work to do. I trusted Ertan instantly. How could I not? He looked, inarguably, like Jesus.

In the Aras office, tables were piled high with scores of books the company had published, all sorts of books about Armenian topics, written in or translated into Turkish. There were novels by Armenian writers, classics and obscure ones, all of which Ertan was able to speak about in admiring detail. There were memoirs describing life in Ottoman villages, volumes of poetry, photography, even cookbooks. Running my fingers over these stacks, I was amazed that just a few steps off one of Istanbul's busiest streets, a world of Armenian culture was flourishing. But as I looked at the titles more carefully, I realized that none of them crossed a certain line: none were directly about the genocide. The reason was obvious: the company would have been shut down immediately. More interesting was the effect: the literature Aras published may have been restricted in its subject matter, but in a different way it was liberated. To my eyes, fatigued by the thought of ever reading another genocide memoir, Armenian culture seemed enriched by this vast collection of books that were not directly about 1915. It was forced to find itself in topics other than the genocide.

ERTAN AND I set off for what was our main purpose that day: to meet his friend Deniz, who had agreed to share the job of being my translator, and to lay out the plans for my project. There were two reasons Ertan wanted to split this job with his friend; the first was that he was already overcommitted, with his work at Aras and *Agos* and a variety of other projects. The second was that Deniz was apparently leagues deep in a procrastination vortex related to his PhD dissertation in sociology, and Ertan thought working with me would help get him out of his rut.

"How is your new flat, Meline?" Ertan asked as we walked.

"It's lovely."

"How much is your rent?"

"Um, well, it's not cheap," I confessed.

"How not cheap?" he asked.

"I don't want to say. It might be embarrassingly not cheap."

"These landlords can really take advantage of foreigners. We can talk to him for you if necessary. But I cannot assess the situation if you do not tell me the price."

A few days earlier, when I had exchanged money and keys with the landlord, I had been a feeble haggler. Armenians have a reputation as penny-pinchers, shrewd businessmen, and although I had not even told the landlord I was Armenian, I could not bear the thought that if he found out, I would seem to fit the stereotype. This notion of some innate Armenian talent for commerce mystified me; I had seen no evidence of it myself. But throughout the Middle East and Russia we were considered Shylocks one and all, always out to cheat and scheme and get a better deal. In the Ottoman era, an American missionary writing in the *Christian Herald* summarized it neatly, reporting that "the people of the East" sized up their neighbors as follows: "two Jews are equal to one Greek, and two Greeks are equal to one Armenian. This means that in commercial shrewdness one Armenian is equal to four Jews. Such people are generally unpopular everywhere."

My landlord was a forty-something man named Sinan who had studied in London and spoke good English. Apart from his price gouging, he had welcomed me warmly, walking me through my new neighborhood and explaining how things worked. First he took me to the grocer on the corner. In a closet-sized shop, four women in head scarves stood behind the counter chatting. Sinan told them that I had moved in across the street.

"They say you should call them if you need something but don't want to leave the house," he told me.

One woman wrote down the phone number and extended it in my direction, her smile encouraging. Stepping back outside, I looked at my new home, only thirty feet away, and tried to imagine a circumstance in which I would feel the need to have groceries brought right to my door.

But it turned out this sort of microdelivery was not treated as a luxury in Istanbul. Continuing up the street, I saw a round wicker basket descending slowly through the air, being lowered on a long rope by a man in a fourth-floor window. As it neared street level, a younger man removed a few coins from the basket and replaced them with a loaf of bread and a pack of cigarettes. The basket then wobbled back up to its owner. I was transfixed.

"I guess you haven't seen that in New York," Sinan said, laughing.

In Istanbul, service like this had a particular grace about it, felt less like exploitative labor than like a matter of the merchant's pride. At a bar or restaurant, if someone ran out of cigarettes, it was entirely normal to ask the waiter to get a fresh pack—not because cigarettes were kept in stock but because there was always a nephew on hand to run across the street to buy them; and when the pack arrived at the table a few minutes later, it might be on a silver plate, the wrapping removed and the top cracked open, with one cigarette pulled halfway out as if beckoning. It was typical, too, to request items not on the menu such as a last-minute birthday cake; the restaurant owner would simply call a cousin nearby who ran a pastry shop, and when the meal was finished an elaborate torte would appear with candles flickering.

At times I would witness Turks uttering food requests so specific, they'd have made the most demanding New Yorker blush: "I'd like a plate of plain, peeled cucumbers, actually. Is that possible? But I'd like them cut in a special way; first lengthwise and then cut in half," one friend said to a waitress, who smiled and brought back exactly that. In a dinner gathering of twenty people, another friend told a waiter that her stomach had been a bit upset all week. "Could you ask the kitchen to prepare a bowl of plain pasta, no oil, but with some yogurt on top? And there should be some herbs, maybe mint, if possible." As for the grocery deliveries deposited into baskets on ropes, if somebody took an aerial shot of Istanbul at just the right hour of a Sunday morning, the streets of every neighborhood would be dotted with round wicker containers moving up and down at various heights.

Around the corner from my new house was a pickle seller, or *turşucu*: in his window sat jars of pickled carrots, tomatoes, artichokes, pumpkin, eggplant—anything that could fit in a jar could be pickled. Across from the *turşucu* was a *ciğerci*, or offal butcher, displaying a skein of kidneys hung above neat piles of liver and brain. We waved at the *ciğerci* as we walked by.

The neighborhood, Çukurcuma, was popular among expats, but many locals considered it blighted and dangerous, in much the same way that longtime Manhattanites had trouble accepting that the formerly crime-ridden borough of Brooklyn had become a desirable place to live. In Istanbul, the elite preferred gated communities far from the city center, or neighborhoods along the Bosphorus coast, such as Bebek, where see-and-be-seen nightspots and twee boutiques could make a person think they were in Beverly Hills. My neighborhood did have sketchy spots, like an alley nearby where homeless teenagers sniffed glue from plastic bags late at night and a tucked-away *hamam* that was rumored to be more brothel than bathhouse. But there were also antique shops and booksellers, boho-chic restaurants, and the ateliers of artisans young and old making pottery and leather goods. And along the steep cobblestone lane where I lived, at least twenty cats of all colors and sizes lounged indifferently.

I don't even like cats, but I was entranced by this stray-animal orgy—and it *was* an orgy, I would soon learn, when night after night the felines screamed sounds not meant to be heard in this life. Like the clocks that appeared to melt over branches and tables in Dalí's painting, the cats of Istanbul draped their torsos over warm car hoods; they hid behind tires, staged complex turf wars on single-file, high stone walls, and guarded doorways, entering and exiting apartment buildings as they pleased. Such a scene would be considered a major pest management problem in much of the West. And Istanbul tried so hard in some ways to be Western. The Atatürk International Airport, for starters, was a monument to European efficiency; it was aggressively modern, with so many moving walkways that if they were laid end to end, they might transport a person all the way to Brussels. But it was the cats of Istanbul that revealed the city's gentle chaos.

In the days to come, as I explored the city center, I discovered that these cats were everywhere, a wonderful absurdity, often twenty or thirty claiming a small block, and that Turks regarded them not as strays but as a communal obligation. Underneath the window of a ground-level flat, one would see a heap of last night's dinner atop a leaf of newspaper; maybe leftover stew with lamb and vegetables, maybe just some noodles or bulgur pilaf. The cats came and went, considering the menu du jour with the caprice of spoiled children. Now and then one saw a bowl of dry cat food; it was not so unusual to purchase a bag to dole out to animals that one did not own.

This collective sense of responsibility, it seemed, was the best thing about Turkey and also the most problematic, for the other side of a shared obligation is the shared weight of liability and even shame, surfacing sometimes over the most trivial matters but at other times, when the stakes were truly significant, hardening into a defensiveness that was impenetrable.

AFTER INTRODUCING ME to an old fellow across from the mosque who wore a prayer cap and sold fresh eggs and yogurt, Sinan took me to meet the *simitçi*. Simit is Turkey's national snack. The classic simit is a ring of bread larger than a bagel and flatter, covered with sesame seeds. A simit vendor could be found every few paces from one end of Turkey to the other. Some pushed simit carts down the street as part of a municipal cooperative, and others carried trays of simit on their heads: the trays were twice the size of a large pizza pan, and the simit was piled as high as a wedding cake. When the *simitçi* encountered a customer, he would stop and squat slowly, until the tray on his head was low enough that the person could select a simit from the stack. The random passerby was entrusted to choose even at the risk of toppling the entire pile of simit onto the sidewalk.

There is another kind of simit: dense, bite-sized butter biscuits, their surfaces tanned with egg and sprinkled with black seeds. These could be savory or sweet; *tuzlu* or *tatlı*. Sinan asked the woman at the simit shop for half a kilo of each kind, and after she gave him two brimming gray paper sacks, he handed them to me. I tried to give him money but he refused.

"A welcome gift," he said. "You're still tired from traveling and need something to eat until you do your shopping."

Turks and their glorious hospitality; what it meant was that nearly every foreigner who set foot in Turkey fell in love with the place within minutes. In Islam, guests were considered messengers from the almighty; an unexpected visitor was called *tanrı misafiri*, a guest from God, and to treat them as anything less was a spiritual failure. Before I had spent time in Turkey, it drove me crazy when American friends or acquaintances made a trip there and returned with stories of the generosity they encountered. I didn't want to hear it. It felt like a big con, designed to distract from abuses both current and historical. But I was quickly seduced, too, and that particular enchantment never really broke; it only stretched to accommodate new realizations.

Taking in the delights of the neighborhood with Sinan, I had nearly forgotten where I was—or rather, who I was. My reverie was interrupted by a thought: would Sinan be as kind to me if he knew that I was Armenian? I felt almost guilty not having told him, as though he had the right to know what he had gotten himself into by renting an apartment to me. This wasn't just paranoia; if the label "Armenian journalist" would never have been neutral in Turkey, in the weeks after Hrant's murder it evoked actual danger. Would my phone be tapped? Would my windows be watched? And if something went wrong, whose side would the landlord be on?

I DECIDED TO tell Ertan what I was paying in rent, but I rounded the number down by about 20 percent, wanting first to gauge his reaction.

"Is that liras or dollars?" he asked.

"Euros," I admitted.

"That is very, very expensive."

With the landlord I had worried about seeming like an Armenian cheapskate, but with Ertan I felt the burden of being American, as if I carelessly tossed money around everywhere I went. The truth was, I had arranged to rent the apartment before I'd even arrived, using a fancy online brokerage service, knowing full well I'd be paying too much, because it promised to be a more or less anonymous transaction. If there was one thing I needed at least the illusion of in order to feel comfortable taking up residence in Turkey, it was anonymity.

"You should have asked me for help," Ertan said, sounding irritated. "That is really too expensive."

I figured I might as well understand the full cost of my cautionary measures. "Would you say it's grotesquely expensive?" I asked.

"Yes," he nodded, smiling appreciatively now. "*Grotesquely.*"

Because Ertan translated literature for a living, he took pleasure in certain words I used in English, and I, in turn, took pleasure in introducing them to him. Both of us had an endless attention span for etymology and linguistics, which was a nice but inefficient point of compatibility for a journalist and her interpreter. One day he called me from his job at the publishing house to ask about the word "whitewash." We chatted for a good fifteen minutes as I explained the many different connotations. It could mean concealing the truth, I said, as in "Turkey whitewashes the story of what happened to the Armenians." Or, in the American context, it could be a metaphor for issues of race relations, implying that white was somehow purifying, or that black culture was being undermined. Ertan listened patiently throughout my lecture, offering an "I see!" or "That's very interesting!" now and then. Also, I concluded, it could simply refer to a kind of thin, white paint. I gave the example of a scene from *The Adventures of Tom Sawyer* in which Tom whitewashed a fence. "How is it used in your text?" I finally asked.

"It is used in reference to building materials. The people in a village are painting a wall in the traditional whitewashed style."

* * *

DENIZ HAD TOLD us to meet him in an out-of-the-way pastry shop. As we waited, I asked Ertan to tell me more about his friend. I had been fortunate to find Ertan, but it seemed unlikely there would be too many more people like him: fluent in Turkish and English and comfortable talking about the Armenian genocide with strangers.

"Deniz is very, very smart," Ertan said. "He is much smarter than me, and his English is much better."

Just then, an olive-skinned fellow appeared at our table, grinning. It was a grin that looked mischievous, then and ever after, because his upper lip peaked higher on the left side when he smiled. He had thick black eyebrows, black eyes, and the soft black curls of a Middle Eastern cherub. Wire-rimmed glasses added a hint of gravitas. Deniz had arrived.

"What's up, dudes?" he said, shaking my hand. Deniz had completed part of his doctoral course work in New York, and could have just as easily been discussing Lacan in English. He delivered his favorite bits of American slang with an extra-heavy accent, intentionally making fun of himself for trying to sound colloquial. He sat down and placed a silver tobacco case on the table, opened it to reveal a jumble of brown shreds and white filters, and began to roll a cigarette. The three of us sat silently as he rolled and rerolled until it was just right.

The purpose of our meeting was to discuss my plans for interviewing people about the Armenian issue: where I wanted to go, who I wanted to meet, and how we would divide the work. I suggested we go down the list so they could get a sense of my intentions, and then we could decide who would join me for each interview.

The first few names I mentioned drew nods and sounds of recognition. A prominent human rights lawyer—"Yes, I know her very well, that will be no problem," said Ertan; or a sociologist noted for his renegade views—"He is in my department at the university, I can ask him," said Deniz. A few newspaper columnists, some activists, various community leaders. They added suggestions of their own, nodding approvingly at each other as I wrote down the names.

I had organized my list into two categories: minority views and mainstream views. As I passed from the first list to the second, suddenly the affirmative murmurs from Ertan and Deniz ceased. I continued reading names. I thought I noticed a smile taking shape on Ertan's face, and then—just after I said, "Yusuf Halaçoğlu, the president of the Turkish Historical Society"—Deniz burst into a high-pitched, nervous laugh.

"What?" I said.

"Why do you want to talk to those people?" Deniz asked, now giggling like a schoolgirl.

"Don't you think it would be fascinating to understand what goes on in their minds?" I said.

"Why do you think anything goes on in their minds?" he said, laughing more, now joined by Ertan, and finally by me, the three of us soon clutching our stomachs and rattling the cups on the small table between us.

"Okay," I finally said. "But the whole point of my project is to find a way to connect with people who don't already think the same as me."

"Yes, you may be right," Ertan said, getting serious again. "It is important for you to talk to people with different opinions. My parents live in Ankara. We can go there to interview Yusuf Halaçoğlu and we will stay at their house. It will be a good excuse to make my mother happy."

I continued on with the list of nationalists and known Armenian-haters, they snickered a few times and made some jokes, and then I reached the last name on my list.

"Kemal Kerinçsiz."

Nobody said anything.

"He's that lawyer, you know, the one who—"

"We know who he is," said Ertan.

Neither of them was smiling now. Kemal Kerinçsiz was the lawyer who brought charges against Hrant. He was the one who distorted Hrant's comments and set off the smear campaign that led to his murder. More direct connections to the murder would surface later. He was also the head of the Great Union of Jurists, a group of lawyers who sought to revive the dream of a pan-Turkic empire that would stretch all the way to China.

"I'm sorry," said Ertan. "I cannot participate in that interview."

"Why?" I asked. "Are you afraid that you could get in trouble?"

"I am not afraid," Ertan said.

"So what's the problem?"

"It's simple. I will not sit in the same room with that monster."

I looked at Deniz. He shook his head.

MY INTERPRETERS BELONGED to a tiny but vocal outer fringe of Turks, a cohort of activists, journalists, sociologists, historians, and lawyers who, for reasons much broader than the Armenian issue, had nonetheless taken up the Armenian issue, had accepted that Turkey needed to acknowledge what happened in 1915. Risking lawsuits and death threats, some of them freely called it genocide; others did not necessarily embrace the word, but pushed for more openness on the subject anyway.

The genocide, however, was only a small piece of the picture: these people were committed to a larger vision of a democratic society. They favored greater cultural rights for Turkey's Kurds, drastic changes to the way women were treated (even though Turkey's secular elite liked to believe that Atatürk's fascistic decrees for gender equality, like ordering police to rip the head scarves off old women, had settled the issue), and saw a society-wide need to acknowledge the hardships that minorities, including Greeks and Jews, had faced in Ottoman times and throughout the decades since. They considered the power of the military a fundamental problem, and the consequent obsession with national security—used as an excuse for all sorts of prohibitions—as the greatest symptom of this problem.

These views would seem unsurprising to many Westerners, similar to the ideals of liberals in any society. But in Turkey, people like Ertan and Deniz were radicals. They needed to be understood as completely distinct from another type of liberal, a subset that confounded the assumptions of, say, an American journalist: this subset was popularly known as "White Turks."

For the first few months I spent in Turkey, I tried to flesh out the particulars of what it meant to be a White Turk, asking Ertan and Deniz small anthropological questions nearly every day. The label had nothing to do with skin tone. It described somebody who had all the superficial trappings of the West: stylish clothes, stylish interests (photography was a big one, along with yoga), and most likely an academic degree from somewhere in Europe or the United States—but despite these surface signs of being open-minded, believed strongly in Turkey's staunchly nationalist, secularist old guard, also known as the Kemalist establishment, after Mustafa Kemal Atatürk. This old guard fetishized the goal of modernity—Atatürk's great project for Turkey—but was often intolerant and even tyrannical in service of it. The Kemalist doctrine was inhospitable not only to ethnic minorities but also to excessively pious Muslims, whose head scarves and baggy pants the White Turk found embarrassing.

The White Turk might have gay friends, and might like edgy contemporary art, but he would also do entirely un-edgy things now and then, like replace his Facebook photo with a Turkish flag or a favorite image of Atatürk gazing down upon the world. Baskın Oran, the *Agos* columnist, described White Turks as people who were "appropriate citizens according to the State." (At the time I was in Turkey, Oran's summary still perfectly described the power dynamics there; but a sea change was taking shape. Before long, pious Muslims would have unprecedented power, while White Turks would be left feeling like underdogs.)

Most Americans and Europeans would be captivated by the White Turks they met—how seamlessly they embodied that elusive East-West balance—until they made the mistake of bringing up one of three untouchable issues: Armenians, Kurds, or the fact that there was a picture of Atatürk in every store and office across the nation. Then their new friend's fuse would blow and the complexities of the typology would reveal themselves.

* * *

DENIZ WAS AN Alevi Kurd from the province of Tunceli, formerly Dersim. Alevis were Muslim, but practiced a more liberal variant that was influenced by Sufism. Alevis could be Turkish or Kurdish; either way, they faced persecution from the mainstream Sunni Muslim community, which considered them heretics. If the two most problematic identities in Turkey at the dawn of the twenty-first century were Armenian and Kurdish, Alevi was in third place. As an Alevi Kurd, Deniz had two of the three categories covered, and to make it a hat trick, he also had an Armenian girlfriend, a woman from Istanbul who was completing her PhD abroad. This made me see him as something like a cousin. When he introduced me to his mother, a modest, elderly lady, she hugged me over and over and said to Deniz, "Are you sure she's not from Dersim? She looks like one of ours."

One Friday night a couple weeks after I arrived, Deniz invited me to go out with a group of his friends. He met me at my front door; Deniz and Ertan both insisted on doing so for weeks before they would let me meet them at locations more mutually convenient. This was a latent chivalry that occasionally possessed them even though they were nobody's definition of macho. Along the same lines, they tried to pick up the tab whenever we went out, despite the fact that I was technically employing them. (Such gender expectations were hardwired in me, too; I was raised in a Middle Eastern family, after all. But I was also filing occasional stories for the *Times* under a freelance agreement in which I swore never to accept gifts on the job, so the payment issue was one of many arenas where I struggled to balance conflicting roles.)

As Deniz and I walked down İstiklâl Street, he pointed out numerous "passages" that specialized in different sorts of retail goods. These bustling arcades in grand stone buildings housed tradesmen and merchants selling everything from discounted H&M irregulars to electronics and housewares. Until the early twentieth century, this neighborhood, then known as Pera, was largely the domain of Armenians, Jews, Greeks, and European traders. Many of the buildings were constructed in the Ottoman era by Armenian architects, and accordingly some of the passages had Armenian names. I walked by one of these for the better part of a year before I noticed its tiny sign, faded and outdone by bright ads for tailors and law offices, announcing Tokatlıyan Pasajı. The name itself was a passage of sorts: it came from an Armenian hotelier, Mıgırdiç Tokatlıyan, who was originally from Tokat, near the Black Sea. Tokatlıyan erected the building in 1897 as a 160-room luxury hotel, renowned in its early years as one of Constantinople's finest. Now it was one of the shabbier facades on İstiklâl. As for the name of the passage, it was not only inconspicuous but misunderstood by some Turks, who did not know an Armenian surname when they saw one. "Tokatlıyan" looked almost identical to *tokatlayan*, a form of the Turkish verb *tokatlamak*, to slap; thus *tokatlayan pasaj*, although an improbable phrase, would mean "a passage that slaps." People couldn't resist teasing one another when they walked through Tokatlıyan Pasajı: "Watch out, this passage might slap you!"

THE BUILDINGS STANDING shoulder to shoulder along the noble avenue were like sentries guarding access to disorderly backstreets flooded with seekers of nightlife. As we navigated this tangle of alleys behind İstiklâl Street, competing music blasted from the speakers of each café and bar. Deniz stopped in front of a doorway where a Bon Jovi song boomed by way of invitation. It was an Irish pub, complete with a Guinness sign in the window. About ten of his friends were gathered around a long table. Before I knew what was happening, I was seated next to a fellow named Hakan, and Deniz was at the other end of the room. This made me nervous; I wasn't sure what I was supposed to reveal to these people. I didn't want to spoil a Friday evening social gathering by saying something inflammatory. So I decided to forestall receiving questions by asking them myself.

"What do you do here?" I said, turning to Hakan.

"I am a graduate student at Bosphorus University," he said. Bosphorus—or Boğaziçi in Turkish—was known to be a very progressive campus, but Hakan looked conservative to me, wearing grandma glasses and a collared shirt, so I imagined he might be an engineering student or a business major. I asked him what department.

"History," he said. "Late Ottoman history and the situation of minorities."

I looked down the table for Deniz, who was chatting and laughing with his friends. Why had he left me with this character? A student of late Ottoman history was certain to have his anti-Armenian arguments close at hand. Sure, I had said I wanted to talk to such people, but the moment caught me unprepared.

"And why did you come to Turkey?" Hakan asked.

"I'm just doing some research," I said. Now two of his friends were listening to our conversation, and I grew even more uneasy.

"What kind of research?"

"I'm not sure yet," I lied. "I'm still figuring it out."

Hakan looked puzzled. I figured he could shrug off my apparent lack of purpose as just another American with money to burn, a Fulbrighter perhaps. I got up to go to the bathroom.

When I returned, Hakan stood up, pulled my chair out for me, and handed me a beer. "Meline!" he shouted. "Why didn't you tell us?"

"Tell you what?"

"You are Armenian!"

I glared at Deniz.

Hakan led the entire table in a grand clinking of pint glasses. "You are our brother!" he proclaimed. Then he put down his drink and threw an arm around my shoulders. I was completely confused.

"You're Armenian, too?" I asked.

"We are Kurds!"

IN THE MONTHS ahead, I would grow close with Hakan and two of his friends, Murat and Özgür. I learned that in spite of their impressive diplomas and jobs—Özgür worked for a major American consulting firm, Murat at an important Istanbul think tank—they felt like second-class citizens. Like most Kurds in Istanbul, they had roots in the Kurdish towns of the southeast. They were raised speaking Kurdish, and some of their relatives couldn't speak Turkish at all. But between 1983 and 1991—their childhood years—it was illegal to use Kurdish even in private, or to give

Kurdish names to children. Only recently was broadcasting in Kurdish decriminalized. Growing up, they had been forced to pledge their allegiance to Turkey at the start and end of every school week, in an oath for pupils that begins "I am Turkish, I am honest and hardworking . . . My existence shall be dedicated to Turkish existence . . ." and ends, "How happy is one who can say 'I am a Turk.'" My new friends felt their culture, the very basic fact of who they were, was being denied. It was worse than denying history; it was denying the present.

Before going to Turkey, I had envisioned a nation with only one event on its historical timeline: "Turkey, place where genocides are denied," the sign at the border would have read. It was a revelation, however late in coming, to learn that Turks had endured wave after wave of instability: a series of military coups between 1960 and 1980; the rise of a Maoist left given to violence and shock tactics; bloody conflicts between the military and Kurdish rebel groups; clashes between Sunni and Alevi Muslims; fascism, martial law, and mockery on the world stage. Turkey had its own problems, its own grief and fear.

Hakan, Murat, and Özgür, along with Ertan and Deniz and several others I would get to know, formed a network I relied on, the first link of which had been Müge. One to the next, they ferried me around, hosted me in their homes, and humbled me with their energy and insights. Together, they were like some kind of "aboveground railroad"—watching out for me as though I needed protection—but in their willingness to help an Armenian who came to their country as if to enemy territory, there was a paradox: I was not the one with the most at stake. I could leave at any time, whereas my Turkish friends had to live out the consequences of their political and moral positions. Within this paradox was another one: for so long I had feared "Turkey," but all of these people were Turkey.

- 11 -

Language

THERE WERE TWO MAIN TURKISH-LANGUAGE SCHOOLS FOR FOREIGN-ers in Istanbul: Tömer and Dilmer. Tömer was an acronym for "Türkçe Öğretim Merkezi," or Turkish Learning Center. Dilmer stood for "Dil Merkezi," or Language Center. Ertan suggested I try Dilmer; he said he had heard it was somewhat "alternative." The way he phrased this, I imagined Montessori-style playgroups. Then I looked at the Web sites of both schools and realized what "alternative" signified in the Turkish context: free of direct government control. Tömer was connected to Ankara State University. It advertised massive discounts for anyone who had at least one Turkish parent; anyone of any nationality who was married to a Turk; and anyone who hailed from one of the "Turkic republics," which it helpfully specified: Azerbaijan, Uzbekistan, Tajikistan, Kazakhstan, Kyrgyzstan, as well as Tatar, Turkmen, Uighur, and Hazara peoples.

As for Dilmer, if the only evidence of an alternative approach was that course fees were not calculated like DNA tests, that was good enough. (Good enough to get me in the door, anyway: I found out later that Dilmer offered similar discounts but hadn't listed them online yet.)

My teacher for level one was Mehmet Bey, a man in his midforties who wore a proper gray suit every day. He was a picture of conformity, like a harmless middle manager, padded and pink as though he'd gone straight from his mother's kitchen to his wife's without missing a meal in between. His complexion suggested that he'd not smoked a cigarette or taken a drink in his life, and it was only his crew cut of silvering hair and his suits that gave him an air of authority.

I found myself eager to impress Mehmet Bey. I had been fairly insulated from mainstream Turks until then, spending time with Ertan and Deniz or at the *Agos* office. The safety of a classroom seemed like a good place to get acclimated. A language teacher is always, for his students, like an entire country distilled into a person. Besides, I had been poring over grammar books for months, at home in New York, and I was ready to be put to the test.

According to the Turkish Language Association, about twelve percent of words used in Turkish are borrowed from Arabic, Persian, or French; in practice, the number is higher because many Turkish words that were invented to replace foreign ones never caught on. With a rudimentary knowledge of Persian and eight years of French from high school and college, I had a head start on my classmates. Most of them were young Europeans working in Turkey—a Swiss archaeologist, a German teacher, and a Belgian finance adviser among them. There was also a Korean businessman, and a couple of canny Russian women who had met Turkish husbands on the Internet—they disclosed this openly—and were studying the language to communicate with their new in-laws.

On the first day of class, we learned to introduce ourselves. Catherine, a middle-aged French woman weighed down by a cargo of expensive baubles, had been living in Turkey for twenty years, but had never taken a language class. Although she feigned modesty, she was already able to carry a conversation in what Turks liked to call "Tarzan Turkish." She kicked off the exercise: "Benim adım Catherine. Fransa'dan geliyorum." My name is Catherine. I come from France.

Next was a young German student who tried to follow Catherine's example. "Benim adım Liesl. Fransa'dan geliyorum."

Mehmet Bey laughed. "Fransa means 'France,'" he said. "You come from Almanya."

For each student's home country, Mehmet Bey had a ready point of reference. To the finance adviser: "Belgium! Didn't you bring us some chocolate?" About Germany, he offered a slightly fraught commentary on why Turks refer to splitting a bill in a restaurant as paying "German-style," while many other cultures call it "going Dutch."

When it was my turn I said, "Benim adım Meline. Amerika'dan geliyorum."

Beside me, the next student began to speak but Mehmet Bey held up a hand to stop him. "Meh-lee-neh," he said, repeating it slowly, with perfect pronunciation.

I nodded.

Then Mehmet Bey went to the dry-erase board and wrote my name in large block letters with a red pen. After M-E-L-I-N-E, he added a question mark and looked at me for confirmation of the spelling.

I nodded again, beaming. Although my name is distinctly Armenian, Turks did not recognize it as such—the vacuum of knowledge about Armenian culture ensured this. But the sounds and syllables we used were similar, so my name came easily to them, resembling their Emine or Melike, common names for girls. Even the counter clerks at Istanbul's many Starbucks cafés who wrote my name on the sides of cappuccino cups tended to spell it right without asking. This gave me more satisfaction than it would seem to warrant; the very thing that always caused a moment of awkwardness when I met a new person in America gave me a flash of belonging here, in the last place I'd have expected it.

Next, Mehmet Bey erased the question mark with the side of his fist and replaced it with a long blank line where my last name would go. "Soyadınız ne?"

"Toumani," I told him.

"Meline Toumani," he said, in the same measured articulation.

I nodded again.

"But that is not an American name." He spoke in English now, emphasizing the word *not*. "Meline Toumani, what is your real origin?"

My brain started to buzz the way it does on a stage or in a job interview. "I was born in Iran," I answered.

"Ah, Musulmansınız!" So I was Muslim, he said. He liked this.

"Musulman?" he repeated.

I shook my head. In an instant I had gone from feeling slightly smug to paralyzed, like the impotence of a dream in which you cannot will whatever action—run, scream, open a door—you need to take.

Mehmet Bey tipped his head slightly to the right and, with his eyes, invited me to explain.

"Armenian."

"Ermenian!" he exclaimed, pronouncing it the Turkish way—their word was *Ermeni*—and lifting his voice in what sounded like forced nonchalance. I waited to see what would follow, but by the downbeat he had turned to another student.

I couldn't keep track of the next few people introducing themselves; I was too rattled. Looking around the room, I noticed Catherine, the French woman, staring in my direction. As I met her gaze she blinked both eyes tightly with a kind of smile, which I took as a knowing sympathy. I blinked back. It was humiliating the way Mehmet Bey had moved on without comment, as though I had answered the simple question of where I was from with the words, "I like to tap-dance naked in my bedroom"—something a person wasn't expected to disclose to strangers. At least the Europeans understood, I thought, feeling grateful to Catherine for her wordless acknowledgment.

Soon the teacher was on to a new question: where in Istanbul did we live?

Catherine volunteered. She said that she lived in Sarıyer.

Mehmet Bey turned to the class and explained that Sarıyer was a beautiful district way up the Bosphorus, known for its old fishing villages and historic seaside mansions.

Catherine nodded proudly. "And do you know which house is ours?" she said, dropping her *h* and *r* in the French way, *which ouse is ouwz.* "We couldn't afford it but it was too beautiful! I live in Enver Paşa's old mansion." She laughed, a percussive smoker's laugh.

Was I hearing things? Enver Paşa was considered the most powerful leader of the late Ottoman Empire, and one of the three chiefs of the Young Turk government directly responsible for the Armenian genocide. Since childhood, their names had lurked in my mind as a triumvirate of evil: Enver Paşa, Talat Paşa, Cemal Paşa. Could she really have just said Enver Paşa? My name is Catherine, Meline is Armenian, and I live in Enver Paşa's house. The other students looked on blankly. The name meant nothing to anyone in the room except for Catherine, Mehmet Bey, and me.

After class I found myself on the sidewalk with Catherine. I wasn't sure what to say; she had seemed like an ally, but then she had mentioned Enver Paşa with an exuberance that I found inscrutable. Catherine dug around in her giant Chanel bag for a while before asking me for a light. Then she asked what I was doing in Turkey.

"Some research," I told her. "I'm a journalist."

"Ah, but you're an Armenian journalist. So I guess you came here to prove that a genocide occurred." Her smile was pinched now, and the tightening of her cheeks made layers of makeup divide in the creases around her eyes. "You know, it's very bad what the Armenians have done to us French. You made our parliament write that paper, and now Turkey is very angry about anything French," she said. "Eight months I had to wait for my residence permit! It's terrible."

She was referring to the fact that the very energetic French-Armenian diaspora had convinced the French Senate to give preliminary passage to a bill making it a crime to deny the Armenian genocide. The second house of parliament had said it would not move the bill forward to become law, but this didn't stop Turks from taking the gesture personally. Turkish TV stations broadcasted the debates live, and thousands of Turks vowed to go to France just to deny the genocide and get themselves arrested. Prime Minister Erdoğan blocked France's involvement in an eight-billion-dollar gas pipeline that was in the works, and military ties with France were suspended. For a while, anything French was fair game. In central Istanbul, a famous alley of cafés long known as Paris Street was rechristened Algeria Street. A gleaming, new block-lettered street sign installed by the city served mainly to confuse tourists holding suddenly outdated maps.

The subject of my origins never came up again in Mehmet Bey's class, and instead of Catherine, I befriended the German students. But I was attuned to imagined innuendos like a Cold War–era conspiracy theorist might have detected atomic secrets in the morning news. Whatever the day's lesson, my mind could find a connection to the genocide. One day we were learning adjectives in pairs of opposites: hot/cold, black/white, tall/short, and, somewhere down the list, true/false. Mehmet Bey paused on this last example and explained the difference between the usage of the word "false"—*yanlış*—and the word *yalan*, for "lie." Was he trying to tell me something?

When Mehmet Bey reacted to the word "Armenian" by pretending I hadn't said anything unusual, I felt, for the first time, what it was like to be made invisible. Up until that point, I thought invisibility was exactly what I needed; I didn't want anybody to know what I was up to. Hrant's murder had only strengthened the impulse to stay inconspicuous. But being totally unacknowledged felt terrible—maybe worse than if Mehmet Bey said something blunt, like "I don't accept that there was a genocide"—even though he surely assumed silence was the more considerate alternative.

The incident also made me want even more to impress Mehmet Bey. I couldn't help it. I had a fantasy that if I were the best student in his class, he would come away thinking just a little bit better about Armenians in general. "But there was that nice, smart Armenian girl at the language school," he might tell his wife.

His reaction was only one in a vast collection of responses I collected and sorted over time, like a scientist on an expedition; on good days I saw these reactions as butterflies with fascinating patterns; on bad days—more often—I saw them as strains of a virus. As it turned out, I was forced to reveal I was Armenian constantly, without the benefit of preambles or introductions, and the reason was simple: on appearance, I could pass for Turkish, so people spoke to me in Turkish. When I opened my mouth to reply and they discovered that I was foreign, they always wanted to know more.

"Come on, you don't seem American! Is your mother Turkish? Is your father Turkish?" Their sense of recognition was primal in its enthusiasm and had to be gratified with a commensurate explanation. Inevitably, I would end up confessing the truth.

Like Mehmet Bey, many people reacted by ignoring what I had said altogether, or they changed the subject in a farcical manner.

"I'm Armenian!"

"The weather's been beautiful lately, hasn't it?"

But the most complicated response consisted of just one word, a word I learned in level one Turkish but whose nuances blossomed over time: the word was *olsun*. A conjugation of the verb *olmak*, to be, *olsun* is the third-person subjunctive: let it be; so be it. But it's not a defiant "so be it," and not entirely a resignation either. It is the sort of thing you say if a waiter tells you that he's sorry, there's no lentil soup today, but he can offer you tomato soup. "*Olsun*," you reply. You had hoped for lentil soup, but you'll make do. Or if a friend calls to ask whether your meeting can be postponed by an hour: "*Olsun*," you tell her; you're not in a big rush. Depending on the context, *olsun* can mean "no problem," or it can mean, "fine, if you must." Over and over, when I told people I was Armenian, they said, simply, "Olsun." *Olsun*, we'll manage. *Olsun*, it's not your fault. *Olsun*, so you were born into a traitorous and unpleasant people, what can you do? *Olsun*, it's not as if I'm some kind of racist and am going to treat you differently because of this unfortunate new information.

* * *

WORDS HAVE SPECIAL power in Turkey. So many of them need to be used precisely a certain way or not at all.

In 2009, the mayor of Diyarbakır, a Kurd, got a ten-month prison sentence for referring to members of the PKK as guerrillas. The allowed term was "terrorists." Countless others were investigated for calling the PKK leader Abdullah Öcalan "Sayın Öcalan," because *sayın*, an honorific one step more formal than *bey*, seemed to give him too much respect.

Any journalist who failed to refer to a fallen Turkish soldier as a "martyr," or *şehit*, risked his job—and just to be clear, this was martyrdom for the idea of Turkey, stripped of religious meaning (soldiers who went so far as to pray on the job had been charged with lacking discipline).

The letters Q, W, and X had long been against the law, officially because they were not a part of the Turkish alphabet. Strangely, this law was invoked only when the letters appeared in Kurdish words. Kurdish lawyers spent their breath in court pointing out the double standard: "But your honor! Every Web site address uses the letter W at least three times! So should the entire Internet be illegal, too?"

Actually, large swaths of the Internet *were* illegal. From 2008 until 2010, all of YouTube was inaccessible through Turkish Internet providers because a Greek user had posted a video calling Atatürk a homosexual. Wordpress was off-limits for much of that time, too. By 2013, some thirty thousand sites—touching on everything from pornography to the theory of evolution—had been blocked. And, although Prime Minister Erdoğan lifted the embargo on Q, W, and X in September 2013, early in 2014 he banned Twitter for a few days and threatened to prohibit other social media sites if their users did not behave. All things considered, it was no surprise that a multitude of Armenian-related Web sites could not be loaded; in their place one would reach a few lines of text explaining that the site was banned by order of the telecommunications ministry.

The word for genocide, in Turkish, is *soykırım*; its etymology is plain— "soy" meaning race, and "kırım" meaning destruction. But in Turkish, *soykırım* was first brought into widespread use to refer to the Jewish Holocaust. Some Turks, meaning to be helpful, argue that this is part of the problem with applying the word to the Armenian case. They know all about Hitler, and there's no way they can accept the possibility that the word for what Hitler did can be applied to the events of 1915. Nothing could share a label with a tragedy as monstrous as the Holocaust, the *soykırım* of the Jews, they reason.

Unfortunately, this argument falls apart regularly, often on television, because Prime Minister Erdoğan has a habit of referring to every occasion of violence that he personally finds offensive as *soykırım*. Throughout the war in Iraq, he referred to a US-led *soykırım* of the Iraqis. During the Gaza War in 2009, he decried the *soykırım* of Palestinians by Israelis. Later that year, when protests in northeastern China started by the Uighur population—a Muslim group with Turkic roots—turned violent, resulting in some two hundred deaths (many of these Han Chinese, although details on the death toll are disputed), Erdoğan immediately accused China of *soykırım* against the Uighurs and called for an apology.

* * *

OLSUN. DESPITE A stressful beginning, I thrilled to studying Turkish and took language classes daily for over a year. Whereas I had always been shy about speaking Armenian, in Turkish I became irrepressible. Nothing was expected of me. Anything I managed was a bonus. And if learning the language only expanded my awareness of Turkey's darker struggles, it also gave me access to the particular sweetness of Turkish manners.

My favorite expressions were the ones that had an established two-person script, a call and response, like welcome, *hoşgeldiniz*—"it's nice that you came"—and its reply, *hoşbulduk*, "we found it nice." Sure, the word "welcome" had the same underlying meaning in English, but in a new language such deadened phrases come back to life, vital as if crafted by a poet. For me, the unique greetings and expressions of Turkish never ceased to mean exactly what they said: bidding good-bye, for example, the person who is leaving says *hoşça kalın*, "stay well," while the person staying behind responds with *güle güle*—"go smiling" (literally, "smiling, smiling"). When somebody sneezes, you say *çok yaşa*—"live long"—and they respond with *sen de gör*, "may you also live to see it."

Turkish is full of affectionate expressions for strangers. When encountering people busy with work, whether crossing the path of a ditchdigger or upon entrance to a law office, the thing to say is *kolay gelsin*—"may your work come easily"—and after a meal, to the cook, *elinize sağlık*—"health to your hands." To a fortune-teller or any speaker who has said something memorable, *ağzına sağlık*—"health to your mouth." In Turkish, it seemed to me as if everyone was always fussing over everyone else.

Everyone was always keeping tabs on one another, too. This was best captured in the simple expression *afiyet olsun*, a phrase heard countless times every day. Beginning students of Turkish are taught that *afiyet olsun* means something like "bon appétit." The meaning sticks easily because of the wholly coincidental resemblance of the Turkish word *afiyet* to the word "appetite." The words are not related; *afiyet* means welfare, not appetite, and a more technical translation of the phrase would be "may it be sustaining." But the key is in usage, and in this *afiyet olsun* is far more expressive than bon appétit, as any American chowing down on a pastry or a sandwich in public will soon discover. "*Afiyet olsun*," a man on the train may say, with a merry face but an undertone of the slightest judgment, if he spies you so much as eating an apple on your way to work—something a Turk would have taken care of before leaving the house. "*Afiyet olsun*," says a woman in a café, raising an eyebrow, as you tuck into a decadent dessert at the table next to hers. Underlying these weird intrusions, it seemed to me, were complex layers of meaning, telling a person not to be greedy, not to take what they had for granted, not to be too certain that they deserved their pleasure.

Once, a German classmate named Kai came to our morning lesson with a sack of fresh simit, nibbling on pieces he broke off under his desk, apparently oblivious to the way its doughy fragrance was filling the room.

"*Afiyet olsun!*" said the teacher, a fastidious woman named Sibil, striding directly to his desk.

"Thank you!" Kai replied, and continued nibbling.

But Sibil *Hanım* didn't move; "*Afiyet olsun*," she said again, this time separating out each syllable to make her point.

"Thanks?" Kai said again, now uncertain.

Finally Sibil *Hanım* explained that it was very rude to bring simit to class unless you planned to share it with everyone. The poor fellow reached into his bag and extended a simit in each hand to the students around him, sending a shower of sesame seeds to the floor but finding no takers.

Afiyet olsun and all the other expressions that passed between strangers were more than communication; they were random acts of linguistic codependency.

LEARNING THE LANGUAGE was my one pure love in Turkey. Its obvious function was to help me connect with people—to say to every new Turk I met that I was trying to understand them; that I came in peace. But it also sustained me by bringing to life a private Istanbul of my imagination, an Istanbul of sound and music, a place where nobody cared who I was or what I was doing. I got to know this Istanbul, less seen than heard, while lying in bed every morning, and every morning this Istanbul convinced me to stay a little bit longer.

The music began at five a.m. with the *ezan*, or call to prayer. My apartment was within earshot of four different mosques. Their calls came staggered by seconds, a gentle competition five times a day, until I knew every nuance and faltering pitch of each muezzin, and the precise moments when the rise of one and the fall of another would cross in a moment of aggressive dissonance or, occasionally, exquisite harmony.

Shortly after the five a.m. call, all the shopkeepers on my street, their morning prayers finished, got ready for work, yanking up the metal grates that protected their storefronts through the night. One could adjust, after a while, to sleeping through the muezzins' early chants; for the first *ezan* of the day, the speakers were softened just slightly, a small municipal concession. But nobody could sleep through the harsh rattle of the security grates rising up on the shops; one after another they jolted through me every morning, a momentary rasp and then silence, followed by another rasp, and another, until all the neighborhood's unpious were likewise wide awake.

By eight a.m. the street was a carnival of merchants, circling with their wares and their songs, swooping shouts that entered my head and threatened never to leave. Each street porter had refined his unique call, and often these had evolved to the point where they barely resembled words so much as jingles to be recognized.

Every neighborhood had a *simitçi*, who trucked his rings of bread at breakfast time with only a utilitarian cry of "Simit! Simitçim!" But each neighborhood also had its special porters. There was the man who sold socks, *çorap*, and called "*Çoraaaaap! Çoraaaaap! Bayın, bayanın çorabııııı!*" Socks, socks, men's and women's socks! There were people who sharpened knives, others who alloyed the inside of copper pots, guys who hauled junk, sometimes specifying a kind of metal or other material that was their stock in trade. Most of them pushed wooden carts piled with their products, and a few came in pickup trucks, parking on a corner and shouting intermittently for ten minutes or so before driving farther on.

My favorite porter had no cart, and gave a call that I never managed fully to decipher, but I could see what his business was just by looking: over each shoulder rested a bundle of seven or eight brooms and mops; on one side, a bundle of plastic dustpans hung from the broomsticks on a length of twine; in his right hand he carried another mop to which was clipped a plastic pail; and in his left hand he had two rainbow-colored feather dusters with long handles. He was like a department store on feet. Broomstick man, as I came to think of him, did not come daily but perhaps twice a week. While some of the porters depressed me with calls that sounded desperate or heavy with resignation, broomstick man seemed to take joy in his rhythmically complex song, a little number in six-eight time. The only two words I managed to catch after months of listening were *silgi*, which meant "duster," and *arastak*, an obscure word for "roof" or "covering" (I deduced this one because it was similar to the Armenian word for ceiling). In my imagination, broomstick man's anthem translated to something like this: "I-am-the-broomstick-man-with-brooms-mops-and-dusters-for-your-ceiiiiiiling!"

But I worried about him because it seemed to me that brooms were not the stuff of brisk business; didn't everyone already have a broom?

One day when I heard broomstick man's call, I got up and went to the window, watching him for a while, wondering whether anybody ever actually popped out on a moment's notice to buy a cleaning implement. Sure enough, as he passed by a shop that sold mirrors and picture frames, a man appeared in the doorway. Thank goodness! They chatted for a moment and then broomstick man put down his mop-and-bucket set, and from some additional storage place on his body that I could not discern, produced a small squeegee. The shopkeeper took the squeegee, examined it for a moment, handed over some cash, and broomstick man walked on, singing his song.

A few minutes later, as if in mockery of broomstick man's complex operation, another merchant strutted down the street carrying nothing but a bundle of garlic bulbs on long, rough stems, like the bouquet of an unwilling bride. "*Sarımsakçı geldi sarımsaaaaaak!*" The garlic seller has come, garliiiiiic!

The porters had their seasons. In winter, a man pushed a small serving tray on wheels, holding a coal-fired samovar from which he doled out little plastic cups of sahlep, a hot, creamy drink made from orchid root. Although his song consisted of only one word, "sahlep," he fashioned it into something extraordinarily expressive, jumping from the first to the second syllable with an interval of an augmented fourth—known in Western music as the devil's interval because it is so atonal—and then descending in halftones, a lament, as if to say: it's cold and gray, but at least there's sahlep.

Like the passing seasons, my understanding of Turkish, and so of Turkey, moved through phases, cold and warm, fruitful and barren, each tempting me through to another. Every discovery birthed a litter of new mysteries, and before I knew it, the two months I had planned to spend had turned into two years.

- 12 -

Knowing and Not Knowing

THERE WAS AND THERE WAS NOT, TWO MONTHS AFTER HRANT DINK'S death, a development that looked like it could be a real sign of progress in Turkey's modern history: the completed restoration of a tenth-century Armenian cathedral on Akdamar Island in Lake Van. The project was meant to show that Turkey could embrace its multicultural history. Not a secret or any kind of discreet initiative, this was a major, national event, its most central feature the media blitz surrounding it. Perhaps some of the problems might have seemed inevitable to critics less hopeful than I: the sanctimony, the mix of bombast and evasion, and the Potemkin Village–style parading of the press corps before one renovated church that distracted from the presence of a hundred abandoned ones. But who could have been cynical enough to imagine that this entire pageant of televised ceremonies and statements would end without the word "Armenian" once being uttered by a single Turkish official?

THE SIGHT OF an Armenian church is itself a history lesson. Churches built in the ninth and tenth centuries—years when Armenian religious life flourished in what is now southeastern Turkey—are known for bringing innovation to earlier forms. Often hewn from volcanic tuff rock, pinkish or tan in color, they have an asymmetrical aspect, with arches of differing heights topped by gabled roofs of varying widths, all clustered around the main feature, a straight-sided, sharply pointed dome. The church at Akdamar, Cathedral of the Holy Cross, built in 915 by the Armenian king Gagik I Artsruni, featured all these elements, as well as exterior walls that told biblical stories in elaborate bas-relief. For twenty years it served as the primary seat of the Catholicos, or supreme bishop, of the Armenian Kingdom, and from 1113 to 1895 it functioned as a regional outpost under a succession of bishops.

Armenians have thousands of churches around the world, and scores in need of restoration, but the one at Akdamar—Akhtamar in Armenian—is special, due in part to a folk legend immortalized by the writer Hovhannes Tumanian in a long, metered poem published in 1891. As the story went, a maiden named Tamar lived on the island in Lake Van. She was madly in love with a young man who lived across the water. Each night, Tamar lit a fire so that her sweetheart could swim across the lake and find her. In Tumanian's telling, the stars and the waves took to gossiping about the couple's shamelessness, and soon the locals became angry and extinguished Tamar's fire. That night, when her suitor swam to find her, he got lost in the dark. He drowned in the waves, calling out for her until the end: "Akh, Tamar, akh, Tamar!" When I was a child, my mother liked to read me Tumanian's *Akhtamar* now and then, and each time she reached the climax, she wept as if she had only just learned of the lovers' fate.

As it happened, the poem's themes of longing and helplessness eerily presaged the fortunes of the island in real life. In 1895, one thousand years after King Gagik's men laid the first stones, the last Catholicos of Akhtamar died, never to be replaced. In the wake of the genocide, the diocese he had governed was gone, too. Thereafter, the cathedral fell into ruin, and its walls were used for target practice by locals and soldiers.

The state of this church was one of Hrant Dink's pet issues. A decade before he died, Hrant had made a prediction: if the Turkish government would one day restore the ruined cathedral at Akhtamar, Armenian youth from all over the world would come to lend their energy to the rebuilding effort. It was already a rite of passage for diaspora Armenians to spend a summer during their college years rebuilding churches in the countryside of Armenia. Surely they would also want to help preserve ancient Armenian sites in Turkey, he reasoned.

Hrant's article, "Akhtamar Labor Battalion," was an open letter to the Ministry of Culture. "Rather than creating monsters in an attempt to draw tourists"—he was referring to the giant green and yellow statue of the mythical Lake Van Monster, Turkey's answer to Loch Ness, erected to ludicrous effect in the Van city center—"try to take care of the artifacts that are right before your eyes. . . . What you call Van is an ocean of historical artifacts. Why is it that no one thinks of sitting down properly and restoring the region in its entirety? They say, 'but then the Armenians would come.' So let them come. Let them see the places where their ancestors lived. Let them satisfy their longing. So what? If there is any need for help or labor . . . [Armenian] youth from Turkey, Armenia and even the diaspora are ready to volunteer. . . . Come, do not let the Akhtamar restoration be solely the restoration of a building; let us also restore our dilapidated spirits."

The letter did not inspire the Turkish authorities to spring into action, but a few years later, in 2005, a European Union committee proposed that the medieval church should be a UNESCO heritage site. It also suggested that Turkey show some goodwill toward its minority populations in order to bolster its EU membership bid. In short order the Turkish government embarked on a restoration that would cost two million dollars.

It was only a matter of bad luck that the two-year-long project was ready for the cameras mere weeks after Hrant's assassination—or ideal timing, if you were a Turkish politician looking for a way to mitigate criticism. Invitations were sent to Armenia's officials, diaspora leaders, the entire Turkish press corps, and a long list of European Union dignitaries. But Hrant had miscalculated: when he waxed poetic about the healing that could come from a renovation of Akhtamar, he did not account for his own murder or the fact that Armenians worldwide would boycott the event.

"No Self-Respecting Armenian Should Accept Turkey's Invitation to Akhtamar." This was the headline of an editorial written by Harut Sassounian, publisher of a weekly Armenian newspaper, the improbably named *California Courier*, which reached a devoted diaspora audience. Sassounian called the renovation a "cynical ploy" by the Turkish government to distract from its genocide denialism on the eve of yet another April 24. In fact, the opening was originally planned for April 24, but then the Armenian Patriarch informed the authorities that no Armenian would attend if it were held on that date. Turkish nationalists were enraged by the choice, too—better not to draw attention to that date—which led to a fight in parliament. The date was changed twice more, finally landing on March 29.

As the big day approached, problems multiplied. First, news got out that the church was going to be opened as a museum rather than as a house of worship. This made some Istanbul Armenians question the sincerity of the effort, and a debate ensued as to whether a cross would be placed atop the dome.

"The pictures we used as a guide for renovation did not include a cross," said the minister of culture, "but if you show us evidence that there was a cross we will put a cross." Photographs showing the cross were duly provided.

"But if we add a cross it might be struck by lightning," said the lead architect, despite having learned his science in a nation of ten thousand minarets. Armenians provided technical suggestions involving lightning hazard lines.

"But isn't it disrespectful to put a cross on a building that will not be used for services?" said the head of the Turkish Historical Society.

"Then let us use it for services," said the Armenians.

Every last detail was subject to argument; even the spelling of the name of the island became controversial. An Armenian-American from the Dashnak Party pointed out that in the Turkish rendering, Akdamar, the first syllable, "ak," means white, as in pure, while "damar" means vein; did the name secretly have racist connotations?

WHEN I HAD traveled to the southeast with Müge and Sarkis Bey two years earlier, we had visited Akhtamar to check on the progress of the renovation, then in its early stages. The architect in charge, a Kurd from Van, had spent an entire day showing us around the area.

Now I wanted to attend the opening ceremony, but covertly. As word trickled in that every diaspora leader had rejected the invitation, the Turkish authorities were scrambling to find diaspora Armenians who would show up for the ribbon cutting. After all, what was the point if not good PR? A delegation from Istanbul would attend, and a small group from Yerevan, too, but no community leaders from the United States or Europe. I worried that if I wound up being the only diaspora Armenian on hand, I might be turned into some kind of unwitting poster girl for Turkey's great strides toward reconciliation. I had come to Turkey to seek out and describe such efforts—to contribute to them, even—but if I was optimistic, I was not entirely naive. I would have to pass as a local in order to evade notice and participate on my own terms. So I called Sarkis Bey for help, and in short order he made me an *Agos* press card and hitched me to one of his reporters, a young man named Aris.

"Finally, we'll get you to write for the paper," Sarkis Bey teased.

He himself was not planning to go. He offered a variety of reasons—he had concerns about how the work was handled, he was busy, he was no great fan of the Armenian Patriarch, who would be speaking at the event—but I had a feeling that at the heart of the matter was the fact that Sarkis Bey had no interest in visiting Van as anything but an intrepid explorer. A press conference at Akhtamar, even if it counted as a major event in his life as a Turkish citizen, threatened to diminish his private relationship with Van's Armenian treasures.

Aris, my new colleague, had been one of Hrant's protégés, a fixture at the paper since he started there as a teenage intern. Now, at only twenty-seven, he was the news editor of *Agos* and assumed responsibility for much of the action in the office. He didn't look the part; wearing slouchy jeans and a hoodie nearly every time I saw him, with a perpetually burdened, sleep-deprived sag to his eyes, he could have passed for a kid trudging to first period in his senior year. His role at the paper—and as a representative of the Armenian community in the wake of Hrant's murder—was evident in the number of calls he fielded. All the Turkish journalists who used to phone Hrant for information or quotes about minority politics now pestered Aris. He had a reasonable command of English and a dutiful if not quite enthusiastic attitude about helping me navigate the Akhtamar ceremony.

"Will this really get me in?" I asked Aris, studying my press card, a rectangle of paper on which I'd handwritten my name and contact information.

He nodded. "Since Hrant died, if you show you're with *Agos*, nobody can say anything."

SURE ENOUGH, FROM the moment we arrived in Van, everybody treated Aris like a VIP. About fifty journalists waited outside city hall for the arrival of the press secretary, who then ignored the clamoring reporters and strode directly to Aris to thank him for coming. When the other journalists realized Aris was from *Agos*, they approached him to shake hands or offer words of acknowledgment. And before anybody else was allowed onto the bus chartered to carry the press corps to the event, Aris and I were ushered aboard.

As the bus filled up, a clerk walked down the aisles dowsing our hands with *kolonya*, a lemony ethanol perfume traditionally offered at the start of any bus journey. Moments later we were given a choice of Fanta or Coke in small plastic cups. The drive was less than half an hour, but no detail had been overlooked in a day that relied entirely on ceremony.

ONLY TWO YEARS after my first visit to Van, everything looked different. The entire city was covered in posters bearing the slogan "Respect the history, respect the culture." Hundreds, maybe thousands of these posters were tacked up on storefronts, in hotel lobbies, restaurants, and walls all over town. Sometimes twenty or thirty of them were pasted in a row, each one bearing a photo of the beautifully restored cathedral. This seemed promising at first. The Ministry of Culture had also produced a thick, glossy booklet explaining how the renovation was done, telling about the features of the church, how the architects had adhered to its original style, and how much money had been spent on the project.

But some things had not changed at all: the booklet managed to detail the renovation endeavor at the length of twenty pages without using the word "Armenian" once. Instead, heavy usage was made of the term "Anatolian," a mealy, general word without any agreed-upon definition, a label that offended not because of anything specific it meant but because of what it didn't say. Anatolian culture, the peoples of Anatolia, Anatolia's climate, geography, richly diverse past. Carpets, textiles, pottery designs—all Anatolian. I looked through the booklet again and again. No Armenian. Just those other words: Respect the history, respect the culture.

Meanwhile, a few new kinks had surfaced. An ultranationalist group, the Great Unity Party (BBP), had brought in members from all over the region to protest the Akhtamar opening; they were planning a demonstration in front of our hotel, because the Patriarch's delegation was staying there. The hotel manager had to hire extra security. In the lobby, I watched him, a round, balding man pacing from one telephone to another behind the reception desk. How did he feel, I wondered, being thrust into the position of protecting a group of Turkish-Armenian visitors, bound by the requirements of commerce and hospitality to take care of them even as nationalists threatened a riot?

There had also been some last-minute administrative changes: the governor of Van had been transferred just days before to a post in a distant city, despite having been involved in the restoration all along—before it had gained such a high profile. A new governor, one more likely to uphold Ankara's expectations, had been installed. Similarly, the authorities had appointed a new mayor of Gevaş, the district responsible for Akhtamar.

THE EVENING BEFORE the ceremony, Aris and I had watched a special broadcast on CNN Türk about the church renovation. It had been promoted as the big event on television that night, treated with the kind of importance that the American media gives, say, the State of the Union address. This seemingly minor event was in fact a matter of great curiosity in a country where Armenian history was seldom mentioned at all.

The program featured a panel discussion with the architects, the Armenian Patriarch, and the Turkish minister of culture. This was a cast of characters if ever there was one. The minister of culture, Attila Koç, variously nicknamed Sleeping Beauty or Sleepy Smurf, was narcoleptic; people watched his TV appearances eagerly, in hopes of seeing him nod off midsentence, and he often obliged.

Then there was His Beatitude the Archbishop Mesrop Mutafyan, officially still titled the Armenian Patriarch of Constantinople. Since Ottoman times, the state had treated the religious leaders of minority groups as governors of a sort. They were invited for discussions of political developments and concerns—concerns of the state, that is. And they were expected to keep their communities under control. As the closest thing the Armenians of Istanbul had to official representation, Mutafyan also had to answer the calls of journalists, domestic and foreign. *No,* he told them, one after another, *there is no problem, Armenians live peacefully in Istanbul. No, there is no discrimination. No, we don't think it's necessary to talk about 1915. We should focus on the future. No, we do not approve of the way that diaspora Armenians talk about Turkey.* The same diaspora Armenians disparaged him nastily for this kowtowing rhetoric.

Meanwhile, he was constantly under fire from *Agos* for behavior that was seen as cronyism; the Patriarch had a small circle of trusted confidantes, mostly wealthy Istanbul Armenians who donated to the church, but he was opaque to everyone else. I had interviewed him on my first trip to Turkey, and was struck by his failure to project any of the warmth one might hope for from a man of the cloth. His was a cold, realpolitik sort of diplomacy, an affectless response to the no-win situation in which he found himself. Generations of Armenian Patriarchs of Constantinople before him had had similar problems.

As Koç delivered official banalities and the architects eagerly discussed their technical standards, one could only wonder how Archbishop Mutafyan would handle the following day's high-stakes spotlight.

It was a gorgeous morning at the tail end of winter. When our bus pulled up to the boat landing on the edge of Lake Van, hundreds of people were trying to gain entrance to the event. Strings of pennants and bundles of balloons encircled the area. The pennants, with their random stripes and symbols in various colors, seemed designed to lend some ambiguous international spirit, but they reminded me of a used-car dealership. The hills behind the dock had become a kind of amphitheater where throngs of townspeople squatted and watched the festivities. It was not every day that crowds of people from Istanbul and Ankara descended on Van. Buses filled with politicians and other dignitaries arrived, and disgorged their well-dressed passengers. These visitors had likely been to all the capitals of Europe, but probably 90 percent of them had never before been more than a few miles east of their own capital. From the dock, we could see across the rippling water to the island, where an enormous Turkish flag blanketed the sloped shore, appearing nearly as large as the church itself.

As we entered the boat, our hands were doused with more of the reeking *kolonya*. Aris was approached by a friendly fellow who introduced himself as the president of the Van Association of Turks Who Were Killed by Armenians. Aris smiled politely and chatted with him. Aris was a pro. Meanwhile, women in colorful, nebulously ethnic dresses ("Anatolian costumes") served tea and *mezze*-style appetizers. Just like our overtaxed hotel manager, all of these people—tea girls and boat captains, bus drivers and security guards—had been drafted into this celebration, and no matter what they called it or didn't call it, this felt significant. Everybody knew that in some basic sense, their labors today were on behalf of the country's Armenian history.

When we disembarked at the island, a line of people two or three deep had already formed a long, zigzagging procession up the hill toward the church. Aris darted away for a minute with his camera. He shifted from one spot to another to capture this cortege from the best angle. Watching him, I had the feeling I knew what he was thinking.

"You know what this looks like?" he said when he returned to show me his photos. Yes. The people may have been wearing suits instead of rags, heels and oxfords instead of bare feet, and they were walking toward the church instead of away from it. And they were Turkish. But there we were in Van under an intensifying sun, and the shuffling queue of humans appeared to any Armenian eye like the lines of deportees we had seen in photos of 1915.

At the top of the hill, a few hundred people were gathered under a tent pavilion facing the church. On one side of the church's entry arch, tacked up against the blush-colored stone, hung a picture of Atatürk and a Respect the History poster. On the other side of the arch? A Turkish flag and an identical poster. A giant video crane hovered over the entire setup.

Then came the Turkish national anthem. Until that moment, I had tried to withhold judgment, and I stood from my seat when everybody else did. But suddenly my throat tightened and my face burned. With the Atatürk poster, the flags, and now the national anthem, the question of whose history was being respected had been answered loud and clear. Next, a Turkish pianist played some self-consciously modernist compositions. That there was no Armenian music in the ceremony—and wouldn't it have been the easiest possible concession?—was intolerable to me.

Several speeches followed. Attila Koç gave a long, unctuous address about vibrant Anatolian cultures living side by side for centuries. By now I should not have been surprised by the absence of the word "Armenian" in his speech. But I was. It was surreal how much effort had to go into speaking about something without naming it, like an elaborate, geopolitical game of $20,000 Pyramid.

Then came Archbishop Mutafyan's turn. After thanking the authorities and praising this step toward improving Armenian-Turkish relations, he went on to say something more forthright than anybody had expected from the famously self-censoring Patriarch. "This building is a church," he said. Well, of course it was. But under the circumstances the statement was momentous. For weeks, debate had gone on about whether this building, this stone house of God that had sheltered Armenian bishops and monks for nine centuries, was still, indeed, a church, if it was no longer being used as a church, and here the Patriarch whose deference had seemed to have no limit had finally reached his bottom line.

"According to our tradition, church buildings have special days." He went on to suggest that if the church were allowed to have an annual festival on one of these special days, it would be "a very good occasion for people who would like to pray here but have been scattered around the world." And with that he was back to the usual euphemisms. *Scattered around the world*; it sounded almost peaceful, like the fluff of a dandelion bobbing on the wind.

Another Disney-in-Anatolia woman emerged holding a silver tray bearing several gleaming pairs of scissors. The ministers of culture, the architects, and the archbishop each selected a pair, and then, in unison, snipped the red ribbon as a hundred flashbulbs captured the moment.

I NEEDED A break. At the edge of the crowd I noticed a reporter who looked European. He saw me, too, and beckoned me over; he needed help with the wireless headset through which we were receiving simultaneous translation. The reporter was from Denmark, it turned out, and he had come as part of a press junket sponsored by the Turkish Ministry of Culture. Apparently the authorities had rounded up journalists from all over Europe, flown them to Istanbul, and taken them to meet a series of historians and officials for lessons about Turkish-Armenian relations. Tensing up at this news, I asked him, as calmly as I could, if the talks had seemed balanced.

"Are you kidding?" he snorted. "It was straight propaganda. I think they rather drastically underestimated the intelligence of journalists."

What a relief that I could speak openly. He asked if I knew of any thoughtful scholars he could call for an interview, and I started to write down names. As we chatted, some other foreign correspondents gathered around us. They had all sorts of questions—about the church, about Armenian history in Van, about Armenian life in Istanbul, and, naturally, about the genocide. Ever since Hrant's murder and those chants of "We Are All Armenian" reverberating down the streets of Istanbul, Western journalists in Turkey were eager to report progress on the Armenian issue. I had counted myself among them; and I had hoped that Akhtamar was good news. But now I could barely contain myself as I took the opportunity to correct for any excessive optimism they may have wanted to take away from the day's infuriating spectacle.

My impromptu press conference continued as we rode the boat back to the mainland, a coterie of European reporters taking notes as I spoke. I told them that everything was off the record. It had become clear that I was, sure enough, the only American-Armenian who had come to the event. Several Turkish reporters had noticed me over the course of the day and had asked to feature me in their articles, too; a story about the renovation of an Armenian cathedral needed to quote at least one Armenian bystander, after all. But I refused. This wasn't only to avoid exposure; it was because what I saw and how I felt clashed profoundly with what I had hoped to discover. Things were bad. Actually, things were ridiculous.

I never regretted going, though. Privately, I still felt angry at the Armenians who refused to attend. Despite the day's indignities, the renovation and the attention it got in Turkey were an important step—marginally better than silence, if more complicated—and an absolutist position against participating was too easy an answer. In an arena already crowded with boycotts and ultimatums that had possibly only made matters worse, I wanted to test the full potential of engagement, no matter how uncomfortable it was.

That night, I wrote a note in my journal, a note I had no intention of sending, to Harut Sassounian, the writer who warned that any Armenian who went to Akhtamar would be a traitor.

Mr. Sassounian, if you keep lengthening your list of conditions that must be met before you will set foot on Turkish soil, then you are guaranteeing yourself it will never happen—not in your lifetime and probably not in your grandchildren's lifetimes. You don't know what you would do, Mr. S., if that day came, because the anger and pain and negativity in your heart is so frozen, so hardened, that no amount of Anatolian sun, the same sun that scorched your ancestors, could melt it away. How could you set foot on this land now, Mr. S.? Your blood would boil even as you bathed in the cool waters of Lake Van. You wouldn't be able to taste the delicious food and enjoy it. And when a little rag-clad, emerald-eyed girl with a space in her teeth grinned up at you and waved as your car rambled past her village, you would need to look away instead of waving back. So what would be the point?

The Akhtamar renovation planted a small seed of possibility—if not in the hearts of most Armenians, then in the logic centers of some Turkish minds, those self-governing reaches of the brain where an unbidden thought might occasionally flicker: Well, if they had been here, and they had *this*, then where did they go, and why would they leave? In fact, I started to notice, gradually, that some Turks put forward such a line of reasoning when they wanted to say something, but did not want to risk saying too much—to say, simply, something doesn't add up.

Other Armenian ruins had been converted into horse stables, restaurants, carpet-weaving factories, and trash dumps. In the town of Gaziantep—Armenian Aintab—I once spent a couple of nights in an extraordinary boutique hotel built from the long-abandoned mansion of a wealthy Armenian family. Since the hotel did not advertise this fact, I was acting on a hunch, and had searched its walls for clues until I found, over a doorway, a keystone carved with the faint but unmistakable Armenian letter "eh," which is the sign Armenians use for God—a symbolic abbreviation of the phrase "He is." Akhtamar, a much larger memorial, bore a similar message: they were.

Or did I have it all backward, then? Turkey already had an abundance of visible evidence of a vanished Armenian population. The rules of "don't ask, don't tell" swallowed it all. Maybe Akhtamar was not progress but just an expensive version of more of the same. Maybe this was even worse than silence, an even more insidious form of denial, because of the way an open secret that has been normalized is then frozen in time.

To deny the truth about a historical event, like a genocide, requires building a raft of justifications, weaving together ideas about the distant acts of unseen players, balancing each component just so, in order that the raft may float under the right conditions. This kind of denial flourishes in books and conversations, in government rhetoric. But such denial has a corollary that is more perplexing—less like statecraft and more like witchcraft, less like euphemism and more like hallucination; the ability to ignore things—tangible objects, even—that are right in front of your eyes. You look at a tree and call it a school bus.

Long after the restoration ceremony had passed, whenever I found myself debating with a Turk about whether Armenians in Turkey faced discrimination, I came back to Akhtamar to make my point; how was it that throughout the entire, exaggerated proceeding, years in the making, officials had been unable to say that the church was Armenian?

"But everyone knows it's Armenian!" they would always reply.

Exactly.

- 13 -

How to Be a Turk

MY FRIEND RAMAZAN TOOK OUT A PEN AND GRABBED A NAPKIN. HE scrawled a map of Turkey on it, drew a large *X* at each corner, then slid the napkin across the café table toward me.

"The first thing we learn in school is that we are surrounded by enemies," he said.

Ramazan was a photographer for a major Turkish newspaper. He had developed a niche for himself traveling to neighboring countries to photograph ethnic conflicts. A pious Muslim, he had a soft spot for religious minorities, such as the Turks living in the Balkans, but he was also broad-minded enough that he had gone to Nagorno-Karabakh and Yerevan to photograph Armenians.

Ramazan didn't exactly look the part of the swashbuckling photojournalist: he was clean-shaven, petite, and as prim and polite as a suitor meeting the family at an old-fashioned courtship visit. His features were strongly Asian; thus alongside his swarthier compatriots, he looked particularly streamlined and compact. And if there were an ideological father for Ramazan's work and worldview, it was neither Atatürk nor Attila, but someone closer to Mr. Rogers: he hoped that if he could frame the picture just so, we could all get along and the world would be a better place.

On this level we understood each other; we had met because of his interest in Armenia, and by disposition we were equally unsuited to conflict. On another level, we didn't understand each other all that well; he didn't speak English. He was one of several friends with whom I spoke only Turkish. This limitation kept our interactions cushioned by a haze of intuition and goodwill; it infused our relationship with patience. Patience was essential because over time it became clear that we disagreed about many things. I'm convinced that if his English had been better or my Turkish more complete, the full force of expression would have made our friendship impossible.

Our ongoing but always well-mannered argument revolved around the fact that Ramazan wanted badly for me to believe that Turks did not hate Armenians, and I wanted just as badly for him to see that he was wrong. I should confess that by the time we became friends I had been in Turkey long enough that I was doing the very opposite of what I set out to do: not listening but trying to persuade. In a Socratic style, I prodded Ramazan with questions that I hoped would make him change his mind.

The question that occasioned his napkin lesson had to do with a popular saying: *"Türk'ün Türk'ten başka dostu yoktur."* The only friend of a Turk is a Turk. What's that about? I wanted to know. Doesn't it seem a bit extreme?

Yes, he admitted. But Turkey's history was a history of betrayals and disappointments. And to understand anything about how Turks viewed 1915, he said, you had to understand this larger story. It went something like this:

Turkish schoolchildren learned that Armenians had lived comfortably alongside Turks throughout the Ottoman Era, because the sultan was generous enough to tolerate them, allowing them the official status *"millet-i sadıka"*—loyal minority. This was seen as something the Armenians should have been grateful for. Loyalty was the main issue, and the Armenians' downfall was that they were not loyal, you see. In the years leading up to World War I, they became traitors.

In this story, no mention was made of a host of complexities that shaped the Armenians' status in Ottoman society: that they were officially deprived of equal rights for much of Ottoman history; that although a wealthy Armenian merchant class inspired envy and suspicion in popular accounts, the majority of Ottoman Armenians were peasants; that they were denied the right to bear arms until late in the nineteenth century; that their testimony in court was unequal to that of a Muslim; that they were charged dramatically higher taxes than Muslims; and that they had to wear different clothes to identify themselves. That this might have made some of them a little touchy.

In the meantime, the Ottoman Empire was losing vast amounts of territory; by the end of the Balkan War of 1912–1913, it had lost 80 percent of its European land, which was about 16 percent of the total empire. That land had been under Ottoman control for five hundred years. The way Turkish children learned it, in the midst of this tragic dissolution culminating in the First World War, just when the Ottoman Empire needed the loyalty of its subjects the most, Armenians began to form armed bands who terrorized their Turkish and Kurdish neighbors.

The theme of loyalty cannot be overstated: beginning in 2003, the Ministry of Education called for all schools to hold student essay contests on why the Armenians were traitors, why genocide claims were baseless, and why Turkey needed to secure itself against minority claims to preserve its unity as a nation. Teachers were sent to special conferences where they rehearsed talking points on the matter. These were merely refinements to the existing curriculum. In the lessons students learned, Turkey was always under attack, always in danger of being dissolved.

This belief is so strong that scholars have given it a name: Sèvres syndrome, after the 1920 Treaty of Sèvres. This treaty, a peace agreement between the Ottoman Empire and the Allies after World War I, would have given large sections of what is now Turkey to Armenia and Greece, and would have granted France, Italy, and Great Britain significant influence over various zones of the formerly Ottoman lands. It was a raw deal for Turks, and could explain their modern-day paranoia about dismemberment, but for one detail: the treaty was never implemented. It was a disaster averted—a ghost treaty, a shadow self for a Turkey whose insecurities never quite healed.

The treaty was annulled in the course of the four-year Turkish War of Independence, in which General Mustafa Kemal brought his nation a decisive victory, kicking out the European occupiers and putting Turks back in charge. Sèvres was replaced by the 1923 Treaty of Lausanne, as well as smaller treaties such as the Treaty of Kars, which confirmed the border with Soviet Armenia, and the stakes were shifted completely—in

Turkey's favor. Turkey remained large and intact, and Armenians and Greeks, along with Jews, got the consolation prize of official minority status, a dismal rehashing of what they had had all along. The nation moved forward. Mustafa Kemal became "Atatürk," and led the way to modernity, and the new Turkey was soon the bearer of every cliché about being a bridge between East and West.

But the ghost of Sèvres haunted the country still, and no element of that dead treaty's promises caused more paranoia than the Armenians, who had not gone quietly into the night, but instead popped up again and again, in the halls of governments the world over where they sought to blame Turkey for a so-called genocide, and in a decade-long spate of terror in which they gunned down Turkish diplomats everywhere they could find them, from Los Angeles to Geneva to right there at home, in the Ankara airport (where civilians were murdered, too).

Until the law was relaxed in 2012, Turkish high school students were required to take a course on national security—a course taught by military officers and enlivened by standing in rank and saluting. Its main themes were Atatürk's accomplishments, the importance of national unity, and the internal and external threats facing Turkey. Indeed, in every subject, from history to literature to music to science, there are reminders that the state is to be protected and the individual's main purpose is to help uphold its integrity.

A social studies textbook for fifth graders tells them: "The principle of nationalism serves to keep our nation in full unity against external hazards. . . . Certain neighboring countries are attempting to obstruct this aspiration of the Turkish society to develop and modernize rapidly. These countries are striving to expand their lands and to achieve dominance in the seas. Under these circumstances our duty is to eliminate all subversive and divisive threats directed to our country."

A high school linguistics textbook uses as an example the phrase, "It is worth sacrificing our life for the motherland."

In a science class, a lesson on preventing soil erosion reads: "The purpose of erosion prevention is to know that the soil is the most important element of our motherland. . . . This is a fight that will be carried out by courageous, militant citizens who love their soil, nature and homeland."

As for Armenians, when they are mentioned in schoolbooks at all, they are portrayed as in this high school geography text: "Actually

Armenians were neither innocent nor loyal to the state. Their activities concerning the state in which they lived after the end of the nineteenth century were beyond all tolerance, fully treacherous and hostile."

Thus it was important to understand that even if some of Turkey's positions on what had happened to the Armenians in 1915 sounded patently false, if not absurd, to the rest of the world, in Turkey these arguments had real power. They were planted in a field that was already well tilled with suspicion and fear.

And on a good day, I felt sympathetic. Yes, I was Armenian, but I was also American, and my decisions were generally not caught up in a web of distrust and defensiveness. I did not take it personally if somebody said that America still had not paid its debt to African-Americans for the horror of slavery, and I was perfectly willing to assume that whatever we had done to the Native Americans was probably a genocide, too, even if I knew rather little about it.

I had the luxury of relative security, if not existential—no nation could guarantee that—then at least geopolitical. And my conscience seemed to function rather independently of anything George W. Bush had stirred up or, for that matter, anything George Washington might have said or done. In short: *L'état, ce n'est pas moi.*

* * *

I am of Armenian origin but I have no information about this topic. How can I learn about my religion, especially how to practice it? I am at a crossroads. I am looking for someone to guide me.

A young man, barely twenty-one years old, posted this query, in Turkish, in the comments section of a Bolsahay community Web site. This young man had been raised as a Kurd, in the western city of Bursa. As a teenager he had moved with his family to the opposite side of the country, Diyarbakır, where his parents were originally from. Lacking the temperament for university, he found work at the utility company. For his job, he drove to tiny villages all over the Diyarbakır region to read electricity meters. As he worked, he liked to spend time with the elders in the villages, asking them questions and listening to their stories. Little by little, he started to realize that many of the people he spoke with mentioned having Armenian roots. He also sensed they were uncomfortable talking about it.

One day the young man told his father about his discovery and asked him what had happened to all the Armenians who used to live in the area.

"If only you could look into your own grandfather's eyes," his father said.

That was the first time he heard an acknowledgment of what he'd begun to suspect, even to hope: that he, too, had Armenian ancestors.

His grandfather was no longer alive, and his parents didn't have any details to offer, but they did not stifle his curiosity. His father had taken a turn as a leftist and understood his son's burgeoning sense of commitment to a larger cause. His mother was glad to see him enjoying his work, and encouraged him to learn what he could, as long as he didn't get himself in trouble. They had seldom seen their boy take such an interest in anything.

There were ruined Armenian churches all over the Diyarbakır region. One of these, the shell of a cathedral that had lost its roof, had intact stairways, mysterious carvings, and even a blue-tiled baptismal bath molded into a wall. The young man began spending time at the ruined church. Soon he was acting as a caretaker of sorts, self-appointed, keeping the grounds tidy and chatting with tourists who found their way to the captivating site. Eventually, he met an Armenian priest who hailed from his grandparents' village and now worked at the Armenian Patriarchate in Istanbul.

With the priest's guidance, he moved to Istanbul and undertook the steps required for conversion to the Armenian Apostolic Church. For three months, he had daily lessons. He also helped out at the Patriarchate, answering phones and receiving visitors. When people asked where he was from, he liked to tell them Dikranagerd—the old Armenian name for Diyarbakır. Upon his baptism, he accepted a new name for himself, an Armenian religious name. For the purposes of our story I will call him Krikor, Armenian for Gregory.

KRIKOR'S CONVERSION ANTICIPATED a small but undeniable trend in Turkey—a trend of people discovering that they had Armenian roots. The movement found its foothold in a book published by a woman named

Fethiye Çetin, a human rights lawyer who would go on to represent the Dink family in Hrant's murder trial. Çetin's book, *Anneannem*, or *My Grandmother*, told of how her grandmother had confessed, shortly before dying, that she was born Armenian. Separated from her family during the genocide, never to see them again, she had been taken in by a Muslim family when she was nine years old, and married their son, living out the rest of her years as an upstanding Muslim woman. The author, Çetin, was the only person her grandmother told about her true origins.

The book gave voice to an open secret: around one hundred thousand children—most but not all girls—had survived the genocide only because they were brought into Kurdish and Turkish homes, usually as wives or maids, and converted to Islam. Some families spoke of this among themselves but concealed it from outsiders. Others knew in vague ways but never acknowledged it even in private. Many had no idea at all. Çetin's book nudged the taboo open just enough that in the aftermath of its publication, some Turks started to admit that their grandmothers had been Armenian, too. It wasn't a national coming-out; the shift was quieter than that. One man wrote in *Agos* that after his mother died, he discovered a tiny cross sewn into the collar of her nightgown. This was the start and end of what he knew. Several people told me privately that they had an Armenian ancestor, but unlike Krikor, nobody else I met had any interest in converting.

And why would they? One of the worst and most common insults in Turkish was to call somebody *Ermeni dölü*—Armenian sperm. In polite conversation, it was translated as "Armenian seed." People used it to accuse each other of lying, to scold children for mischief, and even, publicly, to criticize politicians for unfavorable decisions.

Which begged the question: was Krikor crazy?

By the time I met him, he was back in Diyarbakır. Istanbul was expensive, and besides, he had not felt particularly welcome in the Bolsahay community. Armenians eyed him warily. They knew better than anyone how strange it was for a young man to willfully join their ranks. And when Krikor started wearing a cross outside his shirt, instead of tucked beneath the collar, people thought he was reckless, maybe even dangerous.

"How can you live when you hide yourself?" Krikor said. "They are so oppressed." Then he corrected himself. "*We* are so oppressed."

Istanbul Armenians were paranoid as a rule. But Krikor was also cautious, in his own way. It took weeks of phone calls and several days of in-person coaxing, with Deniz at my side, to convince him to talk to me about his decision to convert. When we finally spoke, in a large, crowded tea garden in Diyarbakır, he made us change tables four times before he was satisfied that nobody was eavesdropping.

I asked him why he had wanted to take on the burden of being Armenian.

It was not a burden, he said. He searched a long time for the right word, and finally said it felt to him like *asalet*—Turkish for "nobility," a term with ancestral connotations, hints of something bygone and beautiful.

What about his Kurdish identity? Didn't it mean anything to him?

"What matters to me is to feel that richness of all those people from the past. Muslims, Jews, Christians, all of them used to live together in peace. If people all over the world only understood this . . ."

The problem with Krikor's sentiments was that they were based mostly in myth. And the same myth was used by people with the opposite intentions: to insist that Armenians could not have been persecuted because everybody had lived together in harmony. Of course ordinary people of all backgrounds had, in many cases, at many moments, on many blocks of many quarters, lived together without problems. But the age-old interreligious prejudice of the region was not unique to Turkey and could not be denied. I said this to Krikor: it was a nice idea, but it wasn't really true that people of different religious and ethnic groups had always lived side-by-side in peace.

"It was true in Diyarbakır," he said. "I am more than one hundred and ten percent certain of it."

Later, I heard rumors that had spread around the Bolsahay community, rumors that Krikor, by appointing himself in charge of the church ruins in Diyarbakır, had been siphoning off donations from occasional visitors. Some people defended him: there was nobody else who spent time at the church, tending the shrubs and giving little tours. He had even built a Web site with photographs and stories about the church and the formerly Armenian villages.

I couldn't confirm whether Krikor had stolen money. And I would not have been surprised if his desire to become Armenian had more to it than a spiritual need or a passion for history. He was desperate to get out of the country to avoid military service, and he had become fixated on the idea that if only he could find an Armenian bride overseas, maybe in France or Canada, he would have a ticket out. He asked me for help applying to Armenian organizations for scholarships to pay for college abroad.

Every year hence I would receive greetings from him on January 6, for Armenian Christmas, and again at Easter, with the requisite expression in Armenian script: Christ has risen, blessed is the resurrection of Christ.

Maybe Krikor was bonkers. Or maybe he just couldn't live with the sense of rupture inherent to life as a Turkish citizen. Maybe Krikor hoped that by converting, he could embody, within himself, a wholeness—a Turk, raised as a Kurd, now Armenian by some distant drops of blood—a wholeness that the current situation denied everyone.

* * *

MANY PEOPLE I met seemed to have developed some kind of coping mechanism to manage the rigid requirements of Turkish identity, each according to their own circumstances and character—but none were as extreme as my friend Tunç.

Tunç was ethnically Turkish. He grew up in İzmir, with typical middle-class parents and a typical elementary school education, then went to high school, college, and law school all in France before moving back to Turkey as an adult.

When I met Tunç (at a Lenny Kravitz concert in the Tünel district, as it happened), he was living alone in a stylish apartment in Nişantaşı, one of Istanbul's tonier neighborhoods. On the surface, he had White Turk written all over him. He had no interest in politics and preferred to talk about film or a prospective trip to Thailand. His wardrobe looked like a J. Crew window display, and his home had all the latest features; he had installed radiant-heat floors throughout the condo and liked to make himself coffee using a high-end espresso machine. He afforded this comfortable lifestyle easily, because he worked as general counsel for the Turkish division of a leading American tobacco company.

But ideologically he was as far from being a White Turk as could be. Actually, he was in a category of his own.

After I had hung out with Tunç a few times, I asked him what he thought about the genocide.

"It happened," Tunç said.

"How did you come to believe that? Was it something you read that convinced you?"

"I don't need to read anything," Tunç said. "It's obvious from the way Turkey denies it that it happened."

"But how come you see it that way, when most Turks don't at all?"

"I don't consider myself Turkish."

Here was a person whose job was to defend, in courts, a giant, international cigarette maker, a company that spent billions of dollars peddling a drug known to hold its users in thrall no less than heroin (a drug, I should note, which Tunç himself never sampled, despite keeping cartons stacked up in his living room for visitors). He spent his waking hours in the legal department of an organization whose chief activity was to lie about what everybody knew to be true: that smoking kills. There was something bitterly nihilistic in Tunç, maybe even sociopathic, and yet something utterly, exhilaratingly pure.

And Tunç did not consider himself Turkish. He insisted on this whenever I asked him questions about things Turkish people said or did.

"I don't consider myself Turkish," he would repeat, as if the matter had been resolved and the only complication was his birth certificate.

In Tunç's nihilism there was a clue as to what motivated everybody else. He didn't ask for anything from Turkey, so he didn't feel the need to offer Turkey—the idea of Turkey—anything in return. It was as if this distance between himself and his ethnic identity was the reason he was able to say something so remarkably simple about the genocide: *I don't need to read anything. It's obvious from the way Turkey denies it that it happened*. There were no scales to fall from Tunç's eyes. He didn't consider himself Turkish.

But then we would stop to buy a couple of döner kebabs from a cart on the street, and Tunç would address the vendor as *abi*, brother, and offer an *eyvallah*—a bit of homey, religion-inflected slang calculated to reduce the chasm between a street food–seller and himself—and I would catch a glimpse of the child of a neighborhood in İzmir who hadn't earned fancy diplomas in Europe just yet. Or he would give a disquisition on the relative merits of different styles of börek pastry, or marvel at the view from a particular point on the pier near Üsküdar.

Tunç didn't consider himself Turkish, but he *was* Turkish. It wasn't a choice, and I am not talking about something as meaningless as the components of his blood. Turkey was the place of his birth, the language he spoke, and the home of the only family he had. He was Turkish, and why shouldn't he be? It was unfair, and heartbreaking, that the label had become so narrowly defined that he felt his only option was to refuse it entirely.

- 14 -

Official History

THE ATATÜRK MAUSOLEUM LOOMED OVER THE CITY OF ANKARA. High on a hill, angled so that it seemed just above your head no matter where you stood, it was a massive block-like rectangle surrounded by close-set square columns, bordered by lights that bounced off the pale limestone and made the structure glow like it was the house of God.

Ankara, Turkey's capital, was as different from Istanbul as Washington, DC, from New York. Ankara meant government, the military, and Atatürk. Like Washington, it was a tidy, functional city where important things happened, but not a place you could truly love. It felt staid and conservative no matter the administration, and a bit too clean, with an early bedtime and all the closed-off dimensions that follow—not to mention quadrants of blight that were excised from its official image.

The official image was what brought me to Ankara: I had a meeting with Yusuf Halaçoğlu, president of the Turkish Historical Society, a state-funded research institution founded in 1930. As president, Halaçoğlu had spent the past fifteen years producing an unending supply of books, reports, and press releases arguing that there had never been an Armenian genocide. He was Turkey's denialist in chief.

I had been naive enough to think it would be difficult to get an interview. I asked Müge's advice about this when she was in town for a

conference; do you think Halaçoğlu would be willing to talk to a diaspora Armenian?

"Are you kidding?" She laughed. "I'm sure he would love nothing more."

When she saw I didn't get it, she explained that a person like Halaçoğlu
was like an evangelist, certain he had seen the truth and eager to share.
He was not burdened by the kind of self-questioning I took for granted
in myself, so being confronted with an opposing view would be a welcome challenge. In fact, there could be no more worthy pupil for his
teachings than a polite, open-minded diaspora Armenian like me. By
Müge's assessment, our meeting would be his pleasure.

Discussing the Armenian issue publicly was the central focus of
Halaçoğlu's career, and he appeared regularly on Turkish television to
announce new findings. Shortly before my visit, he had unveiled his most
creative discovery yet: the notion that almost all those in Turkey who
considered themselves Alevi Kurds were in fact originally Armenian.
With this theory, which occupied the media for weeks, he handily resolved
several long-standing controversies: the inconvenient demographic reality that there were Kurds in Turkey (his new hypothesis helped reduce
their number toward manageable irrelevance); distaste for the Alevi faith
in general (how much easier to explain their apostasy if they were actually Armenians all along!); and—most efficiently—the whereabouts of
hundreds of thousands of Armenians who had mysteriously disappeared
from the Ottoman Empire around 1915. They had simply gathered in the
Eastern Anatolian region of Tunceli and reinvented themselves as Alevi
Kurds, Halaçoğlu explained. This particular report came on the heels of
Fethiye Çetin's book about her Armenian grandmother; the timing suggested that it was meant as damage control in case Çetin's book planted
uncomfortable questions in too many people's minds. Like a spin doctor
for Turkish history, Halaçoğlu was always ready to work with whatever
surfaced, shaping it to keep the official story straight. His efforts over the
years had won him enough prominence that in 2005, the city of Ankara
decided to name a downtown street after him (the plan was later abandoned when a lawyer filed suit defending the street's existing namesake).

The Armenian issue was not just Halaçoğlu's personal mission, but
the Turkish Historical Society's main reason for existence. On the society's Web site, the list of links on the home page went through the typical
administrative categories like About Us and Our Staff until it got to the

only option that concerned a specific subject: "Armenian Studies." As late as 2010, similar non sequiturs were on display on many Turkish government Web sites, especially those geared toward foreigners, such as the portal for the Ministry of Tourism and Culture; their site navigation links ran something like this:

Atatürk
About Us
Contact
Site Map
False Armenian Allegations

I WAS NERVOUS about my meeting with Turkey's head historian in part because I knew how things had gone for those who came before me. Just a few months before my visit, a scholar in Sweden named David Gaunt had tried to engage with Halaçoğlu. Gaunt was widely respected as an expert on the World War I–era massacres of Assyrians and Armenians in Southeastern Turkey's Mardin region. One day in the fall of 2006, something happened that qualified as a major event within Gaunt's precise specialty: residents of Kuruköy, a tiny village near Mardin, found a mass grave inside a cave. The villagers took photographs and alerted the media; they said they had found similar graves before.

Some Turkish journalists contacted Gaunt for his analysis, and when he reviewed the available evidence, he circulated a statement saying that while the location of the mass grave was used for defense works and underground storage as far back as the Roman Empire, it "was turned into a killing field during the summer of 1915. With great probability the cave should contain Armenian, but with some likelihood also Assyrian-Syrian and Chaldean, victims. But only a site investigation could tell."

In response, Halaçoğlu called a press conference and assured reporters that no further investigation was necessary; indeed, the grave *was* a Roman site, he pronounced. He challenged Gaunt to prove otherwise. So Gaunt sat down and wrote Halaçoğlu a letter. Acknowledging the politically sensitive nature of the case, he suggested they appoint a delegation of historians and archaeologists entirely disconnected from the ethnic tension—Latin Americans, perhaps. He and Halaçoğlu and other Turkish and Armenian scholars could participate, but would not lead the project. It could be a model for how a Turkish-Armenian research coalition could proceed responsibly in the future, Gaunt proposed.

Halaçoğlu wrote back saying that before they went any further, another press release was in order.

I spoke to Gaunt while this correspondence was in progress. Of course he was aware of Halaçoğlu's "abysmal track record," he said, but he could see no way to work around him. And he cringed at the thought of involving the media before a real investigation had begun. The most important issue was the intactness of the "find"—that nothing had been taken away from the site since its discovery, or, for that matter, added. He described his worst nightmare: a TV news spot in which Halaçoğlu might kneel down, scratch a bit of earth, and—*Eureka!*—pick up a Roman coin that he'd cadged from a nearby museum, flashing it for the cameras.

Gaunt persisted, writing another letter about budgeting, scale, necessary qualifications for the investigative team, the cooperation of local universities to store remains, and the possibility of a search for DNA among the living to match with those buried in the grave.

In the Turkish newspapers, meanwhile, Halaçoğlu promised that if his Roman theory was proven wrong, he would publicly apologize to Gaunt.

"Please," Gaunt wrote, concluding his letter, "you do not need to do this for me and I don't understand the necessity of your odd promise, which seems more suited for film-version samurai warriors than down-to-earth researchers. In scientific circles we are daily confronted with new interpretations, new facts, new materials, new techniques and unexpected results—and as scientists we learn from them and are not embarrassed by new knowledge. As fellow historians, I believe that our first priority must be to pay our respect to the past and honour the memory by identifying whoever is enclosed in these long lost graves, whatever ethnicity they happen to have had." No reply came.

At around the same time, a British-Armenian historian named Ara Sarafian, head of London's Gomidas Institute, had been invited by Halaçoğlu to undertake a cooperative study of 1915. Sarafian was a specialist in archival scholarship of the late Ottoman era. He was known as something of a renegade, as critical of Armenian scholars as of Turkish ones. Now he, like Gaunt, tried to anticipate the problems inherent to working with Halaçoğlu by proposing a highly focused test case: a team of scholars could examine the fate of the Armenians who had lived on the Harput Plain before World War I. Halaçoğlu believed that they had been deported in an orderly manner as a necessary wartime precaution. Sarafian argued that the fate of the Harput Armenians had been significantly less orderly and significantly less benign. He outlined an examination of the sets of records that each side had been using as evidence. "What are the strengths and limitations of these materials?" Sarafian wrote in a statement describing the project. "And how can we assess these two sets of information? How far do they agree or disagree with each other?" But this project, too, was over before it started: Halaçoğlu claimed the necessary records were not available, and Sarafian moved on.

These foiled attempts by serious historians to work with Halaçoğlu were important because Prime Minister Erdoğan had recently taken to calling for a joint historical commission to analyze the events of 1915. It was a trick play, implying that the events had not yet been adequately studied: nobody who understood the territory could take such a call seriously. But because Erdoğan kept repeating the idea to foreign reporters and in diplomatic meetings, he had the rhetorical upper hand, making it seem as though Turkish scholars were eager to cooperate if only the other side would step up to the plate.

Sporting metaphors were irresistible: Müge had told me of yet another failed project that she referred to as a "boxing match of documents." Under the auspices of a group called the Vienna Armenian-Turkish Platform, Halaçoğlu had offered to bring to the table one hundred documents that proved the genocide had never happened. And two scholars from Armenia's National Academy of Sciences would chip in one hundred documents that proved it had. A group of scholars of various ethnicities were to adjudicate the battle. Papers came and went; at some point the document cap was raised to 133. Eventually, the Armenian participants pulled out. "I don't know why they even tried," said Müge. "I would never go into such a thing. That's not how scholarship works."

In fact serious scholarly cooperation was well under way, but Halaçoğlu was not part of it. And despite Erdoğan's calls for more research, his own administration initially shut down the first attempted conference in Turkey that sought to discuss the 1915 massacres outside the official framework. That groundbreaking event was eventually held at Istanbul's Bilgi University in September 2005, but only after participants passed through a crowd of nationalist protesters hurling eggs and tomatoes, and after the minister of justice Cemil Çiçek accused the conference organizers (a group of progressive historians and sociologists, all Turkish) of "stabbing the nation in the back."

In the United States, meanwhile, Müge and two of her colleagues—Ronald Grigor Suny and Gerard Libaridian, both ethnically Armenian—had convened the WATS group, whose conferences and online discussion boards were equal parts rigorous academic exchange and group therapy for Armenian and Turkish scholars.

As for scholars of the subject who were neither Armenian nor Turkish, they were few and far between—and almost all those in this category had, at least, an Armenian or Turkish spouse. The two most prominent American supporters of the Turkish position, Heath Lowry and the late Stanford Shaw, were both married to Turkish women (whether those marriages were the result of their work or its inspiration is a study for a journalist more intrepid than I).

The relevant point is that the political drama surrounding scholarship on 1915 meant that hardly anybody without a personal stake in the matter had the energy to get involved. A shocking proportion of Ottomanists and scholars of World War I stayed out of the debate entirely, glossing over the subject on the last page of a chapter or in a disclaimer-style footnote after a suspiciously vague passage. If the book is five hundred pages long, look for a paragraph about the massacres of Armenians—they may be generalized as "the empire's Christian subjects"—around page 498.

This reluctance to enter the fray was somewhat understandable if you considered what happened to the late American historian Donald Quataert. A respected scholar based at Binghamton University, Quataert specialized in the social, economic, and labor history of the Ottoman era. He was on the board of the Institute for Turkish Studies, a research center on the Georgetown campus. In 2006, after a long career that carefully side-stepped the Armenian question, Quataert made a bold move: he wrote in a book review that more Ottoman scholars needed to take the risk of studying the Armenian genocide. He noted that although he considered the term a distraction, he did believe the events fulfilled the definition. And it turned out that even this passing comment tucked into an article was a bridge too far.

Quataert's review was met with a stern warning from Turkey's ambassador to the United States, Nabi Sensoy. According to Quataert, the ambassador told him that his comments had angered Turkish leaders and they had threatened to revoke the Georgetown institute's funding—three million dollars from the Turkish government, which at the time constituted the institute's entire budget.

Quataert resigned from the board of the ITS and was followed by a few colleagues. The president of the institute, David Cuthell, referred to the Armenian issue as the "third rail."

Meanwhile, Western scholars who supported the Turkish thesis, such as Lowry and Shaw, had faced a threat far worse: assassination attempts by Armenian terrorists against them and their families.

In this politicized, even dangerous academic climate that scared off all but the most hardy, the influence of a government-appointed historian like Halaçoğlu—a defender of the faith whose resources and energy seemed inexhaustible—could not be simply dismissed.

Passing through the lobby of the Historical Society, which occupied a large, modernist building, Ertan and I stopped to take in a relief of Atatürk's face on the wall, accompanied by an homage. Translating it for me as a receptionist watched us, Ertan forced a straight face and a businesslike tone: "Dear Eternal Atatürk, the things that you expect from the Historical Society, we and those who come after us will follow your wishes always."

Moments later, I shook Yusuf Halaçoğlu's hand with as much willful positive feeling as I had ever mustered. He looked about my father's age, with a sharp, triangular chin shooting up to high, wide Mongolian cheekbones. His hair was opaque and smooth, shaped like a helmet. He had a permanent squint in his eyes that reminded me uncannily of George W. Bush. He appeared delighted to see me.

Halaçoğlu showed us to one of the six leather couches in his office. He did not speak any English, so I signaled to Ertan that I was ready to begin. I had prepared my introductory comments at some length, but before I could say a word, Halaçoğlu began to orate, and Ertan had no choice but to go along: "When the subject is Turkish and Armenian relations," Halaçoğlu said, "the issues go back to history."

I interrupted. "Before we start, I want to let you know a bit about myself, and the reason I'm here." I told him that I was an Armenian from the diaspora. I was doing research in Turkey about the "difficult issues" in our "shared past" and the way that those issues played out in the present. "I know that it's not easy for Armenians and Turks to speak to each other naturally about this subject, but I really hope that we can have an open and comfortable conversation."

"Just a minute," he said, holding up his palm in front of him. "For me it's not hard at all. I have many Armenian friends. It's not necessary that we do not have a comfortable relationship because of an event in 1915. After all, we're living today."

I had Turkish friends, too, I told him brightly. I added that I was having a lovely time in Turkey. "So that's all good. But I'm talking about how Turks and Armenians feel about one another in general."

"Now of course, because of the recent events, from 1915 on, there are people who say that there was a genocide, and those who come out against that," Halaçoğlu said. "And because of all these rumors, our Armenian youth—I mean young Turks with Armenian origins—feel a trauma. There's a similar trauma in the Turkish young people. That's why I think that at this point it is necessary to bring together young people with Turkish origins and young people with Armenian origins."

I, too, believed that we needed to bring young Turks and Armenians together, I told him. I was surprised to find common ground so quickly. I asked if the point would be for the youth to talk about their stereotypes of one another, or perhaps to exchange stories about their families' experiences.

"No," he said. "It would be something like a summer camp; a chance for them to meet each other, but also a chance to educate them about certain issues. To counteract the effects of negative ideas that come from the outside to the minds of these young people."

"Like what, for example?"

"When you bring people together and they face traumas simultaneously, then it's easier for them to see things."

"What things?"

"So if you were a person always saying that, for example, 'This many Armenians were killed there at this moment'—and if I was a person saying, 'That many Turks were killed at that moment,' then from our debates, at the very least we would relieve some tension. But it's not only that. There are many positive things to talk about, like what good neighbors they were to each other." He meant Armenians and Muslims in the Ottoman Empire.

"How many nice things happened between them. It's not only bad things that happened in 1914, 1915, and 1918."

I had been determined *not* to talk about history with Halaçoğlu, but as our conversation progressed, he tried to squeeze in a historical red herring at every turn. I began to see how truly confusing it would be to talk to him without a total grasp of both the history and the historiography of the Armenian issue, to understand the myriad ways that the events of the late Ottoman era could be used to serve different agendas.

Simplistic tropes such as the great, unsung harmony between Christians and Muslims, as Halaçoğlu liked to think of it, were obvious enough. Another transparent tactic was to imply that everyone had suffered equally. More complex and insidious were his frequent allusions to evidence and records. The government orders for the deportation and extermination of Armenians were known to have followed two tracks: the Interior Ministry issued official, written instructions to deport the Armenians of a given province, citing such reasons as protecting them from unrest; at the same time, unofficial commands—sometimes written but often only verbal—were delivered through party secretaries and other trusted messengers, indicating that the goal of the deportation was extermination, to be effected by a brutal Special Organization that operated outside normal channels and drew on refugees and convicts to carry out the massacres. The dual-track orders continued to serve their obfuscating purpose decades later, inviting misinterpretation by researchers. Even population records, which could seem to a casual observer like a relatively neutral form of documentation, were rife with controversy because it was in the interest of the Ottoman authorities to manipulate the numbers in order to control minority representation in local or national councils. Demographic records from the Armenian Patriarchate—which had its own interests—regularly clashed with official numbers. Population counts were of particular importance, of course, when historians looked back to assess the scale of massacre.

For years, Turkey's official position on the events of 1915 had created for Armenians an imperative to *prove*—resulting in a single-minded, juridical drive to show that there was a genocide. Consequently, the dominant scholarly energy on both sides had gone to answering the question of *whether*, instead of *why* or *how*. Even less subtlety trickled down to the level of popular conversation. There was or there was not—this was the realm of faith and fantasy, of childlike thinking. As if one morning, for no reason whatsoever, a big bad man in a palace woke up and ordered that all the Armenians be shot dead. Or as if one morning, the terrible Armenian traitors began fighting for the enemy and the poor Turks had no choice but to send them away.

One reason why the WATS group represented such a sea change in critical analysis of the genocide was because it openly acknowledged the politicized landscape but attempted to move beyond it—to move away from *whether*, toward a more complex understanding. The group proceeded from a basic view that Armenian civilization in Anatolia as it had existed for hundreds of years had been, in effect, annihilated in the World War I era, but that many aspects of that annihilation called for further study. How far in advance had the Ottoman authorities considered such radical measures? Were earlier pogroms against Armenians, in the 1890s and 1909, isolated events, or were they part of a long-term radicalization of the government's approach to national security leading to 1915? Events unfolded differently in different regions, with some local commanders following orders while others refused to obey: what did local variations reveal about the larger picture? To what extent was violence from Armenian nationalist committees perceived as a real threat or used as a pretext? How did wartime pressures and the intervention of European countries influence Turkey's decisions? Was there a meaningful difference between actions that resulted in genocide and actions planned with that explicit goal? The questions were as rich as they were problematic.

The goal of WATS was not to embrace some kind of bottomless relativism in which all interpretations were equally valid, nor to parse out some sort of compromise. The purpose was to develop a mature reckoning that could hold multiple, tense factors side by side in one analysis: to acknowledge that Armenians could have been actors in their own fate while also being, unequivocally, victims of genocide. That Turks could have been absolutely besieged by the demise of their once-massive empire, and indeed suffering the hardships of World War I, but that their leaders could have nonetheless made ruthless calculations that later could be called genocide.

It was easy to see why Turkey would benefit from a more nuanced understanding of the genocide, but perhaps less obvious what the Armenians stood to gain from complicating their own story. One of the

Armenian founders of WATS, Ronald Suny, explained succinctly: if we don't ask questions about why and how the genocide happened, we are left with the explanation that most Armenians have settled on—that "Turks are just the sort of people who *do* these things." In other words, racism.

I had become something of a WATS groupie. But as the saying went, "The more you know, the more you know how much there is to know." I knew this much: talking to Halaçoğlu, I would not have the mental stamina to go point-for-point on history with somebody whose entire career was devoted to sowing confusion. Instead, I spent much of our interview trying to reorient the conversation.

"Why did you decide to become a historian?" I asked.

"Oh!" he exclaimed. "In fact, I was drawn to two professions—one was agriculture, the other was history. I chose the second one. I was thinking it would be nice to know about the past." He leaned back and spoke with a fond, nostalgic tone.

"And when did you first learn about the Armenian issue? Did you hear about it when you were a child?"

"No, not when I was a child. When I was a docent at the university in 1985." That would have been right at the end of the ASALA era; his mention of a specific year seemed deliberate.

"But when you were a child, did your family tell you any stories about Armenians? Did the word 'Armenian' mean anything to you?"

Halaçoğlu seemed to like this question. "I was born in the region with the old name of Kilikia, in the town of Sis"—modern-day Kozan—"a place where many Armenians used to live. And well, there were—unfortunately this is a fact—there were two ovens there." He referred to *fırın*, the deep, barrel-like kilns that were used to bake bread, which was tossed against the hot stone walls. "And they said that in those ovens Armenians had burned the Muslims. Those two ovens were still there."

I nodded. This may have been true. That was terrible. I was intent on showing empathy for such a possibility.

"And, well, my grandfather was born a very long time ago, in 1876, so he knew all the events. But you know, he never spoke about the Armenians in a negative manner. He only spoke negatively about the Armenian rebel gangs. As a child, I never heard the word genocide; that is, I didn't hear it from either side. I was never brought up as anyone's enemy."

Of course, the term genocide hardly existed in common parlance when Halaçoğlu was a child. He was born in 1949. The term was coined in 1944 by Raphael Lemkin, a Polish-Jewish lawyer whose life's work was to devise a way for the world to punish the perpetrators of race murder. Lemkin's campaign resulted in the United Nations' passage, in 1948, of a treaty to define such an atrocity. Titled the "Convention on the Prevention and Punishment of the Crime of Genocide," it said that a group had suffered genocide if, because of its nationality, ethnicity, race, or religion, its members had faced any of the following: killing, serious bodily or mental harm, conditions of life calculated to bring about the group's physical destruction in whole or in part, the imposing of measures intended to prevent births within the group, and the forcible transfer of children to another group. Lemkin cited the massacres of Armenians as an example in creating his definition, but Armenians themselves did not start campaigning for use of the term until decades later.

"Were there still Armenians living in Sis when you were a child?" I knew the answer to my question already; I was simply trying to make a point: where do you think they went?

"No. But sometimes those who had emigrated from Sis to Lebanon and Aleppo would visit. And because they spoke in Turkish we used to stroll around with them and talk."

"What kinds of things would you talk about?"

"Oh, they used to speak about their old houses where they had lived, and how they used to live together with the Turks and had such good neighborly relations."

Those who had emigrated. They used to tell about their old houses. He made the visits sound like casual sightseeing excursions. In fact, most of the Armenian deportees had been forced to leave their homes and assets, sometimes significant holdings. Many survivors who wound up in nearby Aleppo tried for decades to return and file claims to get their property back, almost entirely without success.

The other subtext to Halaçoğlu's anecdotes was: *Many Armenians survived. So why would you call it a genocide?* Indeed, Armenians from areas close to the Syrian border, like Sis, were disproportionately more likely to have survived the expulsions. Whereas deportees from Eastern Anatolian cities had a survival rate of only about 20 percent, deportees from provinces farther west, including Kilikia, had the comparatively better fate of only walking for weeks to disease-ridden refugee camps in the Syrian desert.

Halaçoğlu went on, obsessed with the idea that everyone had gotten along. "They always wondered how it could have happened that two peoples living in the same place could become enemies. They talked about how they never wanted to leave this place. . . ."

One of the most beloved Armenian folk songs mourns the Armenians' dispersion from the Kilikia region in painful detail. As Halaçoğlu kept going with his spiel, I remembered the first time I heard "Kilikia." One of my favorite uncles (by marriage), whose Kilikia-born mother had survived the genocide and settled in Lebanon, sang the song from the end of the table after a family dinner. "I've seen the plains of Syria, the peaks and cedars of Lebanon. I've seen prosperous Italy, Venice and its gondolas," went one verse. "But none of them are as beautiful as my Kilikia." The song ends with the hope that if nothing else, they will return to Kilikia to be buried.

"Did anyone in your family suffer from the massacres?" I asked Halaçoğlu.

"Of course, very many. I have a very large family. But people wanted to forget about these things. They didn't want to repeat it, repeat it, and repeat it and make the children remember these things all the time. They wanted to forget."

It occurred to me only much later that Halaçoğlu never asked me if anyone in my family had suffered.

I changed the subject, asking him if he knew Hrant Dink.

"Of course I did." He paused for a moment. "I mean, we weren't really *close* friends."

At this, Ertan, who had been so poised as to seem like a statue, stumbled for the first time. He coughed and rephrased Halaçoğlu's answer four different ways before moving on.

"I was very upset when I learned that he was killed," said Halaçoğlu. "Because maybe he was the only person who could be an intermediary to the Armenian diaspora."

He and Hrant had agreed that Turks and Armenians should not have bad feelings toward each other, he said. A lengthy explanation followed, in which he was intent on demonstrating the precise intersection of Hrant's point of view and his own, hinging on an argument that any bad feelings between Christians and Muslims were created by "imperialists and missionaries in Ottoman times, who tried to make the two groups into enemies." He told me that he had proof of these intentions in the form of secret reports—three thousand documents that he himself purchased from Russia, for five hundred dollars—"because Russia needed that kind of money at the time."

"What did you think about the expression that people chanted at Hrant's funeral: 'We are all Armenian'?" I asked.

"We do not accept in any way such a massacre against Hrant."

"But what did you think about that slogan?"

Halaçoğlu avoided my question and said that radicalization was the result of a constant, one-sided emphasis on a past that was tragic for everyone.

"But could you bring yourself to say this statement in solidarity? 'We are all Armenian.' You personally?"

"We were never brought up in our childhood as anyone's enemies. This revived only in the last few years."

"I'm asking about the 'We are all Armenian' statement. Could you say that yourself?"

"I don't feel the need to say something like that. If I needed to say it, I would, but I don't feel the need."

When I didn't respond, he continued.

"There's no barrier. I mean, I could also say it. So in the end you're Armenian, and I am a Turk, but we are both human beings."

"But it's not that simple," I said. "If it were, I wouldn't be here." And yet, I knew even as I uttered these words, that my own insistence that we were all human beings was precisely what *had* brought me here. Before coming to Turkey, I did not understand that even this, the most innocuous-seeming idea ever to emerge from the mind of man, could be used to promote intolerance. If we were all human beings, Halaçoğlu argued, why should he make any special fuss about someone's Armenian identity?

"I'd like to ask you about something else," I said. At Hrant's funeral, participants had held small, wooden pickets topped with circular posters bearing a life-size photograph of Hrant's face. In coverage of the funeral march, it was repeatedly claimed that one hundred thousand people had marched together. But Halaçoğlu had come forth with a statement that was all over the Turkish papers: he said that the number was inflated, because all those images of Hrant's head had doubled the headcount.

"If your goal is to make people feel more comfortable together, why would you say such a thing at a time like that? I'm speaking from the heart now," I said. "It seemed like a really insensitive comment."

Ertan asked me to repeat this, slowly.

I rephrased. "If we want to find a way to connect to each other as human beings, and if so many people were moved by that horrible tragedy, as an Armenian I felt that was an insensitive thing to say."

Ertan looked puzzled. "Insensitive?"

Something about this word was resisting translation. Was it confusion about the difference between physical and emotional sensation? Or was the notion simply too absurd to repeat? A young journalist, a woman, naturally, using the only power women were expected to employ—the power of the pout, let's call it—telling a sham historian that he had hurt her feelings?

After watching us try to rework my comment a few times, Halaçoğlu leaned forward and held up both hands. "*Tamam, anladım.*" *Okay, I got it.*

Now he claimed that journalists had distorted what he said. This would have been easier to believe if not for the fact that Halaçoğlu had a habit of issuing new press releases whenever prior statements were poorly received. He was like a Magic 8 Ball—if you don't like the result you get, just shake it and try out a different one.

"This is what I actually said. I said that the group that was chanting, 'We are all Armenian, we are all Hrant' did not do anything like this in any other funeral ceremony."

"But was this like any other tragedy?"

"I mean in any other funeral where someone was killed in a similar way."

"Nobody was killed in a similar way," I said. My voice was now agitated for the first time. Neither Ertan nor I could quite keep our cool when the subject of Hrant's murder came up. But my statement wasn't strictly true: many journalists in Turkey had been murdered in similar ways, murdered for their ideas. In the early 1990s, in particular, reporting that could be viewed as pro-Kurdish was tantamount to suicide. Arrests and torture were common, and during that decade several journalists were killed in connection with their work. Fortunately, the pattern had not been repeated in recent years, until Hrant's assassination. But Halaçoğlu apparently saw no threads connecting the murders of journalists, state censorship, and his own bottomless oeuvre.

"What I want to say is that if they had said, in the funerals of these other people, 'We are all Turks,' there wouldn't have been a radicalization in Turkey. We could have prevented this."

"But people already have to say that they're Turks, every day in school," I said, referring to the pledge that schoolchildren chanted in unison. "How can you compare those other deaths to the death of a Turkish-Armenian journalist who was killed because he was Armenian, given the position of Armenians in this country?"

"No, look. I do not accept the idea that Hrant was killed because he was Armenian."

Huh?

"Because his being killed is not good for Turks at all."

Right.

"Who can want there to be more reaction against the Armenians in Turkey? *Who* would want this? Would you or would I? No!"

No.

"So this is being propagated. This is being forced." He referred back to the intervention of "imperialists" in the Ottoman era. "And today in our own time, another state is doing the same thing."

The United States? The EU? Israel perhaps? The paranoia about foreign intervention in Turkey's affairs had a legitimate history, but it had swelled to encompass every single problem the country faced, matters great and small, including some that had nothing to do with politics. Zoology, for example. In 2005 the Ministry of Environment and Forestry renamed three indigenous animals, releasing a statement saying that the old names "were given by foreigners with designs on the country's unity." The name of a red fox known as "Vulpes Vulpes Kurdistanica" was shortened to "Vulpes Vulpes." A species of wild sheep called "Ovis Armeniana" was changed to "Ovis Orientalis Anatolicus," and a type of deer known as "Capreolus Capreolus Armenus" became "Capreolus Cuprelus Capreolus." The statement went on: "Unfortunately, foreign scientists, who for many years researched Turkey's flora and fauna, named plant and animal species that they had never come across before with a prejudiced mind-set. . . . This ill intent is so obvious that even species that are endemic to our country were given names that are against our unitary structure," it concluded.

"What do you think about Article 301?" I asked. This was the amendment to the penal code that made "insulting Turkishness" a crime with a ten-year prison sentence. Judging from the many trials under way in Turkish courts, the law's main function seemed to be to punish the use of the word genocide. There were cases against those who had spoken the word or implied it, then cases against the lawyers who defended them, and, in turn, cases against journalists who wrote too freely about these cases.

"I am in favor of freedom of expression, but with the requirement that you are not harassing others."

"It's difficult to agree on what it means to harass others," I said.

"Well, would it be correct if I insulted you and harassed you because you are Armenian?"

I shrugged.

"It wasn't your choice to be born as an Armenian."

He paused, waiting for me to react.

"The same way I was born as a Turk," he added.

Finally I gathered my wits—only to say something that sounded insane. "I absolutely believe that by law you should be allowed to say whatever you want about me or about Armenians."

He was surprised by this, and scrunched his face in exaggerated disappointment. "But it is not nice to insult, to harass," he said, taking a fatherly, instructive tone. "Would it be correct to say Armenians are low human beings?"

"It would be unfortunate if you said that, but it should not be illegal."

"I think insulting someone's identity should be illegal," he said. "Because one does not choose which nation to belong to."

It struck me as sad that the best argument he could make as to why he should not insult my identity was because I did not have a choice about it.

He went on. "There can be bad Turks, bad Armenians, but we should not harass or insult Armenianness or Turkishness."

"So should insulting Armenianness also be a crime?"

"It should be a crime."

"How about insulting Kurdishness?"

"Any nation." Then he added—as though he was afraid that I was not getting his point—"Nobody should be harassed because he is black."

In the United States, of course, we were more or less free to insult blacks if we chose to. The cornerstone of our democracy, the First Amendment, invited us to insult one another openly and hideously so long as the insult was not accompanied by calls to violent action. To that end, we had Ku Klux Klan marches ambling down Main Street in American towns even after the gains of the civil rights movement. The American Civil Liberties Union had defended their right to do so. An open society calls on individuals and groups to win influence through reason and example, not solely by prohibition. By contrast, in Turkey, the prohibition on insulting Turkishness had been forged into a weapon used in court against Hrant Dink, and the lawsuits and the lynch-mob atmosphere they created led straight to his murder, ennobling a seventeen-year-old from Trabzon with a network of powerful figures behind him to take on the role of assassin. And now, with all of that in mind, I found myself sitting on a sofa at the Turkish Historical Society, face-to-face with Yusuf Halaçoğlu, touting the virtues of hate speech.

But still he was not satisfied that he'd made himself understood.

"How correct, how right would it be if I told you that according to my investigations, I decided that the Armenians are a low-profile people?" he asked.

I said nothing.

"I do not agree that the Armenians, Greeks, or Jews should be in the status of minorities. Because if you give them minority status, they will be second-class people. Armenians were born here in Turkey just as I was. So just like me, they should benefit from everything that Turkey has, as they wish. They can say, 'We are all Armenians,' but they are my fellow citizens."

"That's beautiful," I said. The words came out of me as if from a robot programmed to generate polite remarks on cue. If I hadn't heard my own voice saying this on tape, later on, I would have denied that I ever could have been so mawkishly insincere. I had lost control of the interview altogether, and it was the hint I saw behind Ertan's eyes that told me it was time to cut my losses and go. He looked embarrassed for me.

As we stood to leave, I asked Halaçoğlu if he expected to continue in his job at the Historical Society for a long time.

"No," he said firmly. He was tired. "I don't want to be involved with politics anymore."

Then Halaçoğlu told me he wanted to explain just one more thing.

What followed was less an explanation than a parting souvenir. It was a set of documents that, he believed, would help me understand his views. He shoved a few papers into a clear plastic sleeve, four streaky photocopies of archival documents that were to settle once and for all the debate over what happened to the Armenians at the end of the Ottoman Empire.

What were the documents? A couple of letters from diplomats and a page of a population record. It was as if a historian were merely a cook with a knack for improvising, making some kind of soup with whatever happened to be in the cupboard.

Later, when I recalled the interview, my memories were nearly empty of visual detail, as if I had frozen my senses in order to endure the meeting's peculiar dishonesty—my own as well as his. But one image remained clear in my mind: the sight of Halaçoğlu's unsteady, aging hand trying to maneuver the edges of those photocopied sheets into the soft, transparent cover. He appeared somehow vulnerable—human, finally—as he wrestled with this small secretarial project.

That glimpse of vulnerability reflected my larger confusion about the meeting: all his obfuscations and rationalizations—his own and, by extension, those of Turks in general—seemed on the one hand the very definition of insecurity, of a brittle identity unable to risk questioning the story it clung to. Yet at the same time, he held to his rationalizations with such tenacity that it was he who had control, while I floundered. Thinking back to my conversation with Müge about whether Halaçoğlu would want to talk to somebody like me, I realized that in a match like this, I was bound to be the loser. Certainty is always more powerful than doubt. I had known that once, as a child.

A year later, Halaçoğlu would resign from his post and win a seat in the Turkish Parliament under the MHP—an ultranationalist party—representing the large, industrial province of Kayseri.

* * *

AFTER LEAVING HALAÇOĞLU'S office, I went alone to the Museum of Anatolian Civilizations, which was situated on a hill overlooking the old district of Ankara. What a deep history this region had. The museum was set in the restored structures of a fifteenth-century marketplace and inn, and wandering through its archways and stony nooks, you could learn about the world's oldest civilizations: from the Paleolithic era on to the Hittites, the Lydians, and the Phrygians, they were all there. The museum also covered more recent civilizations: Greek, Roman, Byzantine, and Seljuk. Here and there one might marvel over the involvements of the Medes, the Scythians, the Egyptians, and Persians in Anatolian history. A few years earlier, the European Museum Forum had recognized this as the European Museum of the Year.

I spent several minutes reading a timeline that summarized the shifts and jolts of three thousand years: it began in 1200 BC, describing the aftermath of the Aegean migrations, the vanquishing of Lydia in 546 BC, and so on, as kingdoms displaced one another and morphed and split. There was the divide of the Roman Empire into East and West and the rise of Byzantium, bringing us to the year 330. Then the timeline skipped to 1071, the Malazgirt Battle, which opened the doors of Anatolia to Seljuk Turks. The Seljuks' activities got several entries, leading up to 1453, when Constantinople became the capital of the Ottoman Empire. The next few centuries went by without remark, until 1923, when Atatürk declared the new Turkish republic.

In other words, the hundreds of years that comprised the height of Armenian civilization in Anatolia—the rise and fall of several Armenian dynasties and kingdoms—were left out of the timeline altogether.

I walked through every exhibit in the building, studying captions and wondering if I just hadn't found the right room yet. Peering through the glass at ancient statues and gold earrings, a familiar, self-questioning voice crept into my mind: was it possible that in fact the Armenians were so minor and irrelevant that it was actually reasonable to ignore them in this museum?

I looked around for an information desk or a guide, but the only employee I could find was a young man who seemed barely out of his teens, standing behind the counter at the museum's souvenir shop. Fingering through some postcards and key chains, I tried to sound nonchalant. "Excuse me, I was just curious. Is there anything in this museum about the Armenian people?"

"I don't know," he said, smiling back shyly.

"Is there anybody who would know?"

"Office." He pointed.

But the office door was locked. For the next half hour, I circled the area in front of it, then became paranoid that the souvenir shop clerk had alerted the office staff not to come back because there was a strange woman asking about the Armenians.

A tourist had overheard my question, though. He was a lanky man with a trimmed gray beard and a camera around his neck. He might have been Danish or Norwegian—his accent in English was almost imperceptible in that Northern European way. He stepped over to help me. "Well, it doesn't look like it, according to this map," he said.

The billboard-sized map took up an entire wall in the museum lobby; it showed all the civilizations that had graced Anatolian soil over the past twenty thousand years. A map legend listed each civilization, and you could press a button next to any of the names to make the map light up with red dots showing which peoples had lived in what areas over the course of many empires.

"No, Armenia doesn't seem to be here," he confirmed after another moment of examination. "You see, this would be Armenia," he said to me—pointing to the eastern border of the billboard, where the electronic portion of the map gave way to present-day bordering countries that had not been a part of the Anatolian swath—"but there are no lights there."

No lights indeed, I thought, suppressing a snort as I recalled the daily power outages when I visited Yerevan a few summers before.

"That's today's Armenia," I told him. My question, if it had put the museum shop clerk on guard, had aroused no suspicions about my ethnicity in this European tourist. "But ancient Armenia took up about half of this map. In the second century BC, this"—I swept my fingers from the northeast edge of the Mediterranean across the entire picture, to where it ended, near the Caspian Sea—"was the Kingdom of Armenia."

"Oh, I didn't know that," he said. "Well, maybe you could ask for one of the tour guides who is a local Turk. They seem to be pretty well-informed."

PART FOUR

Armenia

- 15 -

Country on Maps

"Sɪsᴛᴇʀ ᴅᴇᴀʀ, ᴡʜᴀᴛ ᴀʀᴇ ʏᴏᴜ ᴡᴀɪᴛɪɴɢ ғᴏʀ? Mᴏᴠᴇ ᴀʜᴇᴀᴅ ᴏʀ ʟᴇᴛ ᴜs pass!" A burly, middle-aged woman with a beehive of dyed hair that had faded to violet was nudging one of her several checkered, plastic bazaar bags, the square kind, as big as an old-fashioned television set and packed until it was as solid as one, against the back of my knees.

"Eh, who does that guy think he is? We've been waiting much longer than he has!" called another matronly woman from behind me, as a man tried to squeeze into the front of the line.

One fellow, in his thirties, appeared different from the rest—less desperate. He wore a polo shirt and creased khakis, and refused to obey a fellow passenger's insistence that he unhook the rope that was supposed to keep the line in order. As I watched him, reflecting on the fact that he seemed more sophisticated than the others, he turned on the crowd of his shoving, whining kinfolk and shouted, "Have you become Africans? Great, now we're Africans."

They were Armenians, all of them. Armenians from Yerevan, clustered together in Istanbul's Atatürk International Airport, less resembling passengers in a check-in line than practiced Soviets jockeying for the last loaf of bread.

The airport screens showing arrivals and departures made no

indication of a flight to Armenia. A clerk at the information desk had not been able to help me, either. But I found them as if by some deep internal radar, circling the queues of a hundred check-in counters until I heard the jocular plaint of the Yerevan dialect, awakening in me instantly a feeling of comfort and familiarity—of safety?—that I had not realized I was missing in all these months of straining to follow the music of Turkish. It was like taking off an ill-fitting shoe and realizing only then that it had been too tight all day.

The Yerevan group was an island among the Turks and tourists. Instead of head scarves, puffs of blue-black and purple-gray hair were in abundance, an androgynous, chemical hairdo favored by older Armenian women of the working class. Many of the Armenian merchant women who made this trip on a regular basis had gold or silver front teeth and were huskier than Turkish women on the whole, but even so there was a certain effort in their appearance: they wore calf-length skirts and smooth blouses, armored bras aiming their hefty bosoms at ninety degrees, challenging anybody to dare block their path. Standing apart from the merchants, there were usually also a few slender Armenian girls in skintight jeans, amply rouged, with silky long hair, wearing stiletto heels and tank tops, fake breasts distorting fake logos and suggesting a different kind of goods for sale.

Yes, here they were, my people.

This was a charter flight: a mysterious allowance of transit crossing a border that was officially sealed shut. There were no diplomatic relations between Turkey and Armenia; but somehow, for the past several years, without grand pronouncements, with minimal advertising, and lacking even an entry on the airport monitors or the Web site for Atatürk Airport, this charter flight had been carrying a specific subgroup of Armenians from Yerevan to Istanbul and back again. They were overnight entrepreneurs who gathered goods at Turkish bazaars in the Laleli district, stuffed them into plastic bags embalmed with clear packing tape, and shipped them home to Yerevan, where they would get stacked up in clothing shops and beauty stores, "Made In Turkey," for purchase by the consumers of Armenia. This work was done mostly by women—their husbands gone, lazy, or too proud to visit enemy territory.

Armenians could not afford to boycott everything made in Turkey the way their diaspora brethren did. Their border with Azerbaijan was also closed, and the hostility along that frontier was newer and more volatile. Between 1991 and 1993, more than thirty thousand people, soldiers and civilians on both sides, died in the war over Nagorno-Karabakh, and without a resolution to Karabakh's status, the cease-fire remained tenuous. The war had also set off a refugee crisis in the early 1990s, a de facto population exchange: hundreds of thousands of Armenians left Azerbaijan, and an even larger number of Azeris had to flee Armenia and Karabakh, each group leaving behind generations of history.

With blockades to the east and west, Armenia's import and export cargo had to travel across rough mountain passes from Iran, in the south, or via the Georgian border to the north, where goods were exploitatively taxed. Inevitably, when charter flights were established between Yerevan and Istanbul, some intrepid traders were ready to make the trip. In the early days, one might have seen an entire car bumper presented as checked luggage. Now, a few years on, the system had smoothed itself out; larger items procured by Armenian merchants went by trucks driven from Turkey, detouring through Georgia and on to Armenia. The trucks were manned by a special force of drivers who could communicate with everyone involved: they were Hemshin people, inhabitants of a small chunk of Turkey's Black Sea region, where clusters of Armenians and Georgians had long ago converted to Islam and now spoke their own dialect, inscrutable to outsiders, combining Turkish, Armenian, Georgian, and Russian. The Hemshin were said to be a closed community, suspicious of outsiders, but in their way they were also unofficial diplomats.

IT WAS ANOTHER unofficial diplomat who had made the flights possible in the first place. His name was Dikran Altun, and he was an Armenian from Istanbul, a Turkish citizen. For many years, Dikran was the closest thing Turkey and Armenia had to a shared ambassador: he was a travel agent.

I met Dikran by accident. I wanted to get to Yerevan, and after weeks of trying to figure out how to buy a ticket on this semicovert direct flight, I finally found his office, Tower Tur, a speck among the hundreds of travel agencies crowded along a single boulevard in Istanbul's Harbiye district. I had many questions about the enterprise. Who was making use of the flight? Why was it allowed to function? But the woman who processed my ticket would give only one-word answers. Suddenly a loud male voice came from across the room: "I'll tell you about the flights. First tell me who you are."

Dikran and I talked for an hour that day, and again on future occasions when I would drop by for another ticket and another conversation. The story of how he came to establish the route was a long and convoluted tale that revealed much about the small details—chance connections, good or bad interpersonal relationships—that could give rise to significant geopolitical changes.

Dikran was born in Erzurum and grew up in Istanbul, but he left to complete high school and college in Cyprus and Beirut, then lived in Los Angeles for several years. By 1991, he was back in Istanbul, married with children, and working as a gold dealer in the city's Grand Bazaar. One day he received a group of unexpected visitors—three Armenians from Armenia. They were delivering a letter from a relative of Dikran's who lived in Yerevan. And one of these visitors, it turned out, was the brother of Levon Ter-Petrossian, who had just been elected president of Armenia. Ter-Petrossian's term coincided with a brief, critical window of time—the immediate post-Soviet years—when diplomatic relations between Armenia and Turkey seemed possible. Talks were under way, and members of the Armenian administration traveled to Istanbul for meetings. Because of the connection made at the bazaar, Dikran became a kind of fixer for them, translating and helping them get around. Soon he was going to Armenia as well. Powerful people in both countries came to trust him.

After a few years of serving as an ad hoc envoy, Dikran was asked to help with a new initiative, the Black Sea Economic Cooperation (BSEC). With eleven member countries, it was to be headquartered in Istanbul. Since Armenia was the only member without a consulate in Turkey, its BSEC representative didn't have an office. As Dikran told it, none of the Bolsahays wanted to help; they were afraid to get involved with Armenia on any level. By then, Dikran had left the Grand Bazaar and started a travel agency. He allowed the Armenian BSEC representative to use an extra room at the agency, sponsoring this arrangement for two years. He did so, he said, not only for Armenia's sake, but for his own; with an official delegate from Yerevan based in Istanbul, he could hand off the role of middleman.

Serving as an intermediary, Dikran said, had been "a very, very difficult task." Like Hrant and the Armenian Patriarch, Dikran was one of the few people to whom the authorities went for insider information, or whom Turkish journalists called for comments on anything related to Armenia.

"Every night I had to think that tomorrow morning somebody will phone me and ask for my ideas. Sometimes they came from the TV stations for an interview, wanting me to say that nothing happened in 1915, or there was no genocide." There was no way he could talk about the subject while being true to himself and avoid being sent to prison for fifty years, he said.

Dikran presented a sample answer from his repertoire: "I would tell them, 'I'm not educated enough to evaluate the meaning of a genocide against a people. But go look in any museum in Turkey and see that you cannot find anything from the Armenians. You are always saying that Armenians are the best, let's say, goldsmiths, or carpet makers, and so on. So why don't we have anything? Were we so foolish that we couldn't make even one pot?'" He was relieved to put such rhetorical contortions behind him.

He believed that he developed the courage to handle such challenges by living outside of Turkey for a spell. "The difference for me, compared to other Istanbul Armenians, was Cyprus and Lebanon and the United States. It's whatever was given to me by those countries I lived in."

This appreciation for his time in other countries seemed a bit ironic when Dikran told me what happened when he moved from the United States back to Istanbul in the mid-1980s. In those years, most Bolsahays were moving in the opposite direction. Tens of thousands of them were leaving Turkey because of the backlash they faced during the ASALA era. Those who stayed bore the brunt of Turkey's growing fear of Armenians; Bolsahays suddenly became suspect of crimes large and small, and many were framed or threatened.

Dikran, returning from California, was put under arrest, accused of all sorts of illegal activities. While living in Los Angeles, he had become involved with the local community there. He had helped start a choir at one of the Armenian churches, and then, when a school linked to the church needed a new building, he put up money to help—twenty-five thousand dollars, in his and his late mother's names. Someone—Dikran believed it could only have been a fellow Istanbul Armenian trying to stay on the right side of the authorities—told the Turkish police that Dikran had given money to a school that was linked with ASALA. In fact, the school was not even Dashnak-affiliated, much less ASALA; it was a school run by the less-political Armenian General Benevolent Union, like the one Dikran himself had attended in Cyprus and remembered so fondly.

Dikran landed in prison without trial as investigators mined his history for nefarious connections. He was tortured with electric shocks—voltage from an old crank telephone, he said—and also knifed by an inmate who found out he was Armenian. Seven months later, he was released without a charge.

The Dikran before me now looked like a model citizen, a family man. Later, when I searched news archives and other records for corroboration of what he described, I found a mess of bizarre details that contradicted each other and made me wonder for a moment if I'd been hoodwinked, welcomed by someone with a legitimately unsavory record who was eager to clear his name. Seeking some insight, I told the story to a Bolsahay friend, and she nodded as though there was nothing surprising—neither about the confusing news coverage nor about the possibility of a fellow Bolsahay being framed. "That's why Istanbul Armenians had to be so careful about having any kind of relationship with Armenians in other countries, even with family." Anything could and would be used against them.

Dikran summed it up the same way. "It seems very normal to be in these situations when you are living in Turkey," he said. "And I believe that they want us to leave Turkey. So I never will leave."

To make the point, he pulled out an old, expired identification card, showing his city of registration as Yozgat. "I have never seen Yozgat," said Dikran. "Even my father never saw Yozgat. But my grandfather was from Sarıkaya village there." Dikran's father had forced him to put down the old city as his place of origin. "He said, 'If you don't, one day they will say Armenians never lived in Yozgat.'" Dikran waited until his father had passed away before he changed his registration to Istanbul—too many logistical problems, he explained. But he kept the old card in his wallet just the same.

BY THE TIME I met Dikran in 2007, his company owned two planes and ran flights at least twice a week, in cooperation with Armavia Airlines on the Armenian side and Atlas Airlines from Turkey. The Turkish government had allowed Armenian carriers to land in Turkey starting in 1995 but would not let Turkish carriers fly to Yerevan until 2003, when Dikran got what he described as a quiet nod from Ankara. He wasn't sure what ultimately convinced officials to give him permission, but he believed it was the magic words he used: "I told them it would make Turkey look better to foreign countries." He knew there was a risk. "I was sure that if anything went wrong, they would not admit they gave me permission to do it."

More than 80 percent of Dikran's customers were Armenians participating in what was known as "the suitcase trade." They had a strict routine, he said: they came from Armenia once or twice a month, preferring his Monday flights over the Thursday ones so they could avoid paying for a fourth night of lodging. They all stayed in the same hotel in the Laleli district. It had to be that hotel because most of their business happened on one side of a particular street, and they didn't even want to have to cross to the other side. In the hotel basement, a cargo company had set up shop to transport goods by truck to Armenia via Georgia. Traveling back and forth, the Hemshin drivers improved their Armenian. The entire routine had its own perfect logic. It was a Rube Goldberg–style detour around a 166-mile stretch of barbed wire and bad faith.

Other than the merchants, Dikran had some passengers who came to Istanbul to work as maids or nannies—Armenians were reputed to be good cooks, and Turks apparently liked hiring them for household work because they could not understand family conversations. Dikran estimated there were several thousand such temporary workers, many staying illegally. The Turkish authorities had largely looked the other way, but anytime there was renewed tension with Armenia, they issued threats to track down and deport the laborers. Typically, these people overstayed their visas by a few years and then, knowing they probably couldn't return to Turkey again, paid a fine and flew home. The really bold ones changed their names and tried to reenter Turkey. This was a problem for Dikran, because as the air carrier, he was responsible for sending back travelers who arrived without valid papers, and if there was no seat available on the next plane, he had to pay a huge fine himself.

* * *

MY FIRST TRIP to Yerevan was four years earlier, in 2003. I had spent the summer teaching journalism at a university in southern Russia, and one day it occurred to me that I was too near to Armenia not to go. Nobody in my immediate family had visited, even though both of my parents had several first cousins who were born and raised in Yerevan. Branches of the family took root there in the 1930s, when my father's aunt arrived from Georgia to study medicine, and in the 1950s, when my mother's aunt moved from Iran to Yerevan with her husband, who was appointed to a post in the national archives. But throughout the Soviet era, ordinary travel in and out of Armenia was restricted, so although we exchanged Christmas cards and family photos with many of these relatives, we had never met most of them in person.

For that trip from Russia to Yerevan, I invited an American journalist colleague, Gretchen, to join me. For her the visit was a novelty, a funny story to be told even before it had happened. *Armenia? Why not!* For me the company was a buffer against going alone. I had no idea what I would find there.

We traveled from Russia to Georgia—Tbilisi, where my grandfather had grown up. There we found a Georgian-Armenian driver who took us on a six-hour ride through the Georgian countryside to get to Yerevan. At the Sadakhlo border crossing, we had our passports stamped at the lone customs station, which looked like a lifeguard stand airdropped into the mountains. I lingered for a moment and tried to expand within myself what appeared to be a quiet, unremarkable occasion: I, a person who had always called herself Armenian, was actually in Armenia.

We drove on, through the Lori region, home to copper mines and medieval monasteries. It was rocky territory, but that August the landscape was dense with trees such a dark shade of green they looked black. The Debed River seemed to slice right through them, creating just a sliver for itself and the road.

"It's so beautiful," Gretchen said at every turn, and I nodded, proud but silent, trying not to seem like I thought I had something to do with it.

Then came miles of open plains dotted with Soviet-era construction projects that appeared to have been abandoned overnight: cranes stopped midlift, half-built walls of factories that were once destined for more than the weeds and wildflowers that now patched their unmortared crevices. Until 1991, Armenia had been an important manufacturing center for the Soviet Union, and the evidence of this past had not been cleared away.

Gradually, green and brown faded to gray. Instead of apricot sellers, there were makeshift gas stations every few miles—just a bench and a barrel of petrol, a sign in Russian or Armenian hand-painted on a scrap of wood.

Then, before I could register what happened, we were off the main road and driving on small streets, which were empty of people on that muggy summer afternoon.

"Here it is," said the driver, slowing to turn onto Nalbandian Street.

"Here's what?"

"Yerevan."

I was embarrassed. I had lured Gretchen along by telling her that Yerevan was a beautiful city. I had been looking at photos of it all my life, after all—calendars published by the church, postcard sets from relatives on thick, Soviet-era cardstock showing yellowed photographs of monuments, fountains, and elaborate buildings, everything captioned in Russian back then. In recent summers, many of my American-Armenian friends had made the trip, and each one returned beatified as though from a pilgrimage to Mecca or Rome. I couldn't have imagined Yerevan as anything less than extraordinary. But the city I saw now looked shabby and grim on that first glance into the haze.

In the sleepy city center, I found a telephone shop—the developing world's answer to phone booths, where the phones look like the sort you'd find on an end table in a living room, and you pay a man at the front when you're finished. I made two calls: one to my mother's cousin, one to my father's cousin. I had sent word through a chain of relatives that I would be coming at some point that summer, but I did not know whether the message had reached them, or if they would care. And when a woman answered the phone, I spoke Armenian to another person for the first time in twenty years. I was Roubic and Monic's youngest daughter, I said, and I was in Yerevan. Ten minutes later, a car pulled up to retrieve me and Gretchen. She flew home after a few days, as planned, but I was not alone for the remainder of my two-week visit.

FOUR YEARS LATER, when I returned to Yerevan on one of Dikran's charter flights from Istanbul, the city was changing fast. On the road from the airport into town, there was an anticipatory drive lined with casinos boasting names like Nevada's and Rich Man. A law had been passed prohibiting their operation within city limits, so they ordered themselves, obligingly, just outside the boundary, the casinos becoming the first thing visitors saw, and, thanks to their garish, lighted facades, making an indelible impression on the tired eyes of late-night arrivals from all over the world. (Those arrivals, no matter where from, usually occurred between one and three a.m.; given Armenia's economic condition, the inconvenient timing felt like some kind of discount program for use of the sky during off-peak hours.)

Yerevan is said to be one of the oldest cities in the world, officially dating back to 782 BC, when it was called Erebuni. Today, more than a third of Armenia's three million citizens live in the capital and its outskirts. Although much of the population originated in the Caucasus, the post-1915 influx of Armenians from Anatolia is evident in the names of Yerevan neighborhoods: Arabkir, Malatya-Sebastia, New Marash, New Zeytun—towns in Turkey whose names the refugees brought with them. Since most of those places had been renamed in Turkey itself—Zeytun became Süleymanlı, Sebastia became Sivas—these districts were like a Rosetta stone for what had been.

It would be a mistake to imagine a chaotic Eastern city, with shops and kiosks jammed together on small streets. No, Yerevan was orderly and sparse, built to manageable scale, and most of the buildings in the central district were made of the locally abundant tuff stone, pinkish and smooth. This lent a striking uniformity. Still, in the second decade after the Soviet collapse, the urban landscape was transforming as if by the hour. When a boutique opened on an otherwise quiet block, neighbors tended to complain that the new signage was ugly, that the beauty of the city was being destroyed. To my eyes the additions looked like welcome signs of life; to theirs, unseemly capitalist interference.

Yerevan was also a city of a hundred tiny museums, each one devoted to an Armenian painter or author or musician. Streets were named after old poets, and plaques marked the homes where they once lived. And like every former Soviet capital, Yerevan had many parks, overgrown but well-loved gardens filled with pensioners chatting on benches and teenage sweethearts stealing kisses behind mulberry trees, which were everywhere, dropping carpets of ripe, sticky fruit. Of course, all cities have parks and museums, but most cities have more of everything else. Proportion makes all the difference.

I EXPLORED YEREVAN on foot with my father's cousin Rafik and his wife Roza at my side. Strolling was one of their chief forms of leisure, and since Rafik had worked many years as an inspector for the city, he had something to tell me about every bench and building.

"This drinking fountain has the sweetest water in all of Yerevan—no, the world," he proclaimed at one of the many burbling water stations.

Less cheerfully, he showed me evidence of the hardships Yerevan residents had faced. In consecutive freezing winters between 1992 and 1994, during the Karabakh war, blockades and exploded pipelines made electricity, gas, and hot water almost nonexistent. All the front doors along a particular street were made of metal, Rafik pointed out, because the original wooden ones had been ripped away by desperate neighbors and burned for heat.

Roza was a high school biology teacher, and given to commentary on the city's social problems. Everything about their lives was emblematic of a solid, middle-class existence in Yerevan. They occupied the same apartment they'd been granted by the Party decades earlier, and kept it immaculate. Their two sons, near my age, were both working abroad, a doctor and a finance manager; they were part of what was known as Armenia's brain drain—anybody who could get out of the country for work or school did so, and too many never came back.

On my first trip to Armenia, I had gotten to know Rafik and Roza over a dinner that began with shots of homemade walnut liqueur and continued through platters of stuffed vegetables, roasted meat, salads, and cakes until I cried mercy. Then Rafik pulled old maps from the closet, pointing out towns where our ancestors had lived, and Roza brought out photo albums, and read to me from letters my grandmother had sent her forty years ago.

But when I saw them next, fresh off my flight from Istanbul, I had an agenda more journalistic than familial, and at first I feared they'd be disappointed; in a few years' time, I'd gone from carefree long-lost relative to chain-smoking neurotic, prickly with opinions about Turkish-Armenian relations. I made a total of three trips between Istanbul and Yerevan over the course of several months, and each time I had interviews scheduled and appointments to keep. And although my Armenian was not equal to the complexity of my feelings about Turkey, I tried to explain to Rafik and Roza (neither of whom spoke English) what I was doing.

Now, on our walks, Rafik wanted to make sure I surveyed a cross-section of regular Armenians for their views on opening the border. He would stop any acquaintance he spotted on the street. "Zorik dear, how've you been? This young lady has something to ask you," he said when we spotted his old coworker in front of a bookstore. (*Go on*, he nudged me, *ask him what he thinks!*) Rafik never told me what he himself believed; he was diplomatic, choosing curiosity over confrontation. He was the best wingman I could have asked for.

As for Roza, she was also tender with her judgments; she never betrayed suspicion of my motives, but I sensed she was worried that despite my best intentions, I would end up somehow exonerating the Turks. One afternoon, Roza made me a cup of coffee—Turkish or Armenian, call it what you will—and as we sat in the living room, everything haloed by sun pressing through the closed white curtains, she offered to read my fortune in the grounds. Reading coffee fortunes is a tradition usually carried out by women for other women, and it is often a lighthearted pastime. But it can also be taken very seriously—especially when the fortune-teller needs a tactful way to get something off her chest.

Gamely, I placed the saucer over the rim of the cup, held them tightly together and turned them upside down, as is the custom, to let the thickened liquid dribble along the glazed interior. After letting it dry for a few minutes, Roza turned the cup right-side up again and studied the resulting outlines. Then she had me press my thumb into the mud that clung to the bottom, and twist it just slightly, to make a final imprint, which is treated as a sort of punctuation mark to whatever prediction the coffee grounds deliver. She examined it again, and after a long while told me what she saw: my heart was open, she said, but there were two snakes trying to enter it from either side. I would have to be careful to keep them from twisting around me.

Roza was a reasonable but passionate woman, beloved by her students and respected by their parents. Her family had lived in Erzurum, eastern Turkey, before the genocide, and then in Georgia before moving to Yerevan. When we talked about the prospect of diplomatic relations with Turkey, she voiced a view shared by many Yerevan Armenians. She was not above prejudice or pride and did not want to beg Turkey for anything, but her priority was getting access to the world outside; she felt suffocated by the closed border. The verb she used to describe this concern surprised me: *shoonch kashel*, or "to get some air." Armenians needed room to breathe.

- 16 -

Hello, Homeland!

THE VAZGEN SARGSYAN REPUBLICAN STADIUM WAS NAMED FOR THE former prime minister of Armenia, who was murdered in 1999 along with six colleagues when a group of Armenian gunmen, in the name of fighting corruption, burst into a parliament session and opened fire.

Now the stadium's parking lot was filled with thousands of young Armenian athletes. They were in Yerevan for the Pan-Armenian Games—a weeklong Olympics of sorts, where teams of Armenian men and women from all over the world came to compete in basketball, soccer, volleyball, track and field, even table tennis. It was the fourth time this athletic tournament had taken place.

The sporting events themselves held no interest for me, but I was drawn by the prospect of seeing Armenians from so many different countries together in one place, an anthropological full house. I almost hadn't made it on the flight from Istanbul, but Dikran finally squeezed me onboard. The seats were taken by about eighty Bolsahays headed for the games—young athletes who had trained in private sports clubs, as well as their coaches and parents. On the airplane, the athletes had been as boisterous as sixth-graders on a field trip. Now I looked for them in the parking lot, which was mobbed. I had never seen Yerevan quite like this.

It was Friday evening, and the opening ceremony of the Pan-Armenian

Games had been advertised as the place to be. The charm of Yerevan: it was small enough that you could get a feeling hard to come by in a capital city, the sense that there was a single main event. The details could be communicated to the entire population by a few large posters at major thoroughfares, through word of mouth, and by the local television stations (which usually filled their airtime with weather reports every few minutes and commercials for the same three products). In the stadium parking lot, old ladies sitting on overturned oil cans sold snacks for the spectators: pumpkin seeds in cones of twisted newsprint, plastic bags of homemade popcorn.

Each country's athletes could be distinguished by their uniforms: the Paris team wore fitted white T-shirts with "Paris" printed across the back in sparkly cursive; there was Ukraine, looking like a flock of bumblebees in yellow and black; Vienna, indicated by a hip lowercase logo that could have been advertising a skateboard company; a group of women from Tehran in pink and blue jogging suits of cheap nylon; and on it went, Beirut, Cyprus, Georgia, Germany, Russia . . .

Could I tell where people were from by looking at their faces? We were all Armenian, but there seemed to be something besides the varied uniforms that evoked each team's diaspora home. Was it the effect of climate, of fluoridated water, toxic fertilizers? I once read that every language subtly sculpts the facial muscles of its speakers. Maybe the heavy eyebrows and mountainous noses and hooded eyes of my people looked a little bit different on a face that had spoken German, or Hebrew, or Portuguese? Here was Javakh, a team from a troubled region in Georgia; their taupe and navy outfits were surprisingly nice, so nice that I would have thought they belonged to a wealthier city's team, yet I had no doubt the players were from the Caucasus, based on their demeanor: sober, broad, browned faces, like the hardened bark of trees that had stood in the same spot for centuries.

I approached a fellow from the Manchester, England, soccer team. His name was Alex and he was twenty-one. It was his second trip to the games. His father was born in Cyprus, he told me, and his mother in Lebanon. His English accent betrayed nothing of his ethnic roots, and he had an Englishman's reserve; he said he felt relaxed about the competitions to come.

I couldn't hear him very well because a cheer-off had started between

Beirut and Buenos Aires. Buenos Aires! If anybody looked like the cool kids in this sea of faces, it was Buenos Aires. Pounding a drum and singing a rally in Spanish, they wore turquoise and white shirts with the colors of the Armenian flag, red, blue, and orange, as armbands on both sleeves. The Beirut team sidled up to them and hollered the familiar "*Oléee*, Olé, Olé, Olé!" in greeting, which Buenos Aires met with a drawn-out "Beiiiiiruuuuut!"

Yes, there were Armenians in Buenos Aires, more than a hundred thousand of them. The community took root after 1909, when Armenians who fled the Adana massacres in Turkey's Kilikia region went there; they were joined later by genocide survivors after 1915. There was a story for how Armenians had ended up in each of the cities whose teams now swarmed around me. But—did it even need to be said?—it was all one story, really. The majority of them had left Turkey, either after massacres in the 1890s, in 1909, or in 1915. It wasn't news to me that Armenians lived in all these places; what I found amazing was that they were still *organized* as Armenians even as they spoke Spanish and German and every other language, even three generations after their families had made these migrations.

Getting into the spirit, I strolled from team to team like some kind of locker-room sportscaster, sticking my tape recorder in people's faces.

"So are you here to win?" I heard myself asking a twenty-five-year-old guy from the team of La Crescenta, a town near Los Angeles.

"Of course we're here to win!" He beamed. The athletes were enjoying the attention, and I was enjoying the way my presence was taken for granted. I suppose I imagined that my time in Turkey had marked me somehow—a scarlet "T" on my chest. But no, I was welcome here. This was the beauty of being among other Armenians: you were automatically assumed to be a friend—as long as you were Armenian, you were innocent until proven guilty.

Akhaltsikhe, Almelo, Ararat, Armavir, Athens, Barnaul, Beirut, Brussels, Gardabad, Geghart . . . teams were starting to line up in order with the signs they would carry in the Olympic-style opening procession.

I wandered over to Jerusalem and spoke with one of the team managers. He had an accent I have always loved, the Israeli accent, with its burdensome *r*'s and argumentative inflections.

"Do you speak Armenian?" I asked him.

"Of course!"

"Where are your parents from?"

"Jerusalem."

"And your grandparents?"

"Jerusalem."

He told me that at home, there were two Armenian clubs: one Dashnak, the other Ramkavar—those were the political party lines along which Armenian churches divided decades ago—but that for the games the two clubs had joined forces.

"We belong to different clubs but we're not enemies," he said. He seemed sincere, maybe even a little bit sophisticated. But it amazed me that in holiest Jerusalem, where Jews and Palestinians persisted in the most intractable conflict in the world, the Armenians still opted to divide themselves.

I FOUND THE Istanbul team thanks to their impressive outfits. The entire group wore tailored white pants and tucked-in polo shirts; pale blue for the athletes, turquoise for the managers, and yellow for the coaches. Taking in their tasteful ensemble, I remembered something I had read a few years earlier, when I knew little about the Bolsahay community. In a diaspora magazine featuring a long article about the first Pan-Armenian Games, a single point had struck me. A team of Bolsahay athletes had attended the games, but they had problems fitting in. Other teams had bristled on hearing them speak Turkish, the article said. Their outfits might have lent them a subtle class advantage in the eyes of a neutral observer, but here they were more like black sheep.

I wondered if this perception had changed at all since Hrant's murder. I was friendly with the manager of the Istanbul men's basketball team, a thirty-four-year-old man named Nerses whom I'd met in the course of my reporting, and I had asked him about this back in Istanbul. He insisted there were no such problems. Nerses was sentimental about the games, and about Armenia in general. He was the one who convinced me that I had to come see them for myself: "You won't believe how amazing it feels to be surrounded by so many Armenians," he said.

But ever since we had arrived in Yerevan, Nerses had been avoiding me to farcical proportions. Earlier that day he deliberately crossed the street when he saw me coming toward him, and later, when I cornered him at a coffee shop, he got up quickly and insisted he had to be somewhere. If

I was innocent until proven guilty among Armenians from California who knew nothing of me, it was just the opposite with some Istanbul Armenians. While I felt completely at ease with my Kurdish friends, I had not made the same kinds of connections with Bolsahays. I always felt slightly uncomfortable around them, and apparently the feeling was mutual. Some, like Aris, the *Agos* reporter, were reliably helpful when I needed something, but we didn't socialize easily. People in the *Agos* office and at Aras Publishing always greeted me sweetly, but the relationships remained professional.

Just before that trip to Armenia, *Agos* had run a long interview with me, Q-and-A-style, about my work and my experiences. They had titled it—to my chagrin—"The diaspora's 'bad Armenian.'" This was tongue-in-cheek for them—they meant it as a sort of compliment—but I didn't like the way it sounded. Still, I hoped the interview would make other Bolsahays more relaxed around me. But for Nerses it seemed to have had the opposite effect. He hadn't said anything outright, but he was giving me the cold shoulder. He seemed to think I was trying to stir up trouble. He had promised that I could meet some of his players, but now he insisted they were all busy. When I pressed, he finally presented me with Artun, who at 35 was one of the oldest athletes. Artun had attended all four Pan-Armenian Games.

"Do you think life in Istanbul is better than life in Armenia?" I asked Artun.

"Yes, of course."

I asked him if as an Istanbul Armenian, he felt any discrimination from diaspora Armenians.

"Well, we are trying to keep our churches and schools in Turkey, and we have a big responsibility," Artun said. "Armenians in other countries can't understand the importance of our preserving all this history in Istanbul, in Anatolia, so sometimes they see us as a part of the Turkish people. Because they decided to leave"—he stumbled on the word "decided" and then corrected himself—"were forced to leave, and our fathers stayed."

As we were talking it began to rain, a lukewarm, late-summer rain, and we huddled under an archway with hundreds of athletes and coaches. Undaunted, a group of young men in Beirut jerseys started singing a Dashnak revolutionary song, "Arunod Trosh," which means "bloody flag." One of our campfire favorites. They hollered atonally through all five verses.

I asked Artun if he ever learned any Dashnak songs growing up. I had to shout because the noise was so loud.

"Dashnak songs? No! Never!"

"This is a popular one," I told him. The song was so well known among diaspora Armenians that it was strange to realize that it stirred nothing in him.

"We do not have any relation with Dashnaktsutiun," Artun said. "We have no songs of Dashnaktsutiun."

I sensed he was a bit afraid of me, too, as if I was a Turkish military officer questioning him about ties to the Armenian armed bands of the late Ottoman era. I was sympathetic, especially after what Dikran had told me, how Bolsahays had to be careful about their diaspora connections, but it felt awful to be the cause of so much suspicion when in my heart I was on their side.

The singing kept growing louder, and the acoustics of the arch made it deafening, but the rain was also gaining force, so Artun and I had no choice but to stay put. We screamed directly into each other's ears.

"WHAT KINDS OF ARMENIAN SONGS DID YOU LEARN WHEN YOU WERE A CHILD?"

"WHAT?"

"WHILE WE WERE SINGING DASHNAK SONGS IN THE DIASPORA, WHAT SONGS WERE YOU SINGING?"

There was a pause between verses.

"We prefer our traditional music. Gomidas Vartabed's songs, for example. Gomidas's liturgy is very important for us." Gomidas, an Armenian theologian and ethnomusicologist, had arranged a version of the church service unique for its distinctively Armenian motifs.

The Beirut team started up again, this time with "Menk Angeghdz Zinvor Enk"—We Are Sincere Soldiers.

"DO YOU KNOW THIS ONE?" I asked Artun.

"NO."

"ONE OF THE LINES SAYS, 'ISTANBUL WILL BE A SEA OF BLOOD.'"

"OH."

The song tells of a letter arriving from the depths of Iran, telling

Armenians to join their Caucasus brethren to fight. "The battle is about to start from every direction," the lyrics say. "We don't want any limits on our freedom. We've sworn to fight, and we'll die for that cause. We are convinced that Armenian liberation can be won only with weapons."

Artun thought this over for a moment. "The diaspora is so weak," he said. "There is nothing else besides this song."

Then he told me about one problem the Istanbul team has at the games: they cannot carry the Turkish flag in the opening procession. "Every other team will hold the flag of their country, but for us it's impossible."

"Why?"

"It's just impossible."

"Do you want to hold the Turkish flag?"

"It's complicated," he said. "For us, even at a soccer game, for example, if Turkey is competing against another country, well, of course we want Turkey to win. But we also can't fully get behind the . . ." He trailed off because what he might have said next would have been grounds for prosecution in his country.

THE RAIN ENDED just in time for the ceremony to begin. There was a stadium-wide countdown, followed by fireworks, a drum brigade, and a solemn march of men playing the *zurna*, a festive, double-reed instrument from Anatolia. Armenian president Robert Kocharian was introduced, waving from a box above the stands.

Then a series of athletes from various countries made speeches in Armenian:

"I'm Hrant, I'm from Egypt, I'm twenty-one years old. Our uniform is colored black, yes, like the color of our eyes. It's my first time in Armenia. My little brother's name is Sevag. Sevag begged me to give, from his heart, his greetings to our country's president: HELLO, MR. PRESIDENT! HELLO, HOMELAND!"

"I am Maral, I come from South America; our flag is red. Red is also one of the colors in the Armenian flag, which for me is such a precious symbol. I want for all the world's Armenians to come live in their native city! HELLO, HOMELAND!"

"My name is Alisa. I have come from a VERY far place: from Sydney, Australia! Our uniform is green, like the fertile lands of my historic Armenia. Back in Australia, my grandmother told me I am a displaced grandchild of Armenia. I love my homeland. I will never forget you, my native language. HELLO, HOMELAND!"

"I am Massis, and my team's flag is golden, like the golden autumns of my beloved Yerevan. I want for my nation to shine like gold; to shine for the Armenian people from all corners of the world. HELLO, MY GOLDEN HOMELAND!"

An announcer stepped in: "The famous slogan of the Olympics is Citius, Altius, Fortius: faster, higher, stronger! But the slogan of the fourth Pan-Armenian Games is: HELLO, HOMELAND!"

* * *

ISTANBUL AND GLENDALE were on the basketball court. The bleachers on one side of the gym were packed with supporters from Glendale. Some had flown with the team specifically for the games, others just happened to be in Yerevan on their summer vacations. Across the court, a few members of the Istanbul delegation sat together, with Yerevantsis taking empty seats here and there.

I sat alone on the Istanbul side. Both teams were playing hard from the start, and Glendale fans were cheering as if they owned the place, shouting, "Let's go Glendale, let's go!" It could have been a high school game in California.

A man sitting behind me noticed that I was writing in my notebook and leaned over to speak in my ear.

"What you need to write about is the sorry state of affairs here. Write about these thieves that they call our government. They'll go all the way to Karabakh to kill a pig for our dear president's dinner, because he must have the best meat every night, even if the rest of us can't feed our kids. And the way they drive their Jeeps . . ."

His name was Vahan, and he was a local, a middle-aged man with hair on the edge of gray, dressed neatly in slacks and a short-sleeved button-down. He had brought his two young nephews to watch the game, just for something to do.

Vahan moved down a row to sit next to me, and we fixed our attention on the court. I felt a bit silly sitting in the bleachers taking notes; I knew little about basketball, and the only other journalist at the game besides me was a fellow named Onnik, a British-Armenian photographer who had been living in Yerevan for ten years and kept a popular but inflammatory news blog about local politics. Onnik and I had become fast friends a few days prior, when we crossed paths navigating the elaborate and apparently underutilized process of getting press credentials. That we had met each other and could compare notes over the course of the week was the only benefit to having showed up at the Foreign Ministry building to register. Officially, nobody cared who we were.

The score had been nearly tied all along, but at the start of the second half, Glendale was ahead by one. Both teams were playing like their lives depended on it. Then, halfway through the last quarter, suddenly the court was mayhem. A player from Glendale was chasing the star player of the Istanbul team—and since neither of them had the ball, it was clear this wasn't part of the game. Within seconds, people poured onto the court from all directions—referees, team managers, the police. Several men struggled to hold the two players apart.

Just then Onnik ran up to me with gossip. He had been standing among the Glendale supporters before the fight broke out. The Glendale player had made some kind of remark in Armenian about the player on the Istanbul team, and when one of the Glendale fans chastised him for this, he called back, "They can't understand anyway, they're Turkish." Onnik wasn't sure what the Glendale player had originally said.

Vahan, sitting at my side, tried to block my notebook. "Don't write it, don't write it!" he said. "Write that they were so involved with the game that they just couldn't control themselves!" When he saw that I was unconvinced, he tried another theory: the Istanbul team actually had a *bit* of that Turkish barbarism in them, he said, which was why they played so hard. "It's not their fault! You need to explain! It's just something inside them."

At the same moment, a few rows ahead of us, the father of one of the Istanbul players began waving his arms toward the referees and shouting: "Menk Hay enk, menk Tajik chenk!" We're Armenian, we're not Turkish. His face was blazing red.

The final score was Glendale 74, Istanbul 65.

AFTER THE GAME I asked Nerses, the manager of the Istanbul team, what had set off the fight. He shuddered and said, with uncharacteristic openness, that one of the Glendale players had called the Istanbul player *Toork shoon*—"Turkish dog."

Then I found the Glendale player in the lobby of the gym and asked him what happened.

"Nothing, you know. It's just a game. We get worked up sometimes. They were playing really aggressively," he said.

"Did the fight have anything to do with their being from Turkey?"

"No. I don't know. I mean, they're half-Armenian, anyway."

"Half-Armenian?"

"I mean, I guess they have some Armenian in them."

Outside, I approached the father of the Istanbul player, the one who had been shouting in the stands.

He told me that the referees were always unfair to Istanbul players. "It's like this every year. Wherever we go, we're seen differently by other Armenians."

* * *

THE NEXT DAY I headed to the town of Ararat for a soccer game between Istanbul and Rostov. It was an easy choice from the packed schedule of matches: Rostov was the city in Russia where I had worked for a couple of summers, and Istanbul was the city where I lived now. I figured I could be happy no matter which team won.

Ararat town is situated at the foot of Mount Ararat, on the border with Turkey. It was an hour by car from Yerevan, and I needed a driver who could wait around for the return trip. Several taxis refused me, but then I found a driver named Saro who got excited at the prospect: he was born in the village of Vedi, close to Ararat. He said he would drive me to the game and then take the opportunity to surprise his elderly parents for lunch.

Every journalist loves taxi rides for the opportunity to have a spontaneous chat with somebody you wouldn't otherwise meet. Whatever story you might be on your way to cover, whomever you had just interviewed when a taxi picked you up, you could check in quickly with Joe Driver, who might have been a doctor or a professor or a criminal in his other life, but for a few minutes would be your private sounding board.

But in Armenia, for a young, single diaspora woman, taxi rides had special amusements. Even on the shortest drives, cabbies always asked if I was married. Although I had been told I should be more reserved, I delighted in their earnest campaigns on behalf of a "very successful" nephew. (Although once, when I lied and said I was engaged to a man in the United States, the driver became angry—not because I was unavailable, but because I was too independent. "What kind of guy allows his betrothed to roam around the world by herself?" he asked, as if my imaginary fiancé had insulted the both of us.)

There were no right answers where Yerevan drivers were concerned. If you gushed too readily about how wonderful Armenia was, they would huff and tell you that you didn't know the first thing. Since the end of Communism people have turned "uncivilized," they often said. As for the government, it was full of crooks. And housing costs were skyrocketing due to *spiurkahays*—diaspora Armenians—buying homes they used for only a few weeks a year.

But if you dared to point out any of these manifest issues yourself, they would snap and say, "There is not a more beautiful city in the world than our Yerevan! I wouldn't leave this city for anything! You can go to *Los*, and work all day so you can drive a Mercedes, but that's not life!" (*Los* was local slang for the Los Angeles area, which now has as large an Armenian population as Yerevan.) Once, a driver told me that Armenia was the only place in the world he could live with eyebrows like his.

My driver to Ararat town, Saro, did not ask me any personal questions. He only wanted to know if I was planning to pay my respects at Khor Virap, the ancient monastery near Ararat that is credited as the site of Armenia's conversion to Christianity. I told him I'd been to Khor Virap on a previous trip and found it very beautiful, but today I was going to a soccer match for the Pan-Armenian Games.

"Who's playing?"

"Istanbul against Rostov."

"Istanbul? So they're Turks."

"No, they're Armenian players from Istanbul."

"They're not real Armenians then," he said.

"Well, they all speak Armenian," I told him, "and go to Armenian schools, and Armenian churches—"

He cut me off. "Bring me a Turk so I can tear him to pieces."

A Turk: when an Armenian in Armenia says "Turk," he usually means somebody from Azerbaijan. Sure enough, Saro proceeded to tell me that he fought in Karabakh against Azerbaijani soldiers.

"I cut off a man's ears," he said. "Just like that."

I found it maddening the way they used the label "Turk" for people from Turkey as well as Azerbaijan. It's not that it was racist, exactly—Turks and Azeris sometimes did this, too. But for an Armenian to do so was like using an all-purpose word for "enemy." They were different enemies, specific enemies, and this mattered; each conflict had its own dynamics, its own governmental players, and its own geographic border. Eliding the differences only helped guarantee that nothing would change. I brought this up to anyone who would listen, but so far not a soul had agreed with me that the distinction was important.

Our conversation was interrupted by a loud clatter. For a moment I thought we'd hit something, but there was only open road in both directions. Then we realized that the taxi lamp on the roof had fallen off and was banging against the driver's-side door, suspended by a wire. Saro braked just slightly, rolled down his window, yanked the lamp free, and tossed it into the backseat where it landed at my feet, smelling of burnt plastic. "It's the wind today," he said.

As we passed through orchards and sunflower fields, I realized that in a relatively short drive we were covering a significant chunk of Armenia. We drove in silence for half an hour, and then, as we neared the Turkish border, Mount Ararat came into view.

"*Sa mern eh*," Saro said—this is ours. "The entire diaspora should come back to Armenia so that we can increase our numbers. Then if we all gather together and put our arms around it and pull *really* hard, maybe we can get it over to our side."

Just then my cell phone beeped with a text message. It was an automated prompt from Turkcell, my Turkish cell phone provider. "We hope that you enjoyed using Turkcell International Services and that you had a pleasant trip. Welcome to Turkey."

This same device had been connected to Armenia's Armentel network all week. Now we were so close to the border that, diplomatic relations be damned, Turkcell thought I was back. It was not the first time the company had been kind enough to follow my travel plans: on a brief trip to France a couple of months earlier, I had turned on my phone upon arrival at Charles de Gaulle Airport only to be greeted with a different polite notice: "While you are away from Turkey, if you need help, the

Turkish embassy is located at . . ." with an address and phone number. *Always watching out for each other*, I had thought. Then there was a follow-up that informed me I had three free text messages while roaming, and that I should use them to let my family and friends know I had arrived safely. It seemed to me incredibly and endearingly Turkish that a private phone company would remind its customers to call their mothers. Meanwhile, the Armenian network was having problems and I hadn't been able to receive a call for days. I opted not to tell Saro that as far as my phone was concerned, we were in Turkey.

"What about Hrant Dink?" I asked, picking up our earlier conversation.

"What about him?"

"Was he a real Armenian?"

"Of course he was."

"But you said Turkish Armenians aren't real Armenians."

"I'm not saying they're not real Armenians," he said, softening his tone, perhaps feeling sheepish because I'd invoked Hrant.

And in a way I knew he meant it. He wasn't a monster; he was exactly like everybody else. His nasty remarks earlier probably seemed as quotidian to him as talking about the weather. But this was the problem; nobody ever stopped anybody from speaking this way, not in Armenia and not in Turkey, and certainly not in either of their diasporas. Was it really so ridiculous for me to think that the situation could change if only, one taxi driver at a time, it became unacceptable to say such things out loud?

I told him that one of the Glendale players had supposedly called a member of the Istanbul team a Turkish dog during the basketball game.

"Well, that's not right!" he said, suddenly animated again. "They shouldn't have done that. Those are vulgar people who said that." "Vulgar," *anshnork*, was one of the favorite adjectives of Yerevantsis, used liberally along with their other favorite, *shnorkin*, "civilized." "It's not their fault that they have to live in Turkey," he went on. "And that Dink, he did many great things for the Armenian people."

SEVERAL DAYS LATER, after having watched every possible combination of Armenian against Armenian in matches, races, and play-offs, I wondered how anyone could have thought it was a good idea to combine two of the most fierce and maniacal human impulses: patriotism and the animal competition of sports. Was this really bringing Armenians from different places together, or was it only driving them deeper into their microidentities of city and state, of us against them? Sure, the athletes were having fun, and a romance or two had sparked up between players from different teams. But there had also been some serious aggression and violence: a match between players from Yerevan and Cairo had ended in a knife fight, and three Cairo players wound up in the hospital.

Before leaving Armenia, I met with a Yerevan newspaper columnist named Hakob Badalyan, who had written an incendiary op-ed saying that the knife fight was the greatest triumph of the Pan-Armenian Games. What he meant, he told me, was that he was glad it had happened so that the hundreds of athletes from the diaspora could understand that the idea behind the games was a fantasy. "The fantasy that we are one people, that we're all together, unified," he said. "What we need is to have an honest conversation about the *difference* in our experiences, in our realities."

Armenia was a tiny, landlocked country with a corrupt government, a lopsided economy, and a shocking number of families too poor to buy shoes. But for diaspora Armenians, it was a magic kingdom, a repository for their anxieties and hopes. Even if they pointed out problems, even if they were there to fix problems, even if they came armed with giant NGO grants to do so, the fantasy was what drove them—and me. Why deny it? This need for a sense of origin, history, home, was the most powerful force we had. But like love and like hate, it was an inherently irrational force.

THE KNIFE FIGHT was soon forgotten. What lingered was the Istanbul-Glendale "Turkish dog" incident. The day the games were over and the Bolsahay team flew home, the Turkish newspaper *Sabah* ran a front-page story with the headline, "OUR YOUTH WERE ATTACKED!" Our youth. This Turkish phrasing might have been sweet if it were not a gross hypocrisy. The Bolsahays had never been "our youth" to Turkey until suddenly they could be claimed in opposition to the despised diaspora. By the end of the day, the news of the basketball fight was all over the Turkish media.

And somehow this turned out to be my fault. My friend Onnik had written a blog post about the fight. Onnik himself had not spoken to the players or their parents after the match. He had only asked me what they said, and I told him. Without seeking permission, he wrote up my interviews. A Turkish journalist who had not been there at all saw Onnik's blog post, and without speaking to either of us, she fashioned it into a story of her own. But she upped the stakes; in her account, "Turkish dog" became "dirty Turkish dog." And thanks to her employer, *Sabah* newspaper, all of Turkey got to hear about it.

But if you read between the lines, Turks were not angered by this; on the contrary, they were gratified by the news that the diaspora was as obnoxious as they believed. It was the Armenian players from Istanbul who were furious. They called the Turkish papers and insisted that the story was untrue. No such fight had ever happened. Various team members gave interviews trying to mitigate the incident. Everybody was eager to point out that later, after the game, the teams had run into each other at a café and made peace. Suddenly nobody was sure whether anybody had ever said anything about a Turkish dog. *Sabah* ran a follow-up story the next day, saying that the whole thing was made up by a blogger in Armenia to create trouble.

In the midst of all this, I received a phone call from Nerses. He didn't even say hello before he started yelling at me. "You created this whole thing. Why did you even talk to that guy?" he said, referring to Onnik.

Now I was furious, too. I asked him why he was lying to everyone. He himself had told me, moments after the game, that his player had been called a Turkish dog, and now he was acting like I had invented it. Still, he wouldn't budge. He repeated his revisionist account and reminded me (yes, I had heard it ten times already) that they had made friends with the Glendale team later the same day. I told Nerses I understood why he had changed his story. They were in a bad enough situation in Turkey, and making the Armenian diaspora look volatile and anti-Turkish was not going to do them any good. He could say whatever he wanted to the Turkish papers. If I had known Onnik was going to write a blog post, I never would have shared anything with him. But he couldn't just pretend to me that everything we had witnessed was false, that everything he and his teammates had told me, on the record, into my Olympus digital recorder, had not been said.

I felt very alone that day.

Onnik's blog post, meanwhile, stayed online and turned into a field day of comments from the Glendale team and their supporters. The player who had started the fight chimed in and tried to clarify his position. He never called the players Turkish, he claimed. "I said they were playing *in a Turkish manner.*"

- 17 -

Reunions

MY AUNT NORA HAD ALWAYS BEEN ONE OF MY FAVORITE RELATIVES. When I was growing up in New Jersey, she lived in Connecticut, so we saw her often. Nora Morkoor (Armenian for "maternal aunt") was an elegant woman, her tawny coloring and contoured cheekbones like an Armenian Sophia Loren. Savvy about ideas and art and other impractical things that immigrants did not make time for, she had a doctorate in architecture and had worked on a range of public policy issues throughout her career.

Nora Morkoor visited Armenia often, for work and pleasure, and she had recently purchased an apartment in the city. On one of my trips to Yerevan, she happened to be in town. Together, we went to watch old Armenian plays at the theater, to hear jazz at an outdoor café, and to shop for fruits and vegetables at the bazaar.

My aunt had a great talent for this last activity. Shopping at the bazaar might seem simple, but it always left me depressed. As a young woman from America, there was no good way to handle the haggling. If a gold-toothed refugee from a war-devastated village in Karabakh wanted to charge me triple the local price for tomatoes, I didn't have the heart to argue—yet it seemed equally insulting (for her), not to mention annoying (for me), to blithely hand over that kind of money. I loved the sight of the market stalls piled with peppers and cherries and purple basil, the homemade packages of dried fruit decorated with peeled almonds and shelled pistachios in the shapes of flowers. But to avoid the awkward financial transactions, I tended to shop at the soulless new Star Market.

For my aunt, however, the bazaar ritual was an art form. One day we strolled through the marketplace, and I listened as she quizzed an old man about his green beans, a long, flat variety common to the region. Instead of asking the price, she wanted to know his favorite way to prepare them. My aunt was no rookie in the kitchen—she was an enthusiastic cook, and we had a long history of feasting together on her creations. The old man did not pause a moment before launching into a recipe for browning and then steaming the beans with onion and egg, a kind of loose frittata, and spun verses at each of my aunt's follow-up questions about temperature and timing. By the time there was a question of price, money seemed incidental. I loved shopping with her.

On our second-to-last day together, we sat across from each other at the dining table trimming the beans we had purchased. Then, for the first time, my aunt asked me directly about my experiences in Turkey. I knew she felt uncomfortable with what I was doing—all the Armenians in my life did, to varying degrees. We had skirted the issue a few times already, and I was hesitant to plunge in. It was hard—no, impossible—to get across everything I felt, and I didn't want to be misunderstood. Correction: I wanted desperately to be understood.

When I was a child, my aunt had a particular way of taking me seriously that I always appreciated. Once, when I was about ten, she gave me a verbal quiz of sorts, listing words and having me say the first association that came to my mind. I had no idea what she was after, but I had loved it; it just wasn't the sort of thing that happened in an Armenian family. Hopeful that she could hear me out now, I told her about the friends I'd made in Istanbul, the awkward conversations I had about politics and history, the people who helped me with my work, the people who didn't know what to say, and the wonderful food, of course.

She listened for a while without comment, until finally she spoke. "Have you ever entered a Turkish home?"

Sure I had, I said. Too many to count. On a trip to Ankara with my friend and translator Ertan, we stayed overnight at Ertan's parents' apartment. "His parents are schoolteachers," I noted, "state employees. So they're as Turkish as it gets."

She said nothing.

I explained that Ertan had been employed at an Armenian book pub-lishing house for ten years; he was even learning to speak Armenian. He was also working on a project to preserve Armenian liturgical music, and he spoke about Armenian literature more knowledgeably than any-one else I knew. Since Hrant's death, he had been pulling sixteen-hour days at *Agos*. My project would have been impossible without his help.

I could sense that she still did not like what she was hearing, so I elaborated further, concluding with an earnest declaration that Ertan was, in fact, more Armenian than most actual Armenians.

"What was their house like?" she asked.

"It was nice," I said, a comfortable middle-class apartment, three bed-rooms, on a pleasant residential street near the center of Ankara.

"What was his mother like?"

"She was incredibly sweet to me. She kept asking if I was hungry, or thirsty, or if I was cold and needed a sweater." I paused to check my aunt's reaction—her gaze remained fixed on the beans—and went on. I explained that Ertan's mother had made a lovely dinner, cheerfully accommodating her son's vegetarian habits, and made certain to serve me first and to refill my plate after every few bites. I told her about how we fumbled our way through an English-Turkish conversation about my family's origins, how she shyly asked me if my relatives had ever lived in Anatolia, and how we all giggled with relief when I told her that they had not.

"Where did you sleep?"

"I slept in his sister's old room."

"What was the room like?"

"It was very comfortable. His mother made it up for me. Just like my mom would have done"—I paused—"or like you would have."

My aunt went silent again.

I knew from the start that this line of questioning was not innocent curiosity, but now it had escalated beyond even the pretense of being so, and I was getting angry.

"She put fresh sheets on the bed," I went on, becoming theatrical with detail. "The sheets were pink, with flowers. She left an extra blanket for me, and put a glass of water on the table next to the bed, and just before I fell asleep, she knocked on the door and asked me if I needed earplugs in case the noise from the street was too loud."

Had she wanted to hear that they lived in a filthy shack? That they made me sleep in the yard? Actually, I was furious. Nothing I said could humanize Ertan or his parents for her. Ertan's parents! Modest people, civil servants, a couple who had raised a son who had transformed my understanding of dedication and generosity, and of what it meant to question one's identity. Ertan himself had argued at length with his parents about all sorts of political issues, and they had weathered these conflicts better than many parents and children do. His mother could not have been more welcoming to me, a complete stranger. It had been, in fact, the very first time I had visited a home of ethnic Turks—as opposed to Bolsahays or Kurds—and I myself had been nervous about the experience. It had not escaped my imagination, either, that perhaps this was a strange event for Ertan's parents, to have their unmarried thirty-four-year-old son show up with an Armenian girl from the diaspora who needed to stay in their guest room, and that his mother might have felt a confusing mix of hope that I was more than a friend (I was not) and unease that such a candidate, if I were one, would be Armenian. But they had done everything possible to make me feel comfortable, and had insisted that if I ever returned to Ankara, I had a place to stay.

My aunt herself was a generous, gracious person under normal circumstances, and not one to shy away from complex subjects. But when it came to Turkey, nothing I said could move her. Once upon a time—not so long ago—none of this would have surprised me. A terrible but familiar Armenian expression came to mind: "*Turkuh yeteh voski el lini, grpanut mi ktsir.*" Even if a Turk is made of gold, don't put him in your pocket.

THE FOLLOWING MORNING, I took Nora Morkoor to meet Rafik and Roza. They were on different sides of the family, but Nora was curious to meet my father's relatives and they were excited to meet her, too.

Rafik soon had us engrossed in stories about how some of my ancestors were killed amid violence that consumed the Caucasus during World War I. My great-grandfather Garabed, who lived in Tbilisi, had owned a copper mine in Kapan, near Karabakh. He was not involved with politics, as far as we knew, but was murdered on the road during a trip to the mine—either because he was wealthy, because he was Christian, or simply because he was in the wrong place at the wrong time. It was between 1916 and 1917. If we wanted more details than that, we would have to invent them.

This was the first in a series of tragedies that decimated Garabed's family: about a year later, his wife, Natasha, left raising four children alone, died of illness, not yet thirty years old. The oldest son—my grandfather Yeghishe (later known as Aram)—was taken in by an aunt in Tbilisi. Rafik's mother, Mariam, was the next oldest; she and two younger brothers were looked after by another aunt, Zanazan, who worked in a Tbilisi orphanage. One day Zanazan received word that a house she owned in Nukha, 170 miles southeast, was in danger of being confiscated by Azeris. To go and save the house, she left the children at the orphanage, intending to return soon, but on her way back, her coach was attacked and she was killed.

At the time, around 1918, the Red Cross was consolidating orphanages in the region; thus my grandfather's three siblings were moved to an orphanage in Kars, a city at that moment under Armenian control. In Kars they lived alongside Armenian kids from Ottoman towns who had lost their families in the genocide. But soon after, when Kars was reclaimed by Turkish forces, the children were transferred yet again, to an orphanage in Alexandropol (later called Leninakan, now Gyumri). After four more years, Mariam was finally retrieved by relatives in Tbilisi. But by then, one brother, Aleksan, had died in her arms from typhus, and the whereabouts of the other, Levon, were unknown. Rafik believed the Red Cross might have taken him to the United States with a group of genocide survivors.

I knew this story already, but Nora Morkoor didn't, and suddenly we heard a gasp followed by catch-breaths of sobbing. Everybody looked at my aunt. Rafik began to apologize as Nora covered her face with her hands. Her shoulders trembled as she tried to still herself.

"I'm really sorry, I know it's a very sad story," said Rafik, bewildered by this visiting stranger's reaction to a long-ago tale about people who were not even technically related to her. "Maybe I shouldn't have told it," he said.

But I knew that her tears were not only about the story Rafik told; they were about me.

LATER, AS WE drove away from Rafik and Roza's house, my aunt apologized for her breakdown. I asked her why she had gotten so emotional. Now calm, she took a moment, then answered.

"I was reflecting on the fact that even you, an Armenian from Iran . . . even your own ancestors were affected by the terrible things the

Turks did back then." Her voice broke again. "I just don't want you to forget the injustice."

What was I to make of this? Had I forgotten the injustice? I had asked myself this very question many times. But I had never suffered any injustice. I was not immune to the potency of hearing about my family's traumas, not to mention my grandfather Aram's later glories: he was known to his peers as "Kavkasi Marx"—Marx of the Caucasus—and I was more than happy to bask in the tale of his idealistic pursuits, how he got himself to Plekhanov University in Moscow despite all the losses he had known, how he rose in the party ranks as a natural orator, and how he later personally convinced Lavrenti Beria, party secretary of the Caucasus region and one of Stalin's most brutal underlings, to arrange his sister, Mariam's, medical school education. Or so we had been led to believe. I could, if I let myself, follow the dotted lines of my imagination connecting these heroics straight to me. But there was a subtle difference between savoring family history and being blinded by it.

To be moved by a tragic story that had happened to someone, anyone, was natural. It was another thing to take that tragedy upon yourself as a kind of catchall for whatever pain and grief your own life had held, to brandish it like a badge of honor—or worse, like a weapon, to take from it a lesson of hatred that only perpetuated the kind of thinking that created such tragedies in the first place. My aunt was crying because she felt overwhelmed by my entire Turkey project—threatened by the way her niece was tampering with the story we had all agreed to tell.

We were parting ways now—she was off to the airport—and across the front seat of the car we had a tense hug good-bye.

"I just want to ask you one thing," she said. "And you may not like it, but I'm asking you anyway."

It was about Ertan's family.

"Please don't stay with those people again."

* * *

AT HER ARMENIAN high school in Tehran, my mother had studied the map of central Yerevan and claimed she knew the streets by heart. But she had never been there. Neither had my father or my sisters. Finally, after years of saying "next fall" or "next spring," my parents made the trip, and my sister Lily came too. I flew in from Turkey to join them.

On the last leg of their flight, a connection from Heathrow, my mother warned my father and sister of the first item on her agenda: "I want you to know that when we arrive, I am going to kiss the ground, and I don't want either of you to try to stop me."

She was the first among them to emerge from passport control. The new Yerevan airport was designed such that your entrance into Armenia was through the pristine duty-free shop; there was no way to get from the visa checkpoint to baggage claim without walking straight through an assault of Lancôme and local brandy.

But it was Armenia just the same, and my mother began crying the moment she was handed back her stamped passport and ushered in. A young Armenian shopgirl holding a perfume sample intercepted her with a cheerful "Welcome to Armenia!" and leaned in to offer a spritz before she noticed that my mother was in tears.

"Auntie, why are you crying?" she asked in Armenian, returning the perfume bottle to her side.

"Forgive me," said my mother. "It is my first time here and I am just overcome with emotion."

"You are crying because you *entered* Armenia?" the girl asked. "But we cry every day because we want to get out!"

My father emerged from passport control to find his wife locked in an embrace with the clerk.

We teased my mother about her airport incident in the days that followed, but in truth, amusement was the least of my reactions. My parents' arrival shook something open in me that I had resisted on prior trips. Now there was no talk of Turks and no performances about our "golden homeland." There were, instead, glimpses of everything that had been forsaken in favor of thirty years of an American life: an emotional connection to the land, traces of personal history, even a kind of instinctive psychological power.

My mother navigated the city center with confidence; she wasn't exaggerating when she said she knew the streets by heart. Our strolls around town were spontaneous reunions for my parents: on a Saturday evening, rounding a corner, we would be met by a sudden cry: "Oh my God,

Monic, is it you?" or "Roubic, I can't believe it!" They were running into classmates from Iran whom they had not seen since childhood.

Together with my mother and father in a place called Armenia, no longer was I, the youngest daughter, the one with the greater grasp of local culture, the way I was in the United States. In Yerevan, my parents advised me about customs and language, reclaiming their rightful place in the parent-child hierarchy. And soon I was speaking Armenian freely in front of them again for the first time since childhood, a weird reunification of brain and spirit that worked something chemical inside me. (They knew better than to tease me about my mistakes, lest those long unheard sounds went back into their hiding places.)

One day I sat on the balcony of our rented apartment, overlooking Nalbandian Street, waiting for my father and sister to return home from a shopping trip, and I seemed to mistake every passerby for them. Is that Dad? No, it's some other Armenian man. Is that Lily? No, she wasn't wearing that dress. What did it do to a person to resemble those around him, or not to?

What did it mean for my parents to meet cousins they had not known for sixty years, children of their parents' siblings (and how could so many Americans waste this dear connection, not bothering with their cousins at all, I had always wondered)? Decades of family stories had never been shared, and they poured out now over evenings of food and wine and toasts in the Armenian tradition. Those stories were what created a sense of being someone, of belonging somewhere. And this *somewhere* didn't need to be Armenia: my father, for his part, saved these feelings of attachment and belonging for Iran. His siblings felt the same; that was their homeland, where they left their hearts and histories.

Invisible shifts, imperceptible but tectonic, take place when you move across the world; when a nation of people is dispersed, forced to rebuild in a place where it has no foundation. And this was the "injustice" we suffered now. This displacement—the anxiety of immigration and assimilation— was what we, the diaspora, knew of trauma today, but instead of calling it what it was we talked about genocides and government resolutions.

* * *

SOME WOULD SAY I was a bad Armenian because I had taken two previous trips to Yerevan that year and had failed to pay my respects at the genocide memorial. Unlike most of the important sights in Yerevan's small perimeter, it was a place you would not run into without making a deliberate plan; it stood on a hilltop park called Tsitsernakaberd (Swallow's Fortress). For some diaspora Armenians it was their first stop on arrival and their last stop again before departing. On the last day of my last trip, I decided to go, pretending I had interview plans so that I could visit without my family. I thought I needed to be alone if I were to feel anything, and maybe also because I was afraid I would not feel enough.

I had been to Tsitsernakaberd only once before, four years earlier. That had been an especially hot, dusty August day. After taking a taxi up to the complex, which overlooked the entire capital, the first building I entered was the museum, a low-ceilinged underground chamber lit by skylights. Inside, walls were carved with maps of the regions of Turkey from which Armenians were expelled. Six-digit numbers were scattered over these maps indicating how many residents of each town were killed. Down cool stone hallways, I looked at giant black-and-white photographs: rows of skeletons in a field, a line of disembodied heads with pop-eyed expressions topping pikes stuck into the ground, Turkish soldiers posing beside a mound of dead babies and children. Feeling unmoved and unsurprised then, I had barely glanced at the photos. I had seen it all before.

Outside, I had taken a slow walk along the platform surrounding the monument, a 144-foot-tall, narrow stele of granite with a sharp point piercing the sky. Beside it, twelve massive basalt plates lean into a circle, like the petals of a flower turned inward, guarding an "eternal flame." But that day, the monument, like everything else in Yerevan, was under construction. The soaring point was all scaffolding, and the famous "eternal flame" that I had seen in so many pictures was, to my disbelief, out of service and sealed over by shoddy planks.

Now, I returned, alone again, to the monument. As I entered the grounds of the vast complex, I heard Armenian hymns floating into the open air from unseen speakers. The music was morbid and angelic, and the breeze seemed to swirl it around me.

In a small park near the entrance, trees were planted in memory of the victims of the genocide. This was a relatively new addition, and the trees, baby evergreens, ranged from waist-height to about eight feet tall, like a Christmas tree farm out of season. Each tree marked the visit of a foreign dignitary: the late Rafik Hariri, former prime minister of Lebanon;

Bob Dole, the ex–US senator who had been one of the earliest supporters of a genocide resolution in Washington; and Frank Pallone, the chairman of the US Congress Armenian Caucus; past presidents of Romania and Latvia; the Ruler of Sharjah, his holiness Sheikh Dr. Sultan bin Mohammed Al Qassimi; the Deputy Mayor of Issy-les-Moulineaux, a suburb of Paris; and on and on. All this recognition astonished me and reminded me of the world outside of the closed one where I'd been living; how quickly my eyes had adjusted to Turkey.

Inside the museum, a display showed photos, postcards, and quotidian documents from various cities in Anatolia, along with the number of Armenian settlements, churches, and schools in each place. Now I had visited these towns and villages—Dikranagerd (Diyarbakır), Kharpert (Elâzığ), Bitlis, Van, Muş—and I chose to linger. Small bowls of soil were protected under glass, soil from towns only a few hundred miles away from this room, yet as distant as if samples from the moon.

I had come to the museum with a reporter's good intentions, thinking that I would ask a museum guard to describe the typical reaction of a visitor. This was unnecessary. The moment I walked up the steps into the memorial monument, I had to blink through my own tears. The flame was blazing today, and from its heat, the scent of flowers that people had left in tribute ripened and rose. It was near the end of this ordinary weekday in September, and the daily stock of red and white carnations had almost formed a full circle. A man stood on the edge of the ring of stone plates and prayed. Then he disappeared, and I was alone with the echo of Armenian liturgical music. I stared down at the fire until my tears dried to salty traces on my face. When I lifted my head, I saw a white-haired old woman in a navy blue work dress holding a short, handmade straw broom. Where had she come from? She sat on the steps across the circle looking at me.

PART FIVE

Power

- 18 -

The Narcissism of Small Similarities

IN 1947, THE AMERICAN BEHAVIORAL PSYCHOLOGIST B. F. SKINNER conducted a study in which he put hungry pigeons into a cage and fed them repeatedly, at short, timed intervals—15 seconds, one minute, and so on, varying the time in different rounds of the experiment. The feeding schedule had no connection to anything the pigeons did or didn't do, but the birds assumed themselves to have some influence, and began to believe that whatever action they happened to be performing just before they were fed had triggered the feeding. They continuously adjusted their actions, trying to figure out what would do the trick; one flapped in circles counterclockwise; another swung its head like a pendulum. The problem— the point—was that their conduct was irrelevant. The poor birds wore themselves out, "turning, twisting, pecking," Skinner wrote, trying endlessly to determine how to get the result they wanted.

I was starting to feel like one of Skinner's pigeons. I had come to Turkey with the idea—the delusion—that if I could find just the right way to speak and to listen, I would be able to connect with Turks, to create meaningful relationships that didn't depend on agreeing about what happened in 1915. But it wasn't working. I had less control over how these exchanges unfolded than I had fantasized I would. And too often, the space between

"Nice to meet you" and the words "so-called genocide" was only about two minutes long, threatening my composure as well as my goodwill.

When people tried to be polite, I became even more frustrated. Then our conversations were cluttered with bromides straight out of "It's a Small World." For example, Turks were very attached to the notion that Armenians were great cooks.

"One of my favorite foods is topik!" they would say to me.

Topik is a type of *mezze*, or appetizer; a dumpling made of mashed chickpeas and filled with pine nuts, onions, and cinnamon. It is a common menu item at a kind of festive tavern called a *meyhane*; *meyhanes* were traditionally owned by Armenians and Greeks since Muslims were not supposed to sell alcohol. Most of the *mezze* at a typical *meyhane* is considered Turkish food, but at some point, possibly due to its popularity at a famous Armenian-owned *meyhane* in the Kumkapı district, topik came to be seen as specifically Armenian. It was a lovely dish, and unique to the Istanbul Armenians; I had never seen it anywhere else. But it was also the only nice thing that many Turks could think of to say about Armenians.

"I love topik!"

Each person who said it seemed to glow with pride for having found such a graceful detour around his own prejudice. Each person seemed to think they were the only one.

The first few times people told me they loved topik, I had to admit I had never even heard of topik. Soon I had tasted a lot of topik, and then, at least, I could smile and tell them that I loved topik, too. But these exchanges were embarrassing. In place of an acknowledgment of a tragic history, compliments to the Armenian chef. To make matters worse, topik is Turkish for "little ball," as the chickpea paste was often rolled into a round shape. The very sound of the word was condescending. If Turks were oblivious to the patronizing overtones of their love affair with topik, it was all too clear to Istanbul Armenians. A Bolsahay artist had actually put out a small book of cartoons, through Aras Publishing, called *Ben Topik Değilim*—I Am Not Topik.

Armenians were either a curse word or they were the nicest people you had ever known. If the "Good Armenian" wasn't an excellent cook, he was a talented doctor. Or he was like an Armenian girl named Violet, a classmate of Deniz's who had a habit of insisting that she didn't care about politics, that she wasn't interested in 1915, that she "wasn't a historian," borrowing a line typically used by Turks trying to skirt around the genocide issue. The others in their class took well to this and liked to say that if Violet were elected president, all of Turkey's problems would be solved. Violet for president, they would tease merrily whenever she came into the classroom. Violet, the Good Armenian.

IN MY SKINNER-STYLE attempts to make satisfying connections with people, I ended up having an encounter at a coffee shop that I found difficult to classify. The room was crowded, so I had to share a table with a stranger, a Turkish woman, who proceeded to strike up a conversation with me. The woman was visiting from the United States, it turned out; she was a dentist in the Midwest, but she came back to Istanbul, her hometown, every summer. When she found out I was Armenian, she immediately exclaimed that Armenians and Turks were so similar, and proceeded to list the surnames of all her Armenian friends. "Çiçekçiyan, Demirciyan, Avedisiyan . . ."

Then, in the gentlest tone, she asked me to explain to her why, after living side by side with Turks for centuries, the Armenians had wanted to rebel. On cue, I started my song and dance, explaining just as delicately that it was more complicated than that but that we had all learned different stories and it was important to understand each other's experiences—yet suddenly I found myself unable to keep it up. I apologized and told her that I hated to offend, but that the story she learned was built on lies.

She changed the subject abruptly.

"Have you ever had dental work?" she asked.

"I'm sorry?"

"I mean braces, like on your teeth."

"Well, no—"

"Neither have I!" she exclaimed.

I looked at her teeth, and they were in fact remarkable. Blazingly white, and lined up in perfect order along the broad expanse of her mouth. But what did that have to do with anything?

"Look at our teeth!" she said. "We have the same smile! We're from the same people!"

We beamed at each other like two teenagers on Ecstasy.

"You don't see smiles like these in America," she went on. "This is a smile that we share because we both come from this part of the world."

I wanted so much to believe her. It seemed like the most compassionate statement that a Turkish-American dentist could possibly offer to me. For the rest of the day, I sought vain glimpses of my own smile whenever possible; in store windows, mirrors, and in my mind's eye, too. I counted my conversation with the dentist as a positive exchange.

Much later, I happened to read the novel *America America*, by the writer and director Elia Kazan, who was a Greek from Turkey, born in 1909 in Istanbul. Kazan was also interested in the smile shared by people from this part of the world. He called it The Anatolian Smile, the specialty of the Greek and Armenian characters in his book. But for Kazan it was a fake smile, covering complex emotions. He waxed at length about its meaning. The smile of the "minority person," he wrote, is "the only way he has found to face his oppressor, a mask to conceal the hostility he dares not show, and at the same time an escape for the shame he feels as he violates his true feelings."

Were these two different smiles we were describing? Or was it just that I hadn't yet acknowledged, even to myself, how much anger I was in fact holding back, how much frustration, and how much resentment?

I thought back to the woman in the coffee shop. And what if I had crooked teeth, or a cleft palate, or if I simply didn't feel like smiling? Would we still be "the same people" then?

A certain kind of clever intellectual type in calm places like America or England, upon hearing of the ongoing hostility between Turks and Armenians, is likely to shake his head and invoke a bit of Freud: "The narcissism of small differences," he will sigh, chuckling drily at the unruly Orient before going back to his reading.

But maybe the expression has it backward: maybe we should call it the narcissism of small similarities. In clinical terms, narcissism is fundamentally a disease of requiring sameness—of not being able to understand that someone different from yourself can exist according to his own needs and desires, and be entirely worthy of his existence. What could be more narcissistic than needing to believe somebody was the same as you in order for you to tolerate them? "We're so similar, we're all the same!" seemed like a cry of connection, of humanity, and in my strange and stressful Istanbul life, I clung to these attempts at kindness. "We are all Armenian." But although I didn't fully understand it then—couldn't quite let myself—I knew this was incomplete.

An evening spent hanging out with my Kurdish friends, Hakan, Murat, and Özgür, helped me understand why.

One Saturday, they took me to the home of a sociology professor they were close with. She really wants to meet you, they said. But she's tough. Don't take it personally, they warned me.

I wasn't sure what to expect.

Her name was Derya, and she was like a big sister or an auntie for the guys, about ten years older than they were. She lived alone in a huge, modern apartment, where she often cooked them dinner, doled out advice, gossiped with them, and scolded them when they got too rowdy. In return, they doted on her and entertained her with their Three Stooges–style comedy. Derya was ethnically Turkish.

She was also the only Turk I met who asked me this: What is it like for you to be here, in Turkey?

So much was conveyed by this simple question: that my being Armenian was significant—not something to gloss over—but it wasn't Derya's problem to manage; that my being in Turkey was not a challenge to her but a challenge for me. How rare, I suddenly realized, to meet a Turk who did not get defensive or try to overcompensate with excessive enthusiasm. I guess by "tough" my friends meant that Derya was honest. So when we began talking about what brought me to Turkey, I felt comfortable being honest in return.

I told Derya that although I had intended to research and write about Armenian-Turkish relations, with the idea that some kind of "soft reconciliation" was important and valuable—that simply getting Turks and Armenians to interact as human beings would be a major step, more important than forcing anyone to recognize the genocide—I was not sure what I was doing anymore. Not only were people more intolerant than I expected, but my own prejudices had not gone away, either. In fact, sometimes they seemed stronger than ever. And although I had started out looking for a way around the Armenian diaspora's fixation on genocide recognition, I was starting to realize that in my interactions with Turks, if we didn't already agree on what had happened in 1915, the barrier between us was too great to make a meaningful connection.

Derya nodded. "That's why 'soft reconciliation' is bullshit," she said. "Soft reconciliation is all those people telling you that some of their best friends are Armenian.

"It's all about power," Derya went on, looking me straight in the eye.

She realized this one day in a conversation with Hakan and Murat, when she was first getting to know them. They were arguing about the Kurdish issue, and the role of the PKK, and Murat said something that shocked her. "He told me, 'One day *I* want to be the one riding on top of a tank into the streets of Diyarbakır.'" Diyarbakır, the cultural heart of the Kurdish-populated southeast, was under constant military surveillance; and PKK sympathizers there threw grenades and planted car bombs, the only means they had found to express their anger. Attempts at working within parliament had been mostly unsuccessful for pro-Kurdish politicians; for a party to take any seats at all, it had to win at least ten percent of the national vote, so even when candidates from Kurdish parties gained the most votes in their districts, they were usually disqualified. In cases where they managed to win by running independently, thereby circumventing the party threshold, they were harassed by other MPs and tormented by the media. Turks felt like victims of Kurdish terror, but Kurds saw themselves as the victims—and some saw the PKK as the only way to force change. Murat had no wish to commandeer a tank; he simply meant that he was tired of feeling powerless.

The fundamental principles of the Turkish state, Derya continued, could not be changed by anything that was less powerful than the state itself. This was as true for the Armenian issue as it was for the Kurds, she said. The only power Turkey would respond to was power from more powerful countries. To that end, Washington had to pass a genocide resolution.

I challenged her: what about the Armenians in Istanbul and the way the diaspora's campaigns in Washington were making their lives more difficult?

If Armenians in Istanbul suffered in the meantime, it was a necessary price, she said, because otherwise nothing would ever truly change for them here. Their second-class status in Turkish society was a direct consequence of that society refusing to make an honest account of what they had endured.

"I don't care how many people have these little meetings where they bring together Armenian musicians and Turkish musicians, or Armenian filmmakers with Turkish filmmakers. That's all fine, but it's not going to change anything in Turkey."

At first I found this compelling: enough with the sentimental nonsense—it takes power to fight power. But what kind of power? The more I thought about it, the more I doubted whether the top-down kind was what we needed here. In a way, Derya's formulation resembled the right-wing response to the stark increase of school shootings in the United States between 2012 and 2014. They wanted to arm schoolteachers with guns; power against power. But this did nothing to improve the dynamics of the problem; it only changed who had their hands on the levers of power—or the triggers, as it were. Exacerbating the existing power struggle was not a satisfactory solution.

Likewise, even if I found denial of the genocide immoral and toxic, I did not want to entrust historiography to a government body. Living in Turkey made me more certain of this than ever. On October 10, 2007, a perfect object lesson demonstrated the problem: The US House of Representatives Foreign Affairs Committee voted that the events of 1915 constituted genocide, and recommended that a full resolution be considered on the House floor. The very next morning, a high court in Istanbul ruled that Sarkis Seropyan—Sarkis Bey—and Arat Dink, Hrant's son—were guilty of insulting the Turkish nation for allowing the word genocide in their newspaper. The US congressional committee's debate had revolved around the idea that the genocide was a well-documented fact. The Turkish court's verdict centered on an argument that according to its evidence, there had been no genocide. Both decisions had ample precedent and both would be replicated in the future; the noteworthy element, in this case, was their juxtaposition. In less than twenty-four hours, the rulings emerged as mirror images showing how state power could be used and abused.

Alan Dershowitz, the notorious Jewish-American criminal defense lawyer, and an outspoken supporter of Israel, addressed this bind many years ago, during a symposium at Harvard University about freedom of speech and Holocaust denial: "I don't want the government to tell me that it occurred because I don't want any government ever to tell me that it didn't occur." He went on, "I am categorically opposed to any court, any school board, any governmental agent taking judicial notice about any historical event, even one that I know to the absolute core of my being occurred, like the Holocaust. . . . In my experience, government is one of the worst judges of truth."

A French-Armenian scholar, Marc Nichanian, had made an argument to similar effect, suggesting that government rulings on the genocide were inherently problematic because they disempowered the victims, put their suffering, their reality, up for cold, official appraisal. As such, formal recognition campaigns assumed a capitulation to power.

Derya's words rang true for me, but in a slightly different way than she meant. Yes, it was all about power, but not about governmental power, and not about brute force: the issue was the disparity of power between individuals. This was how I came to understand why I had not become genuine friends with Turks who didn't acknowledge the genocide: because if they believed a story in which Armenians were not the perse-cuted but persecutor, they were doomed to discount the current oppres-sion that Armenians in Istanbul lived with every day. If a Turk didn't acknowledge what happened in 1915 he was also denying an entire com-plex of discrimination and power dynamics that defined the minority experience in Turkey.

Which didn't mean government had no role to play, of course. In Turkey, governmental power enabled the disparity of power between individuals. This, finally, was a reason I could get behind: genocide recognition—anywhere and everywhere—for the sake of equality and democracy in Turkey.

UNTIL I TALKED to Derya, I felt disappointed in myself, because although I liked to believe that I could find a way to relate to nearly anyone, I had been keeping certain people at arm's length. A Turkish TV star who prided herself on her interest in Armenian culture wanted to host a dinner party in my honor, but I managed to defer until the offer faded away. I was repeatedly invited out by a Turkish woman named Rüya who had told me that the diversity of the participants in Hrant's funeral march proved that Turks had no particular prejudice against Armenians. I often made up excuses to avoid seeing her. Now I understood why, and it *was* about power: how can you be friends when you are not equals? With the TV star I sensed she wanted to show me off to her peers, a token diaspora Armenian, a defanged, stuffed specimen from an exhibit. With Rüya, I found myself doing strange things—insisting on picking up expensive tabs, for example, even when I was clearly the guest, and this, too, was about power, about me trying to demonstrate some in any way I could.

No wonder I felt so much more comfortable with my Kurdish bud-
dies than with anyone else. They didn't have power either. The same was
true of a Turkish friend I had gotten to know who was crippled, owing to
a childhood bout of polio, and staggered around with a pronounced
limp; and another who was gay, and another who had a disfiguring skin
condition. They formed a ragtag posse who could relate comfortably to
an Armenian because they knew, from their own experience, what it meant
to be excluded from the official story. They could challenge it because they
didn't fit into it either.

My Kurdish friends routinely struggled with this imbalance of power.
On another weekend evening I joined Hakan, Murat, and Özgür at a
popular bar where we stayed talking and dancing until four a.m. After-
ward, we headed for a soup shop, which was the thing to do after a night
out in Istanbul. Every table was full with young people guzzling bowls of
soup, considered a preventative measure against hangovers. The most
effective were made with intestines or cow's feet, but for the faint of stomach like me there was also lentil soup.

We had business to discuss. Hakan was upset because earlier in the
evening, we'd run into a Turkish woman named Dilek whom he had a
crush on. They were classmates at the university, and there had always
been some chemistry between them, he said. At the start of the evening,
she seemed interested in Hakan, but then something had gone wrong.
When we had discussed moving on to a different bar, Hakan had suggested someplace with music, and Dilek had teased him, saying he probably wanted to go to a *türkü* bar. *Türkü* is the name for a style of folk
ballad rooted in Anatolian villages. Despite the name, many *türkü*
musicians are Kurdish and perform songs with Kurdish influences.
The performances tend to draw homesick provincial types or foreign
tourists hoping for a bit of authenticity. Hakan had nothing against
türkü music, but he didn't like what Dilek's comment implied. Despite
the fact that they had many friends in common and supported the
same causes, this passing remark made Hakan feel like Dilek saw him
first and foremost as a Kurd. Which is to say, a villager at best, a terrorist at worst.

We spent an hour analyzing what Dilek could have meant by suggesting a *türkü* bar. Maybe she didn't mean anything at all, we offered. Maybe
she just thought he liked folk music. Maybe—probably—she thought it

was fair game to tease Hakan about his Anatolian village origins because he joked about this himself, telling stories about growing up near the conservative town of Konya that kept us all in stitches. But even as we tossed around justifications, we knew that Hakan's instinct meant something. Dilek may have miscalculated on her humor, and she may have even been interested in Hakan, but she had revealed that his Kurdishness was the first thing she saw.

How could anyone get it right? If your differences were ignored, it felt offensive. If too much attention were paid to them, that felt offensive, too.

Often, when our conversations reached a point of frustration, we turned to joking about "our party." This party had nothing to do with the dance club where we had spent the evening. "Our party" was an imaginary political movement the guys had dreamed up; the Leftist Solution Party, they called it. Hakan would be the party chief, Murat the foreign minister, and Özgür the minister of finance (which basically just meant that he paid for everyone's beer). Deniz, the group's intellectual heavyweight, was the minister of education. When I came along I was elected minister of culture, an honor bestowed after the guys persuaded me to sing some Armenian folk songs for them. Various other friends, depending on who was on hand at the moment, were appointed to a rotation of posts, minister of whatever they happened to be doing when the subject came up.

Our party wasn't just for Kurds, they were quick to say, but Kurds would be among the leading ranks. It was a party for leftists and democrats, for peaceful people who couldn't get behind any of the parties in the current system. Our party was a joke, but a dark one. It was the minority play-acting at wielding power.

After soup, we walked down İstiklâl toward our homes. Other than some flocks of pigeons pecking around food wrappers that were twirling in the wind, the street was empty, a rare sight. İstiklâl was normally filled from morning to midnight with teenagers, families, tourists, and peddlers selling stuffed mussels, corn on the cob, roasted chestnuts, and lottery tickets. Now the sun was starting to come up, brightening blank stretches of cobblestone around us. Hakan took the opportunity to try out his political chops.

"Good morning!" he sang out to the birds, a small-town mayor strolling along Main Street. "Yes, yes, thank you for your vote!" he called into empty doorways. He waved up at darkened windows, first on the right, then on the left, as the rest of us ambled behind him and laughed.

- 19 -

Excess Baggage

EVERY THREE MONTHS, I WAS REQUIRED TO MAKE A "VISA RUN." VISA runs were what foreigners did when they wanted to stay in Turkey a long time but didn't have work papers or a residency permit. Until 2012, when the process was revamped completely, tourist visas were the secret currency of Istanbul's cosmopolitan life. I knew Americans who stayed for five or ten years without any problems; they simply crossed the border to another country once every three months—sometimes remaining in Bulgaria (the easiest choice) for just an hour, long enough for a spinach pie and a new passport stamp—then got another visa for twenty dollars upon reentry at Atatürk Airport.

"Turkey is such a lovely country, I just keep coming back," you would tell the guard with the raised eyebrow in the passport control booth, as he flipped through pages and tried to make sense of your numerous entries and exits. "I love it so much here!" That was all you needed to say, music to a Turkish visa officer's ears, and you had three more months to play with.

I liked the way it felt to say this. Sensing those words come to life in my body and hearing them escape from my mouth—"I love Turkey, I'm having a great time here"—was a way to take on a new identity. Like a psychological version of sky-diving, dangerous but exhilarating.

In the summer of 2009, for my last big visa run, I decided to spend a weekend in Berlin to see some friends. When it was time to return, I stood in line at Tegel Airport to check in for my Turkish Airlines flight back to Istanbul. German efficiency notwithstanding, airport lines for national carriers tend to immediately assume the cultural norms of the passengers. These passengers were all Turkish. Unlike Armenians, who liked to engage in a continuous competition to get to the front even when there was no rush, the Turks seemed relaxed. If you handed people drinks, it would have looked like a cocktail reception; the line had no shape, and the passengers were chatting with whomever was nearby, strangers addressing each other with *canım* and *abi* and *abla*, my dear, brother, sister.

I thought I would be happy enough to see them, the Turks. But as I took my place in the check-in line, the sight of the group brought with it a heaviness that I had forgotten about for a few days. As much as I had grown attached to Istanbul, the reality was that I couldn't go an hour without having to explain that I was Armenian, and it was starting to wear on me.

Just before going to Berlin, I had gotten a pedicure, and the beautician pushed the issue when I told her I was from New York: "But there's something else in you," she said, and then tilted her head expectantly. There was no way I would say I was Armenian at that moment, with my naked pink foot in her hand. It was not merely the physical intimacy of the situation that made such an admission uncomfortable, nor the fact that she was wielding a sharp instrument whose purpose was to scrape the hardened skin from my heels. It was that we were in a setting in which she was supposed to be my subordinate. And I had so internalized the way things were—that as an Armenian, my very existence was a kind of insult to the Turks—that I did not have the courage to tell the truth just then, to subvert the natural order and inform the beautician that she was sitting at an Armenian woman's feet.

The weight of a thousand similar interactions resettled on my spirit when I joined the Turks at the airport in Berlin. But then I was distracted by a cluster of passengers who were whispering and gesturing in my direction. I gave a bit of a smile. A woman in expensive European clothes, the sort of woman who has special outfits just for air travel, looked at me and said to the people around her, "I think she's Turkish." *Bence Türk*, she said. She nodded her head slowly as she said it, and met my eyes almost flirtatiously to see if I was listening.

"Me?" I answered in Turkish. *Ben mi?*

"You see!" she said to the others. "I was right!"

"No, no," I said, laughing. "I'm actually American but I've been living in Istanbul for two years." I held up my US passport, that blue and gold rectangle that is recognized the world over as a kind of dum-dum pass, as in, don't expect much from this person, this is just another pampered, contented American, trotting around the world as Americans do.

But the woman ignored my passport. She was more interested in my small carry-on bag. "Is that all you brought? Most girls your age would need a bag that size just for their shoes!"

Everybody laughed, and I did, too. I told her I had been in Berlin for a short visit to see friends, and assured her that normally I'd have more luggage than this.

Then she stepped closer and dropped her voice. "You see, dear, I can't take both of these suitcases on board." She waved her arm toward two enormous suitcases, the hard-case kind, each large enough to hold an entire wardrobe. "Together they will be over the maximum combined weight. It will be better if you take one of them."

She looked at the people next to her, unrelated passengers with whom she had been consulting on the subject, and they nodded.

So that's what the discussion had been about. The travelers had been scoping out the line to see who could help, and with only a tiny carry-on, I looked like the perfect candidate for the job. But of course it was inconceivable, after years of being battered with questions at American airports—"Does this suitcase belong to you? Did you pack it yourself? Has anyone unknown to you given you anything to carry today?"—that I would even consider checking a stranger's luggage under my name.

Yet suddenly it wasn't so easy to say no. Turkey is the sort of place where, when a car tries to drive down a narrow street, ten shopkeepers immediately step out of their doorways to guide the driver to safety; where friends seem to treat their money as communal, and strangers had helped me a hundred times in ways that I never would have expected in America.

I looked at the other passengers to see if anybody understood my hesitation, but I found no hint. I suggested to the woman that maybe they wouldn't charge her—sometimes, you know, they'll just accept the extra weight, I said.

"Oh no," someone else chimed in, attempting to lift the suitcases one by one. "These are way too heavy for that. It won't work unless you take one of them."

I couldn't believe that nobody else thought the request was strange.

"Let's wait and see," I said, figuring that by the time we reached the front of the line, the woman would sense my discomfort and let me off the hook.

"It's not a big deal," said a tall man, stepping up. He was the woman's brother, and had come to see her off. "Nothing will happen." He told me he used to be a police officer in Istanbul and showed me his old ID card, as though this would put me at ease.

I tried another argument: "I want to help you," I said. "It's just that as an American, since September 11, traveling has become very compli- cated for us. They ask us all these questions at airports . . ."

I waited for somebody to nod or show that they knew what I meant, but instead the words "September 11" drew a few snickers. I tried again to explain what I meant about being American; and then it occurred to me that with my messy Turkish, it probably sounded like I was saying that since 9/11 I didn't trust anybody from a Muslim country anymore. I didn't know what to do. I thought about showing them the page on my passport that said I was born in Iran.

As our turn at the check-in desk neared, the woman actually asked me for my passport, so that she could present us as a pair traveling together. I merely needed to say that the black suitcase was mine, she said.

I held my passport close. Standing there, I knew that if anyone had ever described this situation to me, I would have sworn, without hesita- tion, that I'd never agree to such a request.

At the counter, the woman's brother heaved the suitcases onto the scale, and I made a silent compromise: I told myself that if the German attendant asked me directly whether the second suitcase was mine, I would say no.

What happened instead was that the attendant reached for both of our passports and hit a few keys on his computer. The woman pointed to one of the suitcases and said, "That's mine."

He slid a tag around the suitcase handle. Then, peering at his screen and then at me, he said, "You are Meline?"

I nodded ever so slightly.

"Yours is too heavy," the clerk said. "You need to take some things out."

I had not spoken, had hardly moved, had only confirmed, if anything, that my name was Meline. Nobody could accuse me of more, I told myself, preparing my defense.

The woman's brother hoisted the suitcase and dragged it to a corner, where the two of them began sorting for items to move into a carry-on.

I took my passport back, turned numbly in their direction, and stared at the open suitcase. It held a disorganized pile of unmarked plastic shopping bags whose contents I couldn't discern. Anything could be in those bags. Guns, drugs, cash. Why were there so many bags? I felt miserable. I couldn't stop myself from imagining what would happen if there were explosives inside, and that later, when my parents received the news about the plane that was blown up by a terrorist, they would be told that the suitcase containing the bomb had a sticker with their daughter's name, and nobody would be left to explain what had happened.

That was it. I stood in front of the woman and said, as firmly as I could, "I'm very sorry, but I'm not comfortable with this situation."

Then I grabbed the handle of my tiny rolling carry-on and walked quickly toward the revolving doors that led outside. Fresh air. Germany. I hadn't finished checking in, but I needed to get away from that woman and her luggage. If I waited long enough she would have to go on without me. On the sidewalk, I smoked a cigarette, then walked all the way to a farther set of doors to reenter the terminal out of sight of the Turkish Airlines desk. I stalled for another few moments in a gift shop, my heart pounding, my eyes blurring over souvenirs and stacks of Toblerone. Then, hearing the final call for my flight, I turned to head back to the counter.

When I was still about fifty feet away, I felt a hand on my sleeve.

"There you are! Dear, please, we don't have much time. Everybody else has checked in now. The German man just needs you to go and take your boarding pass. He is waiting," she said.

I couldn't believe it. Walking in a kind of trance, I began to reason to myself that if the suitcase contained something illegal but not lethal, several passengers could bear witness that I had been bullied into taking it, so my sentence might be reduced. And if the luggage contained a bomb, all would be moot because we'd be dead regardless of who checked it in.

At the counter, I handed over my passport again without a word, did not comment one way or another on the giant black suitcase that waited on the scale, made sure not to watch too closely as the clerk wrapped its handle with a sticker bearing my name, accepted my boarding pass, and then shoved my way through the final security line, a too-late surge of aggression directed at everyone and no one.

I had requested an aisle seat when I purchased my ticket, as I always do. But when I got to my row, I saw that, infuriatingly, my boarding pass placed me in the middle seat.

"This is us, dear!" said a familiar voice. Her again, standing beside me.

That's when I realized that we had been assigned to adjacent seats, naturally, since we were "traveling together." After all this, there was no way I was going to sit in the middle. I stepped aside and motioned for the woman to go in first. She looked at her boarding pass and at me, and then shrugged and slid in. I dropped into the aisle seat and tried to avoid her gaze.

But the woman wouldn't stop talking. She spoke about her nieces, about Berlin. She offered me hard candy from a sandwich bag, and I looked at it and wondered if it contained some sort of sleeping potion. I didn't see her put a piece in her own mouth. I refused the candy. I decided to read. But then I realized I had brought with me only a dry history book, which ran the risk of putting me to sleep. I needed to stay wide awake in case something happened.

ABOUT HALFWAY THROUGH the flight, I began to calm down. The woman herself had nodded off, which gave me a chance to take a closer look at her. She was plump, but attractive, with smooth, golden skin and a healthy head of hair whose copper highlights looked like the work of a good stylist. Her hands, clasped across her belly, bore several gold rings of various arrangements, and her long nails were polished in a shimmery rose. She reminded me slightly of Müge, I was surprised to discover—she was about the same age and had that same light coloring, the envy of most Turks—and as I relaxed, I reflected on how much had happened since that first time I nervously dialed Müge's number, since the day I first met her in person in the Istanbul airport. In the subsequent four years, there had been bad moments and good ones, but my adrenaline had been pumping at full throttle all the while. I was exhausted.

I WAS JUST starting to doze when suddenly I heard a voice. "Excuse me," it was saying. "Excuse me."

I opened my eyes. A German stewardess was standing over me.

"Excuse me. Could I know your last name, please?"

Oh God. We hadn't even arrived yet.

"Toumani," I said quietly.

The attendant looked confused. She glanced up the aisle, looked at me again, and then walked away.

They must have searched the bag at Tegel Airport, I realized. Now the passengers were captive in the plane so they could easily pinpoint the offender. I would be arrested on landing. This could not be happening.

A moment later the flight attendant returned. "Miss, your surname one more time?" I repeated it, then from a survivalist reserve of clarity, I managed to ask her why she wanted to know.

"Did you order a special meal?" she said.

A special meal? A special meal! A special meal. My hands went to my face, pressing my eyes shut. We had changed seats. It wasn't me she was looking for. I was not being arrested. There was no bomb.

I turned and landed a hard poke into the fleshy arm of the woman who, after ruining my day, was now resting peacefully, and asked her, in Turkish, if she had ordered a special meal.

"Oh yes, dear, I did! The doctor says I need to watch my sugar, you know," she said with a wink.

"The meal is hers!" I nearly shouted in English. "We changed seats!"

"But you are not supposed to change seats," the attendant said.

I nodded.

"Changing seats is a violation of policies!" The energy with which she delivered this made it sound like something she had waited years for an opportunity to say.

"I know."

"We need to know exactly who is who and what is what."

She waited for me to offer an explanation. I looked over at my companion, who did not understand English, but smiled genially and nodded with interest, as if we were chatting about the latest skin cream.

Then a Turkish flight attendant who had come over to see what was happening repeated the phrase like a recorded announcement: Changing seats is forbidden. *Koltuk değiştirmek yasaktır.*

"Oh, I'm so sorry," my companion replied, her expression turning solemn. "But this poor girl has some claustrophobia so I wanted to help her."

WHEN I GOT back to my apartment in Istanbul, I called my parents in California to tell them I had returned safely from Berlin, and then I recounted what had happened at the airport.

"Are you crazy?" said my father.

"Why would you do that?" my mother said.

"You guys know how it is in the Middle East," I said. "Everybody helps everybody. I didn't want to be that American who only watches out for herself," I insisted. "Come on, do you mean you wouldn't have helped the woman?"

"Never," said my dad.

"Mom?"

"Absolutely not."

My parents had suffered through two years of worrying about their youngest daughter's strange adventure in Turkey. For the most part they had hidden their fears, showing interest in all my stories and proudly describing how they defended me when their friends raised questions about what I was up to. But after the luggage incident their anxiety, as well as my own growing disillusionment, could no longer be ignored.

As we talked, I realized something that I had not seen clearly before. I would not have hesitated to say no to a passenger who was Japanese, or French, or Indian. I had given in to the woman, in the end, not because of Middle Eastern virtue, or American overcompensation, or because I was simply an idiot—but because she was Turkish and I was Armenian. And even though I never told the woman I was Armenian, some part of me, something deep inside of me, wanted her approval, and wanted this only and surely because she was a Turk.

I had absorbed this habit over months and months of smiling and contorting my words and having half-baked conversations with clerks and cabbies about how we're all human beings in the end, and finally it had deranged me. This was the Stockholm syndrome I had heard about and dismissed before I had started my journey. The role I had taken on was incomparable to the lifetime of subjugation endured by my Armenian peers in Turkey, but even this controlled experiment had taken its toll.

My friend Talin, an Armenian from Istanbul who moved to the United States as an adult, once told me she was jealous of the way I was able to love Istanbul. She knew how captivating the city could be, knew it in her very cells, but at some point that wasn't enough, or rather it was too much. Because of who she was, Istanbul could not love her back. We had this conversation when I had been there for only one year; long enough to understand exactly how wonderful Istanbul was but not long enough to realize the price I was paying to stay. She was jealous that I could still love it, but eventually I felt like she did, and in my memories I would not know which Istanbul to think of: the one I fell for or the one where I nearly lost my mind.

For expats, Istanbul was a cosmopolitan dream come true. Yes, it was East and West; yes, it was a bridge between worlds; yes, it was oriental and exotic while still being modern and glamorous. All the clichés were spot-on. For me, it was all of these things, too, but it was ultimately a place where this single dimension of my life, my being Armenian—this feeling of fatigue with the clannishness and conformity of Armenian life that I had come to Turkey hoping to escape, or at least to broaden—had become more a fact of my existence than it had ever been before. If I had to say I was Armenian ten times a day in Turkey, or choose not to say it, but to think it and to wonder about it, and to be a little bit afraid each time, and to twist myself into knots to try to avoid offending anyone, until I had all but lost track of myself entirely, well, this could not go on. That was the day I bought my ticket home.

- 20 -

Soccer Diplomacy

EARLY ON IN MY PROJECT, WHENEVER I TOLD SOMEBODY I WAS RESEARCH-
ing "Armenian-Turkish relations," it was a bit like saying, "I'm studying
unicorns." You could study the *idea* of unicorns, but beyond that there
wasn't much to work with. Likewise with Armenian-Turkish relations:
officially, there were none.

But then a stroke of luck set the stage for this to change.

It was the draw for the qualifying rounds of the 2010 World Cup.
Out of the fifty-three national teams in what the FIFA (Fédération Inter-
nationale de Football Association) soccer league considered "Europe,"
Armenia and Turkey landed in the same group of six countries that would
face off for a chance to advance to the finals.

The first match took place in Yerevan in September 2008. Armenian
President Serge Sarkissian invited Turkey's president, Abdullah Gül, to
attend, making Gül the first leader of the Turkish Republic to visit the
Republic of Armenia. Turkey won, which surprised nobody—they were
seeded much higher in the rankings.

But the match was an opening, an example of possibility, not something to be taken for granted. After all, things could have been worse:
Armenia and Azerbaijan were not even *allowed*, according to FIFA rules,
to be grouped together. (This was a rare exception made for only the most

volatile pairings; Russia and Georgia were also kept apart.) Soccer as litmus test: it is clear that you hate each other, but can you get through one game without starting a war? In the case of Armenia and Azerbaijan, significantly more tame cultural exchanges had proven impossible; a Caucasus chamber orchestra that had recently brought together musicians from around the region for a few concerts was banned from playing in Azerbaijan because it included Armenian members.

Thus when nobody lost any limbs in the 2008 match between Armenia and Turkey, and no bombs went off, the two governments took the next step. With help from Swiss mediators, they began secret talks toward establishing diplomatic ties. And on April 22, 2009, they announced publicly that such talks were under way. Details were vague: the countries had agreed to the intention of developing "good neighborly relations."

"The two parties have achieved tangible progress and mutual understanding in this process and they have agreed on a comprehensive framework for the normalization of their bilateral relations," the statement said. "Within this framework, a road map has been determined."

Decisions to set frameworks to establish road maps to develop agreements. Nothing had been signed, but it was huge news all the same.

In Armenia, the Dashnak Party immediately denounced President Sarkissian for agreeing to a framework based on no preconditions, and ended its participation in the coalition government. The party was in favor of opening the border, but only after Turkey acknowledged the genocide. Most Dashnaks were against any plan that guaranteed the current borders, since they still wanted to reclaim parts of eastern Turkey.

In Turkey, the Nationalist Action Party (MHP in Turkish)—the Dashnaks' hardline corollary—was angry that talks had gone on without the parliament's knowledge. They insisted that no friendship could be established with Armenia until it ended its occupation of Nagorno-Karabakh.

However, third-party countries, especially the United States, France, Switzerland, and Russia, were pushing hard for the new protocols. With their encouragement, talks continued, and on October 10, 2009, a ceremony was planned in Zurich where Turkey and Armenia were to sign a bilateral accord. US Secretary of State Hillary Clinton flew to Switzerland for the occasion. Although not involved in the main negotiations, she was there to show support now that all the details were in place.

But at the exact appointed time, one p.m., it was announced that the ceremony could not begin. Armenia's foreign minister, Eduard Nalban-dyan, had not left his hotel. He was angry about something his Turkish counterpart, Ahmet Davutoğlu, was planning to say in his public state-ment, and refused to go to the University of Zurich, where the proceed-ings were to be held.

Secretary of State Clinton decided to intervene. As correspondents on the scene reported it, she directed her motorcade to the hotel where the Armenians were staying. For two hours, aides raced between the hotel and the university, where the Turkish delegation waited. It was an old-fashioned haggle. Slips of paper were handed back and forth, details were crossed out, edits were made. Clinton canceled her dinner plans in London, the BBC reported. Finally, she emerged from the Zurich hotel entrance with Foreign Minister Nalbandyan at her side, and the two of them got into her car. She admitted later that even then, nothing was certain, and it was dur-ing that tense car ride when the trickiest negotiations were ironed out.

But in the end, as leaders from several countries hovered over them with frozen smiles, the foreign ministers of Turkey and Armenia signed a set of protocols. The key compromise? Neither party would be allowed to make a public statement. Thus what should have been a historic moment was marked with pursed lips.

And the agreement still needed to be ratified by both parliaments.

While the main idea—establishing relations and opening the border—had considerable support on both sides, two factors made full ratification difficult. The agreement called for the establishment of an international commission to examine the "historical dimension" of the relationship, and the majority of Armenians found this clause unacceptable, on the basis that the historical dimension had been adequately examined many times over. In Turkey, meanwhile, most politicians as well as the general public opposed establishing relations with Armenia before progress was made on the conflict with Azerbaijan.

The timing of the October 10 agreement in Zurich was urgent, because four days later, on October 14, according to a schedule determined not by diplomats but by FIFA, Armenia and Turkey would meet again, this time in the Turkish city of Bursa, for round two of the World Cup qualifiers. The game could either be an angry face-off between enemies, or a spir-ited celebration of progress. President Sarkissian had said he would not go to Bursa without an agreement in Zurich.

The game was set for Wednesday night at nine p.m. One of my closest friends was getting married in Los Angeles on Saturday. I would attend the match in Bursa, take a bus and ferry back to Istanbul in the middle of the night, and fly home on Thursday morning—for good. By the time I reached Bursa, my bags were sitting in my foyer in Istanbul fully packed, and I had said most of my farewells.

* * *

MY FRIEND RAMAZAN, the photographer, was from Bursa. He was very excited about the game, since he had already traveled to Armenia to take pictures, and shots of the soccer match in his hometown would make a perfect addition to his portfolio. He had offered to show me around Bursa, so we met aboard the ferry—it was a two-hour ride across the Sea of Marmara—and the first thing Ramazan did when he saw me was hold up a copy of *Milliyet* newspaper, his face exuberant. In huge letters, the banner headline read: "*Sarı Gelin, Hadi Gelin!*"

How to explain the layers of nuance in this perfectly crafted tabloid slogan? "*Sarı Gelin*" was the name of a folk song that became popular—no, mind-numbingly ubiquitous—after Hrant Dink's death, because it was played at so many memorial events for him. It had become a symbol of the multicultural history of Anatolia; the song had lyrics in Turkish, Armenian, and Persian. It was the musical equivalent of dolma, stuffed vegetables: something that everybody in the Middle East claimed as their own, and loved.

Some of the lyrics had completely different meanings depending on which language you spoke. In Armenian, *sarı* sounded like "the mountain." In Turkish *sarı* meant "blond," and *gelin* meant "bride" but was also the imperative of the verb *gelmek*, "to come." An amalgamation: the blond bride comes to the mountain.

In post–Hrant Dink Turkey, "*Sarı Gelin*" had come to be a soft, unthreatening stand-in for all things Armenian. *Hadi* was slang for "hurry up." And so the headline on the day of the soccer match was clever indeed. "*Sarı Gelin, Hadi Gelin!*" Armenia, come on over already!

Ramazan loved it. I had mixed feelings. The phrase appealed to my fondness for wordplay, and there was something sweet about it. The directness was refreshing: not a statement *about* Armenia but *to* Armenia.

Yet in a less charitable interpretation, "*sarı gelin, hadi gelin*" was a bit like saying, "Hey, pansy, get your ass over here." But fine. It was just soccer. I was excited for the game. And Ramazan would be my local tour guide—an ideal way to spend my final day in Turkey.

Unfortunately, from the moment we got to Bursa, things started to turn sour.

The entire city was covered with flags—not just Turkish flags, which were to be expected for a national game, but Azerbaijan flags, too. There might have been tens of thousands of them. Nobody who has not been to a place like Turkey for a patriotic event can imagine what "covered with flags" really means. President Sarkissian had indeed come from Armenia, but the Azerbaijan flag bonanza did not bode well for the tenuous diplomatic connection.

RELATIONS BETWEEN ARMENIA and Turkey had come far enough that for weeks, Turkish journalists had been filing enthusiastic reports about preparations for the match, hopes for great diplomatic strides, and signs of a blossoming neighborly relationship—and a lot of the coverage had the ring of propaganda, but of a sort that had been earned, at least, by the fraught and faulty process, one step forward and two steps back, that had lurched along in the hands of politicians, cultural figures, scholars, and business people for the past few years.

Between Armenia and Azerbaijan, however, there was no such progress. The war was officially over, but there remained unconcealed rage on both sides. Armenians were occupying an enclave that they considered their rightful territory, while Azerbaijan considered this a hostile takeover that would be rectified one day soon. Karabakh declared independence in 1991 as the Nagorno-Karabakh Republic, a status formally disputed by the UN and other international organizations. Officially, it was recognized only by the breakaway republics of Abkhazia, South Ossetia, and Transnistria—and across the pond, by California, Massachusetts, Rhode Island, Louisiana, and Maine. (In 2012, the island nation of Tuvalu was said to be considering recognition of Karabakh, also, and the Azerbaijan press went mad; but then again, reports indicated that Tuvalu might sink below sea level before further decisions were taken.)

I was not a great supporter of most Armenian rhetoric on the

Karabakh issue; it was steeped in an uncompromising arrogance, as Armenians from all over the world went to Karabakh to establish NGOs and other footholds, disguising aggressive resettlement as humanitarian aid. But the fact that Karabakh was now functionally Armenian was indisputable, and there was no obvious way to resolve the situation. Linking it together with Armenian-Turkish relations was like weighting that historic conflict with a lead anchor. Both would go down together.

So the Azerbaijan flags blanketing Bursa on the day of the soccer match meant many things: they were an effort by nationalist Turks to upend any diplomatic progress; they were a reminder that for many Turks, the old slogan still rang true: the only friend of a Turk is a Turk; and they were a guarantee that no Armenian could feel the slightest bit welcome.

A GROUP OF journalists from Yerevan had made the trip, and Aris, the *Agos* reporter, was helping them get around. He had invited me to meet the group a couple nights earlier, when they had arrived in Istanbul. There were about ten of them, almost all women in their twenties and thirties. Most had never been to Turkey before and the Azerbaijan flags were not making a great first impression. But even taking this into consideration, the Armenians struck me as not at all interested in connecting with Turks. Walking around Bursa with them the day of the match, I was alternately amused and disturbed by their running anti-Turkish commentary. It was fascinatingly uncensored, since they were speaking in a language nobody around them could understand, and it was the first time I had heard such talk while standing on Turkish soil.

Aris had arranged a formal lunch for us at a restaurant famous for the Bursa specialty, Iskender kebab, a dish of lamb shavings drizzled with butter, surrounded by red pepper sauce and topped with yogurt. I had tried it the previous night, with Ramazan and his friends, and it was delicious (although too rich, apparently; I was sick in my hotel room later on). But today, the Armenian journalists were staging a lamb revolt. Several of them refused to try the Iskender kebab. One of the men had learned a few words of Turkish from his grandmother and insisted on using them, but only to make demands; he kept barking at the waiter, "*Dana yok!*" What he meant to say was "no lamb"—as in, we don't want lamb. But *dana* means "beef," and *yok* means "there isn't," so the waiter appeared bewildered by this visitor from Armenia shouting, "There is no beef!" like a bad translation of the Wendy's commercial. One of the women was a vegetarian and wanted mushrooms instead of meat, a preference incomprehensible to the chef, and another nearly knocked over the waiter when he tried to douse her plate with a ladle of melted butter.

The proprietor of this famous kebab house had acted delighted to welcome a group from Armenia, and now they were refusing to eat his food. I couldn't blame them for being angry about the flags all over town, but I was surprised by the way that—unlike myself—they seemed to feel no obligation to be gracious even over the simple matter of lunch. Was it because they were not alone but in a group? Because they would be here only for a few days? I was embarrassed by their rudeness, but also a little bit envious of it.

After we ate, the restaurant manager tried to tell the group about the history of the restaurant—it had originally been an animal hospital, opened by a Turkish-Armenian veterinarian named Gregorian. Aris translated, but they showed no signs of paying attention.

"Your friends don't seem very interested," the manager said to Aris.

"Oh, they're just tired." He looked rather weary himself.

FINALLY, AFTER DARK, we made our way to the bleachers. The Atatürk Stadium had room for twenty thousand, and more than sixteen thousand seats were filled. For weeks people had been wondering how the stands would be divided up—everyone wanted to make sure they bought a ticket to sit on their own team's side—until it became obvious that there would not be enough Armenian spectators to bother with sides at all. Only about fifty Bolsahays had come, and they made up the "Armenian section," a little roped-off chunk of seats. It was adjacent to the press section, where I sat with Aris and the journalists from Yerevan.

The pregame festivities began with an announcer reading the names of the players. The moment he started to list the Armenian team members, a chorus of the loudest booing I had ever heard rose up from the stands. I tried to cheer, but it was pointless amid the deafening boos. I could not hear even the faintest sound of my own voice.

When the Armenian national anthem was played, the jeering got even louder. From all directions, an undifferentiated mass of male energy churned with need and rage. Everything that happened next seemed to happen automatically, and I let it happen. I put my hand over my heart. Soon I was shaking with sobs and I didn't try to contain myself. I stared straight ahead, where my eye caught the eye of one of the security guards who was facing the stands. *Let him think about it*, I said to myself. *Let him try to imagine why this journalist in the press section has her hand over her heart during the Armenian national anthem and why there are tears rolling down her cheeks.*

Then the Turkish national anthem started. After two years in Turkey, I could hum the tune from beginning to end, and had even come to feel a certain fondness for it. A good national anthem can stir a listener from any country, if they have the heart for that sort of thing, and I did. But it was different now, as if I had returned full circle to the days when this song made my heart freeze. The volume kept rising as every voice in the stadium joined in.

When the anthems were finished, a flock of doves was released. I turned around to find Aris, and we exchanged a pointed glare. They had released doves at Hrant's funeral. The doves were a mockery here. And it had to have been an accident, but there it was: one of the doves had an Azerbaijan flag stuck in the web of its foot. This unlikely messenger fluttered over our heads with its banner until it found a perch on the eaves high above.

As the game wore on, I stopped watching the field. Armenia would obviously lose. I had never expected otherwise, but it was unbearable to see this happen after the crowd's reaction to the Armenian team. Some of the journalists from Yerevan were live-blogging for their papers or sending text messages to their editors. Over a year had passed since my last trip to Armenia, and if these reporters' wireless arsenal was any indication, things there were modernizing at an astounding rate.

Although a huge Turkish and European press corps had come to the match, the press section still had plenty of extra room, so during the second half about two hundred regular spectators helped themselves to the empty seats, better than the ones they had paid for. Like the rest of the audience, most of them were carrying Turkish flags.

I guess nothing would have happened if it weren't for the fact that, at some point, the ten journalists from Armenia started a tentative cheer. At first, it was as if they were only joking, pretending to behave like real soccer fans.

"HAY-A-STAN! HAY-A-STAN!" The name for Armenia doesn't mean anything to most Turks—in Turkish the name is "Ermenistan"—and nobody more than twenty feet away could hear it amid all the other noise. But little by little the journalists shouted louder, and soon I began to shout with them.

"HAY-A-STAN! HAY-A-STAN!" It was the simplest rhythm of the sporting world, three quarter notes and a rest.

Now and then we swapped in another cheer, "Hayer," which simply means "Armenians." I mimicked the way my Armenian colleagues shouted it, in a sort of fratty drawl, "Hayerrrrr." This sounds very much like the Turkish word *hayır*, which means "no." The call made sense either way. We were almost having a good time.

Then two women grasped the upper corners of a large Armenian flag they'd brought along, and began shaking it to the rhythm of the Hay-a-stan chant. One of the others held a tiny flag, the size of a postcard, in front of his chest. Two flags, that was it.

Suddenly we were surrounded by security guards who were holding up their hands and shaking their heads. "No, no, no," they were saying in English, using the only lingua franca they had.

The Armenian journalists shook their heads in response and kept chanting and laughing and thrusting their flags in the air.

A supervisor appeared in the aisle. "No, no." He made a crossing out motion with his arms. "*Yasak!*" he called out in Turkish, which means "pro-hibited," and then again in English, "No. Excuse me, excuse me. No, no."

I moved closer and asked him in Turkish what the problem was.

"They must not show these flags here. It is forbidden."

"Forbidden? You must be kidding!" I was enraged. "Look around this stadium. Are you saying that in this enormous ocean of flags for Turkey and Azerbaijan, at this so-called historic match between two neighbor countries, that these ten Armenians cannot hold up their flag and say the name of their country? Is this a joke?" I was yelling, really yelling.

The Armenian journalists had stopped chanting and were watching me.

"Think for a moment how we feel," I shouted at the man. "Can you imagine what it's like to come to this place for the first time in your life, this country you have been afraid to take one step toward, and then be surrounded like this, and hear twenty thousand people booing your national anthem? Can you imagine it?"

"This is the official policy. This is the rule," he said quietly. "It is not my rule, it is in the football federation rules. This is the press section. The press section must be objective."

"Who are those guys back there with the Turkish flags?" I said. "They're not press!"

The man nodded nervously. "They are also violating the rules."

"I don't care about those rules!" I screamed. "This is a question of being a person!"

So it happened that a random security supervisor for a soccer stadium became the only person I spoke to honestly and unrestrainedly in all of two years in Turkey.

THEY CREAMED US, 2-0. The instant it was over, the stadium exits were flooded with people, and I was separated from Aris and the Armenian journalists. Outside, I saw the Armenian group from Istanbul. I recognized several faces. There was Nerses, the basketball team manager, and there was Sarkis Bey. I hadn't spoken to either of them in months. I kept meaning to call Sarkis Bey, to visit him at the *Agos* office, to spend a bit more time with him in my waning days in Turkey, but I hadn't done it. No matter what language I tried, communication was still arduous. Nobody else had trouble understanding my Turkish—with my friends who didn't speak English, I spent long evenings chatting, laughing over my improvised vocabulary, jotting down words on napkins, pulling out a pocket dictionary now and then—but with Sarkis Bey, I felt shy about using Turkish, ashamed even. At first, when I was just learning to construct sentences, he would chuckle and offer a "Bravo!" But later, as my Turkish became more fluid than the mash-up of Armenian dialects we had been working across, he seemed to regard me oddly and tended to reply in Western Armenian or to call Ertan or another Anglophone into the room to translate from English. Was my

Turkish so bad? Or did he not, for some reason, want to hear me speak that language?

Maybe I was imagining his resistance. He was never rude, but was never entirely welcoming, either. Or maybe that wasn't a fair assessment; now and then when I ran into him at a community event, he told me I should pay them a visit at the summerhouse. I always nodded brightly, and sometimes my intentions would get me so far as to ask Ertan or somebody else whether they would like to join me for such an excursion sometime soon. But the barrier with the Armenians of Istanbul was still there. It was one of the many complexities of Turkey that I couldn't resolve. And so when I saw Sarkis Bey exiting the stadium in Bursa, on my final night in Turkey, I wondered what I would do. Perhaps the current of people would flow in the right direction and send him close enough that I would be forced to say hello, or, in this case, good-bye. I watched him from a distance and then a crowd of rowdy teenage spectators overwhelmed the forty feet of space between us. There was nothing to do but leave.

I HAD ARRANGED to meet Ramazan postgame at a soup shop where his newspaper colleagues were debriefing. When I told him how upset I got during the match, Ramazan tried desperately to convince me that it was just soccer and not anything specific against Armenians. That this was what happened in any sporting event, no matter who the opposing team was, and that I shouldn't take it personally. But I was beyond consolation, and disappointed that I would have to say good-bye to Ramazan like this, when he had tried to show me a nice time in Bursa, his city.

I needed to catch a two a.m. bus to get back to Istanbul in time to make my flight to California. Ramazan drove me to the bus station. Just before we parted ways, he produced a small bag and handed it to me.

"So that you'll have at least one sweet memory of Bursa."

It was a jar of candied chestnuts, the Bursa specialty. He had been running around all day, covering press conferences and visiting locker rooms and chasing the match from the sidelines with his camera, but he had managed, somehow, to make time to buy a gift. I wasn't sure whether it was okay to hug a man as religious as Ramazan, but I did anyway.

* * *

THE HEADLINES OF foreign papers hailed the progress in Bursa. "Armenian Leader in Turkey for Soccer Diplomacy," announced CNN. "Diplomatic Coup at a Football Match," the BBC reported. Well-meaning readers of the news probably said, "Huh, isn't that great," imagining the players lining up and high-fiving when the match was over.

But the agreement to proceed with diplomatic relations was never ratified. On April 22, 2010, one year after the announcement about starting talks, Armenian president Sarkissian took the project off the table. He was still open to negotiation, he said, but he was not going to let another April 24 pass with Prime Minister Erdoğan making Armenia look like the fool by insisting on Armenia's exit from Karabakh as a precondition.

"We consider unacceptable the pointless efforts of making the dialogue between Armenia and Turkey an end in itself; from this moment on, we consider the current phase of normalization exhausted." Although he singled out Prime Minister Erdoğan for criticism, he closed his speech by expressing gratitude to President Gül for his comportment throughout the entire process. Anyone who had watched the two men would have to agree: Gül was the good cop, Erdoğan the bad cop. Or maybe Gül was just a better politician.

* * *

I REACHED ISTANBUL at four a.m., just in time to race home, brush my teeth, lock up the apartment one last time, and drag my six giant bags down five flights of stairs to the street. I was afraid that the tiny cars that made up Istanbul's taxi force would not be able to fit my luggage. But then a driver pulled up and, seeing all my bags, jumped out and got right to work, heaving them into the trunk and the backseat, prodding and pushing until he had used every spare inch in the vehicle. He was a short, soft-bodied little fellow who looked to be in his fifties. When I tried to help him, he waved me off. My sole remaining goal was to make it to the airport without shedding any more tears, but a sudden surge of gratitude for this cooperative driver threatened to put me over the edge. He slammed the trunk shut with satisfaction and got in the driver's seat.

"Do you have a wet napkin?" he asked. It wasn't as strange a question as it would have seemed to me a couple years earlier; Turks are obsessed with hygiene, and they use wet wipes for everything. Even men carry them around.

"Sure," I said, pulling a L'Oréal eye makeup remover towelette from my purse.

"Oh, that's great, thank you."

He gave his hands a quick ablution and we were off.

It was my last chance to speak Turkish, I suddenly realized. I wanted it to be memorable, but I was too tired to make an effort. My brain was numb from so many sleepless hours, and my stomach felt cavernous. I had tossed out what I hoped was my last pack of cigarettes before getting into the taxi—I did not want to bring the habit home—but the previous day in Bursa I had set a new personal record in the sport of chain-smoking and now my insides felt like they were made of ash.

We were silent for a while, and then, as we crossed the Galata Bridge, the driver turned to me and asked where I was from. "Germany?" he guessed.

This pleased me. I certainly didn't look German, so I took it as a compliment to my language skills; he must have thought I was a diaspora Turk from Germany.

"I'm an American citizen," I said, "but I'm from Iran."

"What languages do you speak?"

I told him I spoke English, French, Turkish, and a bit of Persian and Russian. I didn't include Armenian. There was no point. That science project had run its course, and there was still a twenty-minute drive ahead of us. I didn't want to spoil this final leg.

"Any other languages?" he asked.

Why did he say that? Did he sense I was holding something back? It was always like this: I would tell myself that I did not want to discuss being Armenian, but then some subconsciously generated fairy dust swirling through the air would lead the exchange exactly where I claimed I didn't want it to go.

"I also speak Armenian."

"You're a walking library!" he said.

He betrayed no reaction to the word "Armenian," so I wasn't sure if he had heard me clearly. We chatted about languages for a while. He tried out a few words of English, which led to a long conversation about the difference between "Sit down, please" and "Please, have a seat." He had learned to say these things to tourists at the airport but had been wondering which was better. I explained that one was like a command and the other was like an invitation. He appreciated this conceptually but was confused by the "have" in the second phrasing. Turkish doesn't have an exact corollary for this general form of the verb.

I complimented his accent and he beamed and said he had a good ear but that he could only dream of speaking English the way I spoke Turkish. Trying to be modest, I told him it was easier for me to learn Turkish because in my culture we use a lot of Turkish words. But there I went again, baiting him to ask what I meant; I could not resist bringing it up, again and again, to find out where the limits were, feel out the edges to determine the shape of the thing.

"Which culture?" he said.

"Armenian. I mean, Iranian. I mean, Armenian from Iran."

"What do you think about Obama?" he asked.

Foiled again. I was bored by the Obama question so I asked him what *he* thought about our new president.

"Obama is pretty good," the driver said, "But why does he support Israel so much?"

Oh, Israel. Turks have a bizarre relationship with Israel and Jews. They are incredibly proud of the fact that five hundred years ago, when Spain ejected its Jewish population, the great, generous Ottoman sultan welcomed them with open arms into his multiethnic utopia. Try it if you don't believe me: ask anyone in Turkey what Turks think about Jews and this is the first thing you will hear. They also trot out this defense if you point to examples of anti-Semitism in Turkey. But as far as I had seen, every time there was a flare-up between Jews and Palestinians, Turkish cities exploded into protests during which Israeli flags were laid on the sidewalks for passersby to stomp on, and demonstrations featured banners with cartoon Jew-faces and lines drawn through them.

I explained to the driver that in the United States there are many Jews and that they are an important part of American society. Sometimes, I added, it seems like the rest of the world feels that anything short of hating the Jews counts as excessive support of Israel.

He nodded. I was pleased, thinking he appreciated my point.

"By the way, who lives in Israel?" he asked.

"What do you mean?"

"The people in Israel. Are they Armenians? Or Jews?"

If ever I were to be convinced of such a thing as destiny, this would have been the moment that made me believe. For had it been a different day, with a different driver, or simply fewer bags so that I could have taken the bus to the airport like I usually did, I would have missed out on this final, necessary amazement.

"Are you serious?" I said. "You're asking whether the main group of people who live in Israel are Armenians or Jews?"

Then he was embarrassed. "*Tarihim çok kötü*," he said. My history's really bad.

"Jews," I said. "Jews live in Israel. Israel was created to be a Jewish state. Armenians live in Armenia. Armenians are not Jewish." I tried to control the judgment in my voice. "Armenia was the world's first Christian state," I added, as though a few more details could shore up his unfathomable ignorance.

He said nothing.

I asked him whether he had heard somewhere that Armenians were Jewish.

He shrugged. "I can't remember. You just learn things here and there, you know?"

"I am surprised you thought that," I said finally. "But I guess I can imagine how it would be easy to mix up Armenians and Jews since everyone hates both of them." I giggled at my own joke. He did not laugh.

How could I be offended by this driver? What he said was simply so shocking to me that I could only marvel. I had lived in Turkey for two and a half years and I did not think there were too many things left to surprise me. Certainly I was sure I had heard every possible variation on the themes of anti-Armenianness and anti-Semitism. But this driver was here to offer me one last taste, a special deluxe combo package, before I flew home. And I felt sorry for him—sorry, after he had agreed so cheerfully to deal with my metric ton of suitcases, that I, a woman half his age, a visitor from the wealthy world whom he'd tried to treat generously, might make him feel stupid and small. Sorry that he had never been anywhere or seen anything, and that he never would.

The driver said nothing more, so I decided I might as well squeeze in a few extra clarifications before we reached the international terminal. "Israel is the country that was established after the Second World War, specifically for Jews. They had no place to go after millions of them were killed or forced to leave the European countries they were living in, like Germany."

"*Öyle mi?*" he said. "*Almanya'dan mı attılar?*" *Is that so?* They threw them out of Germany? His voice curved upward with genuine but casual surprise, like I had just handed him an interesting but inconsequential bit of trivia, that I'd told him, for example, that the tallest man in the world was Chinese.

I nodded. "Germany and other places."

We reached the airport. After he finished piling up my bags onto two carts, all three hundred pounds of luggage, he handed me his business card. "When you return to Turkey, please call me if you need a taxi. Happy travels to you."

I thanked him warmly. Then, on behalf of Armenians and Jews everywhere, I gave him a generous tip and went inside.

- 21 -

Terms

In November 2008, a group of four Turkish writers and scholars bought the Internet domain name www.ozurdiliyoruz.com. *Özür diliyoruz*: Turkish for "We apologize."

They created an online petition that read as follows:

"My conscience does not accept the insensitivity showed to and the denial of the Great Catastrophe that the Ottoman Armenians were subjected to in 1915. I reject this injustice and for my share, I empathize with the feelings and pain of my Armenian brothers and sisters. I apologize to them."

A group of 360 Turkish public figures served as founding signatories. Over the next month or so, thirty thousand regular Turks logged on and added themselves to the list.

When I heard about the petition I was impressed—amazed, even—but it was not until I looked at the Web site itself that I really felt something. Have you ever tried scrolling through the names of thirty thousand strangers? Each one had, alongside it, the city where the person lived and their occupation. An architect from Ankara called Ahmet. A lawyer from Mardin named Abdu. A retired teacher from İzmir named Duygu. Who were these people? Who was this potter, Nil Pektaş? Who was this tailor from Köln, Ali? A deejay from Atlanta, a student from Elâzığ, a pharmacist from Diyarbakır, a secretary from London, a customs agent from the border town of Iğdır.

You could sort alphabetically: how many Kemals or Mehmets, Mustafas or Müslüms, each name like a one-word biography. I was sitting in my bedroom at my parents' house, on a holiday visit home to California, and I stared at all these names in wonder. First and last, city, job: all these people apologizing for something they, as Turks, had not personally done, apologizing to me, an Armenian, for something I had not personally experienced. A feeling of gratitude overwhelmed me as I read the names, quietly asserting their humanity on my laptop screen.

For me, the wording of the apology was as good as it needed to be. *Conscience, injustice, insensitivity, empathy.* The first time I read it I didn't even notice the absence of the word that would make the entire enterprise come to naught. They had called it a "Great Catastrophe"—*büyük felaket* in Turkish—not a genocide. The organizers of the petition said that the point was to acknowledge the emotions associated with the events of 1915, and to make it easier for Turks to connect with those feelings. They believed that if they used the word genocide, some people would have shied away from adding their names for fear of legal consequences.

A group of Armenian cultural figures wrote a heartfelt letter accepting the apology completely, without qualification. But they were in the minority. The European Armenian Federation for Justice and Democracy, a lobbying group based in Brussels, sent out a press release:

"While being fully receptive to genuine expressions of sympathy and outreach by Turkish individuals who choose to speak out against their own government's policy of denial of the Armenian Genocide, we must also make clear that the cause of justice with regard to this mass crime cannot be 'apologized' away by populist initiatives, however well-intentioned such actions might seem to be. The recently publicized 'apology' campaign in Turkey is, indeed, a populist initiative, which deliberately avoids the term 'genocide' and which, by so doing, intends to de-criminalize the destruction by the Ottoman Turkish government of 1.5 million Armenians."

Judging anecdotally, many Armenians, at least when called to speak on the matter publicly, felt the same. Nice try, but not good enough.

And some of the angriest detractors of the apology campaign were Turks—not nationalists but radical liberals who felt that the project was merely a ploy to put the genocide issue to rest without having to break through the final taboo, that dreaded word. They considered it not only immoral but dangerous to normalize the idea that there was any legitimate way to acknowledge the genocide without calling it one. In Turkish, the label *büyük felaket* had no symbolic meaning; in theory, somebody could have used the phrase *büyük felaket* to refer to a really bad haircut. The word genocide, however, meant much more than simply the catastrophe to which it referred: it was a proxy for a broader problem, the power of the Turkish state and every small and large oppression suffered in Turkey by anyone who had ever violated the state's written and unwritten rules.

* * *

SOME MONTHS AFTER the *büyük felaket* campaign was launched, Barack Obama encountered his first April 24 as president of the United States of America. When Obama was merely a presidential candidate, he won the enthusiastic support of Armenian-Americans by making it unequivocally clear that he was on their side. "The Armenian genocide is not an allegation, a personal opinion, or a point of view, but rather a widely documented fact supported by an overwhelming body of historical evidence," he said. He promised that as president he would uphold the same view. (Up to that point, our presidents had piled up a great many synonyms for "incredibly heinous event," but none had used the g-word in an official statement.)

But when April 24, 2009, approached, and Turkey and Armenia were on the verge of announcing their secret talks toward establishing relations, Obama's speechwriters came up with an entirely novel workaround used by none of the president's predecessors. He made the following statement: "Ninety-four years ago, one of the greatest atrocities of the 20th century began. Each year, we pause to remember the 1.5 million Armenians who were subsequently massacred or marched to death in the final days of the Ottoman Empire. The *Meds Yeghern* must live on in our memories, just as it lives on in the hearts of the Armenian people."

The *Meds Yeghern*—Armenian for "great catastrophe." Obama had taken a page from the Turkish apology campaign for the *büyük felaket*, using Armenian words with the same meaning. That few people knew what *meds yeghern* meant was precisely the point. With this absurd maneuver, almost grotesque in its contrived, contorted way, the president managed only to infuriate both sides equally. But according to a former ambassador to Turkey, Mark Parris, it was a reasonable solution to an unreasonable problem. "Had the statement contained the word 'genocide,'" Parris said, "US-Turkish relations would have gone into a deep freeze that would have taken years to thaw."

Back in 1948, when Raphael Lemkin stalked the halls of the United Nations until he finally convinced delegates to pass a convention defining and condemning genocide, he believed that when he found the right word, and the word was put to use, things would change. Could Lemkin ever have imagined the way change would be held hostage to his word?

* * *

WHICH ISN'T TO say that Turkey wasn't changing. It was shifting in all sorts of ways, but if some of these developments were good for minority groups, others were worrisome for democracy in general.

Before Prime Minister Erdoğan came to power in 2003, the Turkish military was all-powerful, secularists had political and social dominance, and conservative Muslims, although a majority, were disenfranchised, even oppressed. Well into Erdoğan's second term, which started in 2007, the military was threatening coups and issuing position statements as edicts. But by the start of his third term in 2011, Prime Minister Erdoğan had succeeded in scrambling these long-standing hierarchies of power.

Targeting the secularist establishment, Erdoğan launched a ruthless investigation of a secret network called Ergenekon, which included high-ranking political figures acting as part of what was known as the "deep state." More than five hundred military leaders, security officers, journalists, and private citizens were arrested and accused of participation in plans to overthrow the government. Several unresolved murders of public figures from the previous two decades—including the assassination of Hrant Dink—were believed to be part of the group's plan to foment unrest before staging a coup. The novelist Orhan Pamuk, Nobel Laureate in Literature, was said to be on their hit list too. The Ergenekon network was real and extremely pernicious, and dismantling it was a monumental achievement: by 2013, even Kemal Kerinçsiz, who had bombarded Hrant with lawsuits, was behind bars for his role in the group's plots. But the investigation of Ergenekon was also a mess: justice of the highest order turned out-of-control witch hunt. In this way it resembled Erdoğan's entire project for Turkey: some of what he did counted as essential progress; other changes were alarming steps backward as he remade the nation to suit his own values. By the end of 2013, Erdoğan's open target was a fellow pious Muslim with tremendous influence—Fethullah Gülen, a cleric with a massive network of followers all over the world. Thus even the trusty old binary model of secular versus religious power became shaky. But in consolidating his own authority at any cost, Erdoğan was upholding a long-standing tradition. Like many of his predecessors, he also jailed journalists and squashed public protest. Through all of this, his popularity remained strong among a large base of religious Muslims. Now the White Turks who had been the state's model citizens felt like its unwanted stepchildren, and understandably so.

For minorities, meanwhile, there were some signs of improvement. In 2010, the cathedral at Akhtamar got a cross on its dome at last, and occasional church services were permitted. In 2013, the first baptism in more a century was held there—birth and rebirth, a triumph even if the christening required the presence of eight hundred security officers, bomb-sniffing dogs, and police divers monitoring the waters all around the island. (Sadly, Archbishop Mutafyan, who had blessed the church's reopening in 2007, could not appreciate any of these advances: he was deep into dementia, diagnosed in 2008 when he was only fifty-one. Who could say whether the stress of his position had hastened his mental decline? Who could feel certain it hadn't?)

One of the more shocking changes was the fact that in 2013, Erdoğan abolished the mandatory student oath, "How happy is he who calls himself a Turk," a relic of Kemalist dominance. In a stroke, he transformed the tenor of the Turkish school day. And, like the ruler of a dystopian Sesame Street, he granted freedom to the letters Q, W, and X.

Then, on April 24, 2014, Erdoğan made a statement about what had happened ninety-nine years earlier. The fact that he marked the date publicly was big news in itself, but the content of his speech was an arsenal of strategic verbiage. Its best achievement was that it openly acknowledged that in a democratic society, a variety of viewpoints are not only welcome but healthy. He called for sensitivity and openness to ideas that might feel uncomfortable. He even admitted that the events of 1915 were particularly significant for Armenians. But he also insisted, as his speech's primary theme, that the Armenians were not the only victims of hardship.

"It is indisputable that the last years of the Ottoman Empire were a difficult period, full of suffering for Turkish, Kurdish, Arab, Armenian and millions of other Ottoman citizens, regardless of their religion or ethnic origin. Any conscientious, fair and humanistic approach to these issues requires an understanding of all the sufferings endured in this period, without discriminating as to religion or ethnicity." And as usual, he called for a fair historical accounting, as if one had yet to take place.

His comments reminded me of an essential thing I learned in Turkey: stories, although always important for what they revealed about the storyteller, could be used as a dangerous moral leveler; could be held up to insist on a false equivalence of experience: *I'm human, you're human, we're all human. I suffered, you suffered, we all suffered. Why don't we just put these sad stories behind us and move on?*

There was and there was not—this should not be taken to mean that all stories are equally true, but that all stories are imperfect. Erdoğan's statement was definitely imperfect, but it was the closest any Turkish leader had come to acknowledging the genocide. In the tea leaves, or the Turkish coffee grounds, there were many small signs of hope, and I do believe this was one of them.

Hrant once made a speech in which he used an Armenian expression of optimism: *"Jooruh jampan g'jari"*—Water will always find cracks it can flow through. Water, as in clarity, as in truth. And so while Erdoğan was arranging his words carefully in that ninety-ninth year statement, a few hundred people gathered for a memorial service in front of Istanbul's Haydarpaşa Train Station, an ornate behemoth looming over the water's edge, the same station from which the earliest deportees were sent off in 1915. Several diaspora representatives attended. Such an event would have been unthinkable a few years earlier, and now it was one of several April 24 commemorations in Istanbul.

Across town from Haydarpaşa, a memorial took place in an Armenian cemetery. At that event, Nerses, the Bolsahay basketball team manager— the same Nerses who had yelled at me for speaking too openly when we were in Yerevan—now took the microphone as an activist, and did not mince words. He called for accountability, with a message that wouldn't have been out of place at Times Square in New York: he said he could only accept Prime Minister Erdoğan's statement about 1915 after justice was achieved for all the more recent crimes against Armenians. Fear was losing ground.

Closer to home, a small development in my life felt like important progress. It was another apology, but a private one: my aunt Nora, who had interrogated me in Yerevan and asked me not to associate with Ertan and his family, told me she was sorry for her behavior. One year after our meeting in Armenia, we sat at her dinner table in Connecticut. "I want to apologize," she said. "I realized I don't need to agree with everything you're doing or even understand it. I care about you, so if you have something to say, I want to read what you write, and in doing so I'll be able to understand you better. You are your own person. Why wouldn't I want that for you?" More tears, for both of us—but this time the good kind.

* * *

SHORTLY BEFORE THE Turkish apology campaign, I wrote an article for the *New York Times* about Gomidas, the Armenian musician who had survived the genocide but had lost his mind, living the last twenty years of his life in a mental hospital in Paris without speaking a word. Actually, that's not how I put it. I wrote that Gomidas "lost his mind by the age of 46, a misfortune thought to have been triggered by the 1915 massacres of Armenians in Ottoman Turkey." The copyeditor added the word "misfortune," which seemed to me an annoying understatement, but the rest of it was my phrasing.

The article was about a new recording of Gomidas's music, but I tried to squeeze in a few sentences describing how he was one of the group of two hundred Armenian intellectuals rounded up on April 24, 1915, how he had watched his peers being executed, how he was exiled to a distant town and eventually saved by the intervention of a well-placed Turkish friend in Constantinople. Most of that was cut for length.

I received an e-mail from an Armenian colleague asking me why I had not used the word genocide. He wanted to know whether I had made that decision or whether the paper had declined to use it. In truth, the choice was mine. After thinking about it for a long time, longer than I spent on the article itself, I had decided to avoid the word. Not as a personal policy, not as a new rule for myself; only for this one story. It wasn't my editor, who ran the classical music page, whom I was answering to. I could have said genocide if I wanted; the *Times* had green-lighted the term in its usage guidelines a few years prior.

But that was part of the problem: genocide had become a *term*, a phrasing to be allowed or disallowed, and as such, it was less profound than any other word I might choose to use. It was a secret password, a tool, an emblem—*I am one of those who know*—and a submission to or violation of guidelines set by authorities. To me, the label had lost any visceral sense of what this particular individual, Gomidas, who was a musical hero of mine, whose songs I had been singing since I was a small child, had seen and suffered. When I imagined Gomidas's undoing, when I tried to envision what he had witnessed and what unbearable memories kept him mute for the last two decades of his life, I did not imagine this word, genocide. Genocide sounds clinical, like the textbook name for a chemical compound or a disease, not like a human pileup of misery, monstrous individual decisions to raise a knife or a gun, the mutilation of the human spirit alongside the flesh. Genocide sounds like lobbying and politics.

In Armenian, nobody started calling it *tseghaspanutiun*—the literal translation of genocide, where *tsegh* means race and *spanutiun* means murder—until long after Gomidas was gone: sporadically in the 1960s, then widely from the 1980s onward, by which time recognition campaigns were in full swing in the United States and France.

The word that I and many Armenians heard, growing up, was *jart*. That's a hard *j*, like the *j* in Jesus or jail. *Jart* means "destruction." Armenian nouns for abstract concepts are often compound words, with enough syllables to give the Germans a run. Even ordinary nouns usually get at least two. An Armenian word with a single syllable announces itself. And *jart* stands out for another reason, as an example of what linguists call nominalization—a noun extracted from what had been a verb, in this case *jartel*, to break things open, or its passive form, *jartvel*, to be smashed to pieces. These verbs evoke the very physical destruction of something into shards—the shell of a walnut, the roof of a house. Bones. Sometimes when Armenians talk about the destruction they faced in Turkey, it is a *godoradz* (massacre), an *aksor* (deportation), an *aghet* (disaster). But in English, it is always a genocide. I am not making a case, merely exploring an idea.

As a writer, producing that short article about an Armenian musician—

whose suffering in the genocide had been well documented, indeed whose entire musical oeuvre had been overshadowed by the story of his suffering—I resented the requirement to use a word as a political statement, especially when I was writing about music, the one little corner of my Armenian life that had been safe shelter from politics, lobbying, hatred, nationalism, protests; the one private Armenian pleasure from which I had never felt alienated.

And in my writing, there is no other thing on earth, tangible or abstract, for which I have ever felt forced to use exactly one particular term. That's the beauty of language, description, thought, and personality, of stories— that we describe things in a million different ways and as we do so, we add glimmers of meaning, trying to make them felt and known.

Making things felt and known is essential: for this reason, when President Obama referred to the genocide as the *Meds Yeghern*, it was a mockery of the power of language, a parody: foreign words that were gibberish to the person speaking them. They were nothing more than a strangely shaped puff of air. He said it again every year after, as if repeating *Meds Yeghern* enough times would make it a new tradition—or at least allow him to improve his pronunciation—but instead the offense was compounded anew.

I am not a president, or a lawyer, or a judge, or a member of a human rights monitoring committee. If I were, I would not muse on parts of speech or metaphors; I would be bound by the legal and political power of language, such as it is. Still, in most of what I have written about Armenia and Turkey, and all over this book, I used the word genocide. Just that one time, in that one article in the classical music section that not too many people would read, I wanted to take a bit of expressive freedom back, a bit of individual agency.

This is what it was all about, in the end: to be Armenian had come to feel like an obstacle to individual agency, to being myself, any self, a separate person, and not only a member of a group that had already made all the decisions.

I did not go to Turkey to question history. I didn't write this book because I wanted to decide what the US Congress should do, or because I needed to befriend the Turks, although I am grateful for all the friends I made. I went to Turkey and I wrote this book because I was trying to understand how history, identity, my clan, and my feeling of obligation to it, had defined *me*, and I wanted to understand who I was outside of that obligation—who, if anyone.

What does it mean to be Armenian, or Turkish, or anything else? What does it give you, and what does it keep you from getting?

How much texture and complexity are sacrificed, lost when we retreat to our trenches? We produce a press release instead of a poem or novel. This shrinks us, in the end, makes us less alive. If survival, the future, the avenging of a genocide should be manifested in the flourishing of a people, what makes the soul flourish? Let it all live.

And if we move on from genocide recognition, with or without Turkey's olive branch, what holds us together then? If there is no better answer to this question, maybe the answer is simply, nothing. Nothing holds us together; we are no longer together at all. Now all possibilities are available to us, and that is terrifying. We become individuals.

Acknowledgments

This is my first book. As I finish it, I feel grateful not only to those who helped with this particular project, but to those who helped me build my career and sensibilities as a writer. Susie Linfield, of the Cultural Reporting and Criticism program at NYU, provided unforgettable practice in the art of questioning one's assumptions. Robert Boynton has been an essential mentor and a morale-boosting friend. Michelle Goldberg lent crucial help early on, especially by introducing me to my agent (back when I wasn't even sure what an agent did). Mitch Stephens sent me to Russia for a project that opened my horizons and led to my first Armenia trip. I would also like to acknowledge the late Ellen Willis; her encouragement got me started and emboldens my work still.

James Oestreich warmly welcomed my writing about music, an essential antidote to my writing about genocide. Gerry Marzorati, my boss at the *New York Times Magazine* just before I left for Turkey, gave me important opportunities for which I remain thoroughly grateful. As I developed my ideas for this book, several editors worked with me on articles about Armenia and Turkey that informed the larger project: Keith Gessen, Allison Lorentzen, Adam Shatz, Jennifer Schuessler, Peter Terzian, Charles Sennott, and Thomas Mucha all have my sincere thanks.

In this book's incipient stage, Daniel Menaker's enthusiasm meant a lot. Later, Andy Ward's editorial talents left an impression far out of proportion to the short time we worked together. This book owes some of its spirit to his feedback.

Many scholars influenced my early research for this book. Their names listed here are in no way a suggestion that they agree with any of the opinions I've expressed. Fatma Müge Göçek, a visionary in her scholarship and her handling of the politics around it, taught me not only about Turkish society and history, but about cooperation and keeping one's priorities straight. She was unceasingly generous in sharing ideas and contacts, while also being a delight to spend time with. Ronald Suny and Jirair (Gerard) Libaridian provided insights that shaped my work from the start, and reset my standards for clear, fair thinking about this utterly volatile subject. Taner Akçam was a major inspiration. Donald Bloxham's work added depth to my understanding, especially with regard to larger conceptual issues in historiography.

I benefited tremendously from the fascinating, maddening, game-changing e-mail microcosm that was the WATS listserv. Likewise for the discussions on Reconcile This. If I did not always have the mettle to jump into the fray, I am nonetheless grateful to those who put themselves out there so tirelessly and enriched our larger conversation.

For research input, help making connections, or other favors along the way, I would also like to acknowledge Ayhan Aktar, Armen Aroyan, Melissa Bilal, David Gaunt, Rachel Goshgarian, Sinan Küneralp, Neery Melkonian, Baskın Oran, Razmik Panossian, and the late Aris Sevag.

I do not know how to thank all the people who helped me in Turkey. Some of them are already named in the book and accustomed to being public figures, but for those who are not, I am wary of burdening them by associating their real names with a book that may run into problems in the Turkish legal system. Although in the past few years, the Armenian issue has become less dangerous in public discourse, some risk remains. Most important in this group are my two primary translators: this project would have been impossible without their wide-ranging help on a daily basis and their companionship throughout a vulnerable time. In addition to the two of them, please imagine here a list of the names of other friends and colleagues in Turkey who sat for interviews, invited me into their homes, challenged my assumptions, and, sometimes best of all, met me across a table at a backstreet café called Badehane to ease off the weight of the day. I hope you know who you are, and how much meaning you added to my experiences.

Special thanks to the staff of *Agos* newspaper and the staff of Aras Publishing, circa 2005–2009; they allowed a diaspora visitor to roam in their midst, ask questions, take notes, and sometimes just sit back and watch. Deepest appreciation to Sarkis Seropyan and Aris Nalcı for their help so many times. And although there is no way to thank Hrant Dink, his influence is all over this book.

In Armenia, I benefited from the insights of a range of scholars, journalists, officials, and regular people who were willing to speak with me. My sincere gratitude goes to all of them, and to my Yerevan relatives, without whom my time in Armenia would have been much less rich.

Deepest appreciation to New York friends who added useful perspectives or moral support: Adelle Waldman, not just for her cherished friendship but for one particular intervention without which this book (and its author) might have withered; Evan Hughes, Michelle Orange, Gloria Fisk, Jed Boyar, Carey Kasten, Jared Manasek, Ani Mason, Caitlin Shamberg, Jason Boog, Gary Sernovitz, Carlin Flora, Julie Bloom, Juliet Gorman, Elliott Malkin, James Westcott, Vahram Muratyan, Daniel Kurtz-Phelan, Sasha Polakow-Suransky, Alex Star, Dinaw Mengestu, Julian Rubinstein, Melissa Flashman, Brad Fox, Eszter Domjan, Defne Aydıntaşbaş, Mert Eroğul, Suzy Hansen, Steve Yagerman.

My entire extended family is, in some way, part of the fabric of this book, although none of them should be held responsible for anything contained here. Extra thanks to the wonderful Der-Sarkissians, who gave me refuge and support many times, and to Anouche, for a collection of inspiring notebooks and so much more; to Carina, Melissa, and Meldia for a necessary conversation two summers ago; to Stella for lending me confidence; to Vahan for always cheering me on; to Lena for hearing me out even when it was uncomfortable; and to Sara, for our Shongum days.

My thanks go to my in-laws, Wendy and David Davis and Spencer Bruskin and Lesley Schoer, for showing genuine interest in my project— and for avoiding the words "cry" and "wolf" even after the five hundredth time Alex said that I was just days away from finishing.

My big sisters, Tely and Lily, each supported my work on this book in their own ways: Tely with her lightning-speed processing of the psychological issues at hand, Lily with her core sense of justice and fairness. Love to them and to my brother-in-law Tom.

NOBODY ON THIS list knows how many stages this book passed through as well as my agent, Larry Weissman, who first heard about my intentions at a coffee shop in Prospect Heights in January 2005. Time and again, Larry proved his loyalty, discretion, and spot-on judgment, especially when the stakes were highest; for that I will always be grateful. Thanks also to Sascha Alper, whose suggestions made a difference from the start, and to Elisabeth Alba, who worked quickly and brilliantly to create the map at the front of this book.

From the first time I sat down in a conference room with Riva Hocherman and Sara Bershtel of Metropolitan Books, I was captivated by the dynamic, nuanced, substance-driven yet inimitably merry ambiance of their unique publishing domain. Thanks to Sara for her support all along; to Grigory Tovbis for his competence and gracious communications; to David Shoemaker for designing exactly the kind of jacket I hoped someone would dream up; and to Maggie Richards and James Meader and everyone else at Holt for helping to bring my book to life. But especially, my heartfelt and brain-felt thanks to Riva, who is both my ideal reader and my ideal editor, yet miraculously never confuses the two roles. She was patient when patience was what I needed, and exacting when the time came for that. Above all, she exudes a sense of real commitment to her authors and her projects, including this one, treating books not as products or trends but as contributions to the world.

My parents, Monica and Rouben Toumani, to whom this book is dedicated, have made many things possible for me. But most relevant to this book is the way they modeled—in their own choices, behavior, and guidance—how to think independently and act courageously. They did this while also creating a safety net that allowed me to roam far away without ever needing to question whether I could come home.

And Alex Bruskin, my husband, my partner, my red-pen vigilante, my laughter-maker, and my North Star: you have improved every page of this book and every day of my life.

A Note on Sources and Selected Bibliography

In the course of my research for this book I conducted more than two hundred formal interviews (almost all of them recorded) as well as countless informal ones. I also made use of a wide array of books, journals, reports, and Web sites in English, Turkish, French, and Armenian. The following is a highly selective bibliography of books that I believe will be instructive for readers who wish to learn more about the issues at hand.

Akçam, Taner. *From Empire to Republic: Turkish Nationalism and the Armenian Genocide*. London: Zed Books, 2004.

———. *A Shameful Act: The Armenian Genocide and the Question of Turkish Responsibility*. New York: Metropolitan Books, 2006.

Bloxham, Donald, and Fatma Müge Göçek. "The Armenian Genocide." In *The Historiography of Genocide*, edited by Dan Stone. Basingstoke, UK: Palgrave Macmillan, 2008, 344–72.

Bloxham, Donald. *The Great Game of Genocide: Imperialism, Nationalism, and the Destruction of the Ottoman Armenians*. Oxford: Oxford University Press, 2005.

Çetin, Fethiye. *My Grandmother: A Memoir*. Translated by Maureen Freely. London: Verso, 2008.

Dündar, Fuat. *Crime of Numbers: The Role of Statistics in the Armenian Question (1878–1918)*. New Brunswick, NJ: Transaction Publishers, 2010.

Göçek, Fatma Müge. *The Transformation of Turkey: Redefining State and Society from the Ottoman Empire to the Modern Era*. London: I.B. Tauris, 2011.

Kaplan, Sam. *The Pedagogical State: Education and the Politics of National Culture in Post-1980 Turkey*. Stanford, CA: Stanford University Press, 2006.

Kévorkian, Raymond H. *The Armenian Genocide: A Complete History*. London: I.B. Tauris, 2011.

Libaridian, Gerard J. *Modern Armenia: People, Nation, State*. New Brunswick, NJ: Transaction Publishers, 2004.

Panossian, Razmik. *The Armenians: From Kings and Priests to Merchants and Commissars*. New York: Columbia University Press, 2006.

Pope, Nicole, and Hugh Pope. *Turkey Unveiled: A History of Modern Turkey*. Woodstock, NY: Overlook Press, 1998.

Quataert, Donald. *The Ottoman Empire, 1700–1922*. New York: Cambridge University Press, 2000.

Suny, Ronald Grigor, Fatma Müge Göçek, and Norman M. Naimark. *A Question of Genocide: Armenians and Turks at the End of the Ottoman Empire*. Oxford: Oxford University Press, 2011.

Üngör, Uğur Ümit, and Mehmet Polatel. *Confiscation and Destruction: The Young Turk Seizure of Armenian Property*. London: Continuum, 2011.

Üngör, Uğur Ümit. *The Making of Modern Turkey: Nation and State in Eastern Anatolia, 1913–1950*. Oxford: Oxford University Press, 2011.

Waal, Thomas de. *Black Garden: Armenia and Azerbaijan Through Peace and War*. 10th Year Anniversary Edition, Revised and Updated. New York: New York University Press, 2013.

Zürcher, Erik J. *Turkey: A Modern History*. London: I.B. Tauris, 2010.

About the Author

MELINE TOUMANI has written extensively for the *New York Times* on Turkey and Armenia as well as on music, dance, and film. Her work has also appeared in *n+1*, the *Nation*, *Salon*, and the *Boston Globe*. She has been a journalism fellow at the Institute for Human Sciences in Vienna, Austria, and a coordinator of the Russian-American Journalism Institute in Rostov-on-Don, Russia. Born in Iran and ethnically Armenian, she grew up in New Jersey and California and now lives in New York City.